THE UNIVERSITY OF
WINCHESTER

Secrets beyond the Door

Secrets beyond the Door

THE STORY OF
BLUEBEARD AND HIS WIVES

Maria Tatar

PRINCETON UNIVERSITY PRESS

PRINCETON AND OXFORD

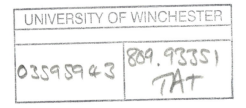
Copyright © 2004 by Princeton University Press
Published by Princeton University Press,
41 William Street, Princeton, New Jersey 08540
In the United Kingdom: Princeton University Press,
3 Market Place, Woodstock, Oxfordshire OX20 1SY
All Rights Reserved

Library of Congress Cataloging-in-Publication Data

Tatar, Maria, 1945–
Secrets beyond the door : the story of Bluebeard and his wives
Maria Tatar.
Includes bibliographical references and index.
ISBN 0-691-11707-1 (cl. : alk. paper)
1. Bluebeard (Legendary character) 2. Bluebeard (Legendary
character) in literature. 3. Women—Folklore. 4. Wives—Forklore.
5. Women in literature. 6. Wives in literature.
7. Women in motion pictures. I. Title.
GR75.B52T38 2004
809′.93351—dc22   2004040045

British Library Cataloging-in-Publication Data is available

This book has been composed in Sabon and
Centaur MT (Title page only)

Printed on acid-free paper.∞

www.pupress.princeton.edu

Printed in the United States of America

1 3 5 7 9 10 8 6 4 2

For Penny and Sandy

First granting, as I do, it was a weakness
In me, but incident to all our sex,
Curiosity, inquisitive, importune
Of secrets, then with like infirmity
To publish them, both common female faults.
   —John Milton, *Samson Agonistes*

I dream of a new age of curiosity.
   —Michel Foucault, "The Masked Philosopher"

CONTENTS

CONTENTS

ILLUSTRATIONS

Secrets beyond the Door

INTRODUCTION

Magic happens on the threshold of the forbidden. Who can forget the moment when Mary Lennox of Frances Hodgson Burnett's *Secret Garden* puts the key into the rusty lock of a door that has remained shut for ten years? After turning it, she pushes back the door, slips through it, and, standing with her back against the door, looks about her, "breathing quite fast with excitement, and wonder, and delight."[1] Disobeying orders, violating bans, and intruding on prohibited terrain may get literary characters into trouble, but these actions also open the gateway to adventure, taking figures on enchanted voyages of discovery. Wonder inevitably produces the desire to wander. Faust's transgressive spirit and his multiple challenges to authority provide him with the means to fly into regions invitingly familiar and exotic. "I love to sail forbidden seas, and land on barbarous coasts," Ishmael tells us in *Moby-Dick*, as he prepares to view the "great flood-gates of the wonder-world swung open."[2] But it is not just the exemplary heroes of modernity who experience an exhilarating sense of liberation and discover new domains for action through transgression. Disobedience turns Pinocchio's life into a series of great adventures. Jane Eyre defies her aunt and refuses to live a life of silent compliance. Even Peter Rabbit enters a forbidden garden.

In an essay on fairy tales, J.R.R. Tolkien referred to the "great mythical significance of prohibition." The "Locked Door," he added, stands as an "eternal Temptation."[3] This book is about the temptations of the forbidden chamber that figures powerfully in a fairy tale that has come down to us under the name of "Bluebeard." It is about the sway of curiosity and the impossibility of resisting its lure. It tells about the seductive power of border crossing, but in this case reversing the conventional spatial coor-

1

dinates of adventure stories, giving us characters who move into secret, enclosed spaces rather than into the vast expanse of wonder-worlds. The Bluebeard story begins on the outside—in the realm of the familiar, common, and quotidian—and moves to the inside—the exotic, dangerous, passionate, and barbaric.[4] Folklorists in earlier times worried about the "vice" of curiosity and were puzzled as to why the "fortunate mortal who has entered an enchanted palace" would ever bother to open the door to a forbidden chamber, especially since it spelled the end to the character's "state of felicity."[5] Today we view curiosity in a different light, recognizing the perils and potentially destructive effects of seeking out forbidden knowledge, yet also acknowledging the pleasures of taking risks and appreciating their role in exploring and mapping the unknown.

The story of Adam and Eve in the Garden of Eden and the myth of Prometheus's theft of fire from the gods link curiosity with knowledge, sexuality, evil, and mortality in powerful ways. These two stories have functioned as compass roses for our culture, helping us to navigate reality, define our values, and reflect on the value of intellectual inquiry. And yet these stories are also powerfully symptomatic of gender asymmetries. The biblical tale tells us that Adam and Eve live in a state of primal innocence until Eve succumbs to temptation and violates the prohibition against eating from the Tree of the Knowledge. After she seduces Adam, the two are driven out of the Garden of Eden, becoming mortal, but also "like gods, knowing good and evil." The Greek myth tells of Prometheus, whose deception of Zeus and theft of fire turn him into a cultural hero who brings to mankind the means for producing civilization. In retaliation for Prometheus's transgression, Zeus dispatches Pandora, the "beautiful evil" known as the first woman, who famously plagues mankind by opening a "jar of troubles."

In *The Sin of Knowledge*, Theodore Ziolkowski reminds us that the story of Adam and Eve is "always with us." Yet as Roger Shattuck points out in his *Forbidden Knowledge*, that story, like the myth of Prometheus, is virtually "invisible" because it "surrounds us too closely." Both Shattuck and Ziolkowski use the biblical story and the Greek myth to reflect on the moral dimensions of intellectual inquiry, to explore the point at which knowledge ceases to enrich and elevate and becomes risky business. Although Ziolkowski is aware of gender trouble in paradise ("Eve is the curious weakling who succumbs to the temptation of knowledge and seduces Adam from the paths of righteousness" and "Pandora is the 'beautiful evil' sent to plague mankind"), his focus is on Adam and Prometheus, men who function as heroic figures, taking on the role of scapegoat and suffering "so that humankind may endure." Shattuck, too, is invested in exploring the stories of Adam and Prometheus as master narratives about the quest for knowledge and as tests of the limits to be set on that quest. Aware of the compelling connection between sin, evil, and femininity in the cultural stories under investigation, these critics nonetheless avoid probing the strange asymmetries that emerge from a comparative analysis of, say, Eve's duplicity and Prometheus's trickery. Eve's curiosity, for example, installs sin, mortality, and suffering into the human condition, while Prometheus's sacrilege becomes a positive foundation for the arts and crafts that produce civilization.[6]

Woman's problematic relationship to knowledge becomes evident in reading the stories of Eve and Pandora, two women whose curiosity leads them to engage in the transgressive behavior that introduces evil into the world. While Western culture has developed many new myths to reflect on male identity and the quest for knowledge and experience—think of Don Juan, Don Quixote, Hamlet, Faust, and perhaps even Frankenstein—it has few compelling female counterparts to those myths. Bluebeard's wife constitutes an exception, and she is, oddly, a figure from the realm of fairy tales.

Fairy tales trace a path from rags to riches, generally staging the conflicts of romance rather than the seductions of forbidden knowledge. "Bluebeard" deviates from that folkloric norm. A fairy tale well known in British cultures and on the Continent, "Bluebeard" not only begins with marriage (rather than ending with it), but also engages with the nexus of knowledge, sexuality, evil, and mortality so familiar from biblical tales and myths. Like many of our foundational cultural stories, "Bluebeard" turns on a woman's desire for forbidden knowledge and, in its canonical French form, describes that desire as a curse. The intellectual curiosity of men may have given us fire, divided us from animals, and produced civilization, but the curiosity of women—as we know from the stories of Pandora, Eve, Psyche, and Lot's wife, among others—has given rise to misery, evil, and grief. And yet in "Bluebeard" hope remains, for the wife of this fairy-tale tyrant survives his death threats and lives happily ever after with another man.

This book will investigate the crimes of Bluebeard and the curiosity of Bluebeard's wife, examining how the story of Bluebeard has been constructed over time and across different cultures. Some wives of Bluebeard are treacherous deceivers, guilty of moral and sexual betrayal; others are resourceful investigators who use their wits to get to the bottom of the dark secrets haunting their marriages. While earlier ages denounced Bluebeard's wife for her "reckless curiosity" and her "uncontrolled appetite," our own culture has turned her into something of a heroine, a woman whose problem-solving skills and psychological finesse make her a shrewd detective, capable of rescuing herself and often her marriage in the bargain. But she can also be seen as a figure who wants to know too much, whose curiosity represents a betrayal of trust, as Edna St. Vincent Millay suggests in a Bluebeard poem: "And you did so profane me when you crept / Unto the threshold of this room to-night."[7]

What, then, of Bluebeard, the figure in the title of the story? Many a commentator on the tale has pointed out that the story, despite its title, is really about Bluebeard's wife, for—like Jack of beanstalk fame or Gretel in the Grimms' tale of sibling solidarity—she is the powerless protagonist who, in classic fairy-tale fashion, must defeat a bloodthirsty ogre, abusive giant, or cannibalistic witch. To be sure, in folktale versions of "Bluebeard," Sister Anne and the brothers of Bluebeard's wife function as agents of rescue. Still, it is the wife who is put on trial with a prohibition, and it is the wife who must contend with the consequences of transgressive behavior. Because "Bluebeard" so often explores the complexities of her behavior, I will lead with her side of the story, although the final two chapters in this volume explore the refashioning of the tale from the husband's point of view.

Bluebeard's wife has been reinvented so many times that she has every right to complain of an identity crisis. In the course of researching the twists and turns of her fortunes, I came across her in many unlikely sources, but none more unlikely than Stephen King's novel *The Shining*. That work has surprising explanatory power for the relevance of "Bluebeard" today and reveals just how robust a culturally invisible story can be.

In *The Shining*, six-year-old Danny Torrance finds himself bored one day and begins wandering "aimlessly" around The Overlook, a posh hotel in Colorado, vacant during the winter months. Danny's father, fired from his teaching post at a prep school, has brought his wife and son to The Overlook, where he is serving as winter caretaker while finishing a play begun some years back. Danny soon realizes that his wandering is not that aimless after all. Drawn by "a morbid kind of curiosity" to room 217, the scene of a gruesome death, he is well aware that his father has forbidden him to enter that room.

In reflecting on his attraction to room 217, Danny recalls a story his father read to him a few years earlier:

> The name of the story was *Bluebeard*. . . . Every day Bluebeard went off to work and every day he would tell his pretty little wife not to look in a certain room, although the key to that room was hanging right on a hook, just like

the passkey was hanging on the office wall downstairs. Bluebeard's wife had gotten more and more curious about the locked room. She tried to peep through the keyhole the way Danny had tried to look through 217's peephole with similar unsatisfying results.[8]

The "morbid" nature of the curiosity felt by Bluebeard's wife does not escape the precocious Danny. Both he and the fabled intruder understand that they are engaging in transgressive acts; both are fascinated by the prospect of the forbidden; and both experience dread and the fear of reprisal as the effect of a shocking visual experience:

> The old fairy tale book had depicted her discovery in ghastly, loving detail. The image was burned on Danny's mind. The severed heads of Bluebeard's seven previous wives were in the room, each one on its own pedestal, the eyes turned up to whites, the mouths unhinged and gaping in silent screams. They were somehow balanced on necks ragged from the broadsword's decapitating swing, and there was blood running down the pedestals.
> Terrified, she had turned to flee from the room and the castle. (183)

Danny further recalls that the fairy tale has a happy ending (in most versions the wife escapes Bluebeard's vengeance and remarries), but he recognizes that the happy ending is effaced by the images of horror embedded in the tale. What the boy finds haunting about the story is "the taunting, maddening locked door with some great secret behind it," along with "the grisly secret itself, repeated more than half a dozen times" (183).

While the locked door arouses a form of "morbid curiosity" that takes an investigative turn, the sight of what is behind the door is calculated to shock, frighten, and alarm the intrepid figure turning the knob. Danny, no less than Bluebeard's wife, is scared out of his wits by what he sees behind the locked door. He shrieks, wheels around, and bolts: "His eyes starting from their sockets, his hair on end like the hair of a hedgehog about to be turned into a sacrificial . . . ball, his mouth open and soundless" (232). There could hardly be a stronger contrast between the boy at the door—curious, introspective, thoughtful, and shrewd—and the boy fleeing the forbidden chamber, out of his mind with fear.

Danny's reaction explains why horror has often come under heavy critical fire. Even as it was being conceived in its modern form, horror, in the shape of the Gothic romance, was seen as a regressive mode, one that reduced readers to the state of abject terror experienced by the characters. "The bulk of readers, the only kind to which we moderns devote our lucubrations, seem now much more pleased to be frightened out of their wits than to be assisted in making proper use of them," Isaac d'Israeli

5

commented back in 1797, emphasizing the profoundly anti-intellectual side to horror.[9]

Often dismissed as escapist, horror stories—including folktales like "Bluebeard"—are designed to frighten us out of our minds, to paralyze our critical faculties as we succumb to the tales' violent delights. Yet these accounts also contain elements that engage our minds with their high-voltage narrative energy, shocking us into responsive awareness. If we look back at oral storytelling traditions, it becomes evident that tales of horror like "Bluebeard" have always had a powerful social agenda. Folk narratives, as Walter Benjamin has emphasized, all contain "something useful." In some cases, the usefulness consists of a "moral," in others of "practical advice," in still others of a "proverb or maxim." "In every case," Benjamin points out, "the storyteller is a person who has counsel for his readers. . . . Counsel is less an answer to a question than a proposal concerning the continuation of a story which is just unfolding."[10] As tellers weave their tales, they also point to different possibilities and destinies, revealing the outcomes of certain kinds of behaviors, negotiations, alliances, and collaborations.

Just as proverbs offer help on how to "size up a situation"—telling us how to cope with perils and how to stand up to adversity—a folktale like "Bluebeard" can provide readers with a kind of counsel about how to manage anxieties that run particularly deep, in this case, those affiliated with romance, courtship, and marriage. A story that turns on weighty events in one partner's past, on the perils of uncovering secrets, and on the quest for intimacy through knowledge, "Bluebeard" can be seen as a particularly potent form of marriage counseling, one that employs melodrama and hyperbole to draw up a map for thinking about the risks of romantic alliances sanctified by law.

Bluebeard's wife is a figure who must size up her situation and improvise a solution, making up a way out as she goes along. Locked in a struggle with a powerful antagonist, she becomes the archetypal fairy-tale figure: at once victim, trickster, and survivor. Her story conveys the lesson that Benjamin saw as the great legacy of the fairy tale: "The wisest thing—so the fairy tale taught mankind in olden times, and teaches children to this day—is to meet the forces of the mythical world with cunning and with high spirits."[11] If Bluebeard's wife is scared out of her wits, her story also teaches listeners and readers how to take the experience shared through the folktale and how to use it to sharpen their own wits.[12]

The story of Bluebeard, which has been encoded with a variety of lessons and inflected in many different forms, has figured as one powerful current in what Salman Rushdie has referred to as the sea of stories. For the Water Genie in *Haroun and the Sea of Stories*, storytelling is a fluid art, with tales constantly combining and metamorphosing:

Iff the Water Genie told Haroun about the Ocean of the Streams of Story, and even though he was full of a sense of hopelessness and failure, the magic of the ocean began to have an effect on Haroun. He looked into the water and saw that it was made up of a thousand thousand thousand and one different currents, each one a different color, weaving in and out of one another like a liquid tapestry of breathtaking complexity; and Iff explained that these were the Streams of Story, that each colored strand represented and contained a single tale. Different parts of the ocean contained different sorts of stories, and as all the stories that had ever been told and many that were still in the process of being invented could be found here, the ocean of the Streams of Story was in fact the biggest library in the universe. And because the stories were held here in fluid form, they retained the ability to change, to become new versions of themselves, to join up with other stories and so become yet other stories; so that unlike a library of books, the Ocean of the Streams of Story was much more than a storeroom of yarns. It was not dead but alive.[13]

The Ocean of the Streams of Story represents a kind of collective cultural archive from which we draw strands of narrative to construct our own experiences. "Bluebeard," as a story in the "library of books," has lost much of its visibility, even if it is not dead. But as a tale in the "streams of story," it is perpetually revitalized by writers and artists who take up the theme of intimacy, showing how the desire for disclosure is always also hemmed in by the need for concealment.

This book does not aim to create a comprehensive catalog or archive of works that have stood in the long shadow cast by "Bluebeard." Instead, it seeks to map the cultural circulation of the Bluebeard story by showing how it left its mark at specific historical moments on the stories we tell and the pictures we look at. To paraphrase Rushdie, this is a book that will observe how "Bluebeard" has changed, created new versions of itself, and joined up with other stories to become yet other stories.

"Bluebeard" has an extraordinary cultural elasticity, in part because its folkloric history is so richly nuanced, with Bluebeards as French aristocrats, Oriental tyrants, and Greek Lords of the Underworld and with wives who are sometimes anxious and passive, sometimes intrepid and resourceful. I will begin with a chapter on Perrault's master narrative "Bluebeard" and its relation to folkloric counterparts the world over. From the start, Perrault's story was framed as a tale about transgressive desire, as a text that enunciates the dire consequences of curiosity and disobedience. This first chapter will also explore the reception of Perrault's story, analyze its dissemination in other cultures, and investigate its links with stories about female curiosity. In addition, it will consider competing narrative traditions, among them the Grimms' "Fitcher's Bird" and "The Robber Bridegroom," in which women are less curious than bold, courageous, and clever.

"Bluebeard" entered literary culture in the aftermath of the Gothic vogue, shaping marriage plots in novels ranging from Charlotte Brontë's *Jane Eyre* through Daphne du Maurier's *Rebecca* to the latest Harlequin Romance. Chapter 2 will explore how the Bluebeard plot competes with the Cinderella story as our culture's paradigm for romantic excitement and how it provides opportunities for reflecting on the play between intimacy and distance, between disclosure and repression. The secrets harbored by men with mysterious backgrounds endow them with sexual charisma, but they also divide marriage partners and give rise to a new type of heroine who must engage in both detective work and psychoanalytic investigation in order to secure a happy ending for herself.

Jane Eyre and *Rebecca* both entered cinematic culture in the same decade, and chapter 3 will examine the migration of the Bluebeard story from novel to film. In the 1940s Hollywood witnessed the premieres of over a dozen movies drawing on the Bluebeard story. Each of these films staged marital trouble turning on the suspicions of a woman who fears that her husband is trying to kill her. The vogue was brief but intense, with Cukor's *Gaslight* (1944), Hitchcock's *Notorious* (1946), and Fritz Lang's *Secret beyond the Door* (1947) among the most prominent examples. In these films husbands are positioned as figures with terrible skeletons in forbidden closets. Their wives may be terrorized victims, but they also take on the role of investigator, detective, or psychoanalyst, working hard not only to unlock the domestic space forbidden to them but also to discover the key to the traumatic mystery feeding their husbands' homicidal urges. In the cinematic context, "Bluebeard" functions as a cultural blueprint for building plots about troubled marriages, a topic particularly pertinent during the war years and after.

From these films, I will turn in chapter 4 to the ways in which the Bluebeard story was reworked in the literary and visual culture of the last decades of the twentieth century. The new cultural investment in an old tale about a bad marriage dates back to the 1960s and has something to do with a feminist effort to reclaim the folklore of old, to rely on the stories once told by women to women as they shared experience and communicated values and beliefs. Feminist rescriptings of "Bluebeard" stress the resourcefulness of the heroine, yet they also reveal the degree to which women are complicit in perpetuating the fatal repetition of patriarchal values, foremost among them the self-immolating nature of romantic love. Margaret Atwood, who weaves fairy-tale motifs throughout her narratives with almost unprecedented insistence, unsettles the traditional story of "Bluebeard" and challenges us to understand the complexities of what she calls "power politics." Like Atwood, Angela Carter rewrites "Bluebeard" from the point of view of the wife, letting us see inside a mind to which we do not have access in the fairy tale. Cindy Sherman's *Fitcher's Bird* and Jane Campion's *The Piano* reveal just how powerfully the death drive is embedded in uneasy marital alliances from a variety of cultures.

If the story of "Bluebeard" cried out for revision to women writers, artists, and filmmakers during the last decades, it has also not escaped the attention of male writers, librettists, and filmmakers, who, if somewhat less passionate and partisan in their engagement with the story, seem equally committed to understanding and reinterpreting its terms. Chapter 5 begins with Chaplin's *Monsieur Verdoux*, a film that identifies Bluebeard as both con man and cultural hero—a decent, if not quite law-abiding, fellow who is just trying to make a living. For Uncle Charlie, in Hitchcock's *Shadow of a Doubt*, murder is less of a business than a passion, one that turns him into a disruptive, yet also profoundly alluring Bluebeard figure in the dull routines of a sleepy town. A social outlaw who is both glamorous and sympathetic, he falls victim to the investigative energy of agents of law and order. Both Monsieur Verdoux and Uncle Charlie follow in an operatic tradition of Bluebeards who are subjected to deeply invasive measures taken by women who want to know too much. Figures of dark existential loneliness, these men are presented as quietly heroic in their effort to ward off the insistent prying of women in search of enlightenment.

While the husband's point of view has been embraced many times in the folklore, fiction, opera, and film of the past century, Bluebeard has also been the target of rehabilitation by a number of writers who see in the folktale an allegory of artistry. Chapter 6 interrogates the relationship between murder and art and identifies the strategies used to collapse the differences between them. Often cast as aesthete, artist, or writer, this misunderstood figure of Bluebeard has, in Vladimir Nabokov's phrase, "only words to play with." Seeking redemption from the beastly violence of real life, he finds the promise of immortality—the permanent happily ever after of fairy tales—in the enthralling surface beauty and moral depth of fairy tales. Yet even as writers as different as the Russian Nabokov, the German-American Kurt Vonnegut, and the Canadian L. M. Montgomery celebrate Bluebeard's artistry, there are others who chart a decline in Blue-

9

beard's fortunes, showing how he has lost his menacing mystery, romantic allure, and potent masculinity. This latter-day Bluebeard may remain a haunting presence in our collective imaginations, but he has become a figure who finds it increasingly difficult to live up to the reputation that has been built by words and images disseminated across our own contemporary cultures and those of other times and places.

This study seeks to restore to adult cultural consciousness a story that we are in danger of repressing, even if not of losing. The tales we tell each other and our children not only reflect the lived experience and psychic realities of another era but also shape our lives, enabling us to construct our desires, cope with our anxieties, and understand how those desires and anxieties are profoundly enmeshed with each other. The story of Bluebeard may not be one of the canonical fairy tales (like "Cinderella," "Little Red Riding Hood," or "Snow White") to which we ceaselessly refer in our culture, but it remains in brisk circulation, ensuring that it remains part of what Roland Barthes famously declared to be the "tissue of quotations" in every literary text. The appendix includes eleven different versions of "Bluebeard," each recasting the story in dramatically different terms.

In "Grimms' Remembered," Margaret Atwood recalls the experience of reading fairy tales, in her case, the "complete" Grimm, in which "every bloodstained axe, wicked witch, and dead horse was right there where the Brothers Grimm had set them down, ready to be discovered by us." She concludes her essay with words that hold true for readers today: "And where else could I have gotten the idea, so early in life, that words can change you?"[14] It is that transformative power, both within the tale and beyond its narrative limits, that I wish to investigate.

1

CHAPTER

The Attractions of "Bluebeard": The Origins and Fortunes of a Folktale

> You had the sense to see you were caught in a story, and the sense to see that you could change it to another one . . . for many things may and do happen, stories change themselves, and these stories are not histories and have not happened.
> —A. S. Byatt, "The Story of the Eldest Princess"

"There are only two or three human stories," Willa Cather once declared, "and they go on repeating themselves fiercely as if they had never happened before."[1] Although each of us might have different candidates for those two to three tales, many of us would come up with the usual suspects: the stories of Oedipus or Hamlet, Eve or Cassandra, Odysseus or Jack, Cinderella or Snow White. Much has been written about the seemingly timeless and universal nature of these master narratives, which we encounter in print, on screen, and in performance as poems, myths, films, operas, fairy tales, and plays. Yet the stories rarely repeat themselves, certainly not word for word, but often not even idea for idea. Instead they are constantly altered, adapted, transformed, and tailored to fit new cultural contexts. They remain alive precisely because they are never exactly the same, always doing new cultural work, mapping out different developmental paths, assimilating new anxieties and desires, giving us high pathos, low comedy, and everything in between.

If Cather recognized the resilience of certain tales, she also implied that we are doomed to endlessly repeat history through certain plots. But if we tell one of these "human stories"—say, Cinderella or Jack and the Beanstalk—to someone from another part of the world, it quickly becomes evident that traditional tales exist in many different versions, in at least as many versions as there are cultures and in perhaps as many versions as there are people who know the tale. Fairy tales, for example, have an extraordinary cultural elasticity, rarely repeating themselves even when recited verbatim from a book—every voice puts a new inflection on each episode. Their expansive range and imaginative play are so powerful that they never seem to bore us. Italo Calvino once said of storytelling that the tale is beautiful only when something is added to it.[2] Each telling of the story seems to recharge its power, making it crackle and hiss with renewed narrative energy. Or as Tolkien put it, drawing on a different metaphorical regime, "the Cauldron of Story has always been boiling, and to it have continually been added new bits, dainty and undainty."[3]

This book focuses on one of the tenacious cultural stories to which Cather refers, showing how it has repeated itself but also reinvented itself over the course of the past centuries, taking unexpected twists and turns as it makes its way into different cultural settings. "Bluebeard," a tale that is now found between the covers of fairy-tale collections for children, began as adult entertainment, and although it seems to have fallen into a cultural black hole, it has left profound traces on our cultural memory. Even if many of us are supremely unaware of it as story—we may not be able to reproduce it the way that we can recite Hamlet's dilemmas or identify the rivalries dividing Cinderella's household—we are familiar with many of its chief ingredients: a barbaric husband, a curious wife, a forbidden chamber, a blood-stained key, and corpses in the closet.

The Bluebeard plot, in its standard folkloric form, features a sinister figure whose wealth wins him the hand of two sisters, each of whom mysteriously disappears. The third and youngest in the trio of young women reluctantly marries Bluebeard, who arranges a test of her fidelity when he hands over the keys to all the rooms in his mansion but expressly forbids entering one remote chamber. As soon as Bluebeard leaves for an extended journey, his wife rushes to the forbidden chamber, opens the door, and finds the corpses of her husband's previous wives. A stained key, a blood-spattered egg, a withered flower, or a bruised apple betray the wife's transgression to the husband, who, in a murderous rage, is about to behead his wife, when her brothers come to the rescue and cut Bluebeard down with their swords.

The story of Bluebeard and his wife has a cultural edge so sharp that it continues to be recast, rewritten, and reshaped even though the name "Bluebeard" often elicits a blank stare or an erroneous association with piracy on the high seas (the wealthy Frenchman is often confused with the seafaring Blackbeard). Despite the prominent position that "Bluebeard" occupies in the cultural archive of the West—the number of writers and artists with Bluebeard skeletons in their closets is staggering—most adults seem only dimly aware of the plot outlines of the story. Dismissed as an obscure tale belonging to another time and place, it seems of little more than antiquarian interest.

How do we account for the way in which "Bluebeard" has kept so powerful a hold on our imagination, yet at the same time fallen into cultural oblivion? Charles Dickens offers a clue in his childhood memories of a story called "Captain Murderer," which was told to him by a nursemaid incongruously named Mercy. This Captain Murderer, as the adult Dickens realized, was an "offshoot of the Blue Beard family," and he terrorized the young Dickens over a period of many years. That "Captain Murderer" was not really a story for children becomes evident in Dickens's account of his response to its telling:

> Hundreds of times did I hear this legend of Captain Murderer, in my early youth, and added hundreds of times was there a mental compulsion upon me in bed, to peep in at his window as the dark twin peeped, and to revisit his horrible house, and look at him in his blue and spotty and screaming stage, as he reached from floor to ceiling and from wall to wall. The young woman who brought me acquainted with Captain Murderer had a fiendish enjoyment of my terrors, and used to begin, I remember—as a sort of introductory overture—by clawing the air with both hands, and uttering a long low hollow groan. So acutely did I suffer from this ceremony in combination with this infernal Captain, that I sometimes used to plead I thought I was hardly strong enough and old enough to hear the story again just yet. But, she never spared me one word of it.[4]

"Bluebeard" is one of those stories that did not travel well in the great eighteenth-century migration of fairy tales from the fireside and parlor to the nursery. "The ugly story of the famous or infamous French Count" should be "cast out of the society of fairy-stories," Aline Kilmer declared. "It is not folk-lore but yellow-journalism."[5] A tale that centers on marriage and focuses on the friction between one partner who has something to hide and another who wants to know too much, it did not prove attractive to tale collectors, who were eager to assemble stories that would appeal to adult sensibilities about what was appropriate reading for children. And so while "Bluebeard"—an anomaly among "Little Red Riding Hood," "Cinderella," and "Jack and the Beanstalk"—got lost on its way from adult storytelling cultures to children's books, the tale managed to lead a powerful literary afterlife without our ever being fully aware that its constituent parts belong to a narrative whole.

In his autobiography *Black Boy*, Richard Wright tells us exactly why "Bluebeard" is a story that has refused to go away. "Once upon a time there was an old, old man named Bluebeard." These are the words read by a "colored schoolteacher" named Ella from a book containing a story called "Bluebeard and His Seven Wives." In this coming-of-age portion of Wright's autobiography, we learn how the folktale about Bluebeard introduces the boy growing up in the Jim Crow South to the world of adult secrets and intrigue. The European folktale about Bluebeard elicits what is described as a "total emotional response." When Wright's grandmother cuts the narrative short, denouncing the tale as "Devil's work," the boy is distraught. "I hungered for the sharp, frightening, breath-taking, almost painful excitement that the story had given me." The "whispered story of deception and murder" feeds a "thirst for violence" and "for intrigue, for plotting, for secrecy, for bloody murders."[6]

What Wright discovers as a boy is that narrative can elicit a somatic response, sending a chill up his spine and taking his breath away. Nothing is as irresistible as melodrama, and the "Devil's work" has always proved more compelling than pious feelings and saintly behavior. "Bluebeard and His Seven Wives," with its solemn mysteries, grim carnage, and damsel in distress, produces the suspense of all stories in which an enigma about a killer must be solved by one of his potential victims. And by casting the killer as husband and the victim as wife, it adds the ingredients of intimacy, vulnerability, trust, and betrayal to make the story all the more captivating.

It is above all the pathology of the husband—"intrigue," "plotting," "secrecy," and "murder"—that captures the young Wright's attention. "Bluebeard and His Seven Wives" fascinates because it stages secret anxieties and desires taken to a criminal extreme—anxieties and desires that are foreign yet also fascinating to those on the threshold of becoming adults. Beyond that, it produces in exaggerated terms what the young often long for in literature, and sometimes in life as well: not Wordsworth's sweet serenity of books but the excitement and revelation that keep them on the edge of their seats while they are reading.

"Bluebeard" and its variants enjoyed widespread circulation in European cultures, and the tale is broadly disseminated in England, France, Germany, Italy, and Scandinavian countries, even reaching into Slavic traditions. Via trade routes, the story found its way to Africa, India, and Jamaica, where Bluebeard sported beards of different hues, sometimes red, occasionally green, and even blond.[7] In Italy Bluebeard is a devil who hires young women to do his laundry; in Germany he is a sinister wizard who dismembers his brides; in Norway he is a mountain troll who twists off the heads of women who spurn his advances. It was in France that the story seems to have originated and taken particular hold, and Paul Delarue, in his magisterial study of French folktales, lists dozens of versions of the tale.[8]

Margaret Atwood once warned that we should never ask for the "true story," for it is always "vicious and multiple and untrue."[9] Nothing could be closer to the truth about folklore. When it comes to folktales, there is no authoritative, original version. We have only variants, "multiple" and "untrue," each unfaithful to the previous telling and inflecting the plot in a slightly different way. And yet all these variants—oral, literary, or a hybrid of the two—can lay claim to unwavering fidelity to their own time and place. As Italo Calvino put it, while he was preparing *Italian Folktales* for publication, "I too have the right to create variants."[10] In every sense, we are right to perpetually reinvent the story, for the true one fails to ring true to our cultural values. "Why do you need it?" Atwood shrewdly asks.

And yet understanding how "Bluebeard" has engaged in shape shifting over the centuries challenges us to think about the ways in which stories that we think of as "timeless" and "universal" constantly have to reinvent themselves in order to ensure their survival. For that reason, I want to look at multiple untrue stories that have emerged over the past three centuries. I begin with Charles Perrault's "La Barbe Bleue," for no other Bluebeard story has been invested with as much cultural authority as this French variant from *Tales of Mother Goose* (1697).

CHARLES PERRAULT'S "BLUEBEARD" AND ITS LESSONS

"Bluebeard" made its literary debut in a collection that drew on a culture of oral storytelling for adults to craft stories that would appeal to children.[11] For the peasants who distracted themselves from the monotony of manual labor through gossip, banter, and tale telling, "Bluebeard" did not fall short of the entertainment mark. In an age without radios, televisions, or other electronic diversions, farm laborers and household workers demanded fast-paced narratives with heavy doses of burlesque comedy, high drama, scatological humor, and freewheeling violence. "Bluebeard" seems to have escaped the heavy editing to which Perrault and the Grimms had subjected stories like "Little Red Riding Hood" and "Rapunzel" (the one story had featured a striptease performed for a lecherous wolf, the other a young woman wondering why her clothes were too tight after indulging in daily romps with a prince up in her

15

tower). Perrault's "Bluebeard" retained the dark mystery, suspense, and horror of versions told by adults to other adults around the fireside. It does not mince its words about the bloodied bodies in Bluebeard's chamber of horrors and invests much of its narrative energy in exposing the title figure's wife to terrors of extraordinary vividness and power.

Just who was Bluebeard and how did he get such a bad name? As Anatole France reminds us in his story "The Seven Wives of Bluebeard," Charles Perrault composed "the first biography of this *seigneur*" and established his reputation as an "accomplished villain" and the "most perfect model of cruelty that ever trod the earth."[12] Cultural historians have been quick to claim that Perrault's "Bluebeard" is based on fact, that it broadcasts the misdeeds of various noblemen, among them Cunmar of Brittany and Gilles de Rais.[13] But neither Cunmar the Accursed, who decapitated his pregnant wife, Triphine, nor Gilles de Rais, the marshal of France who was hanged in 1440 for murdering hundreds of children, presents himself as a definitive model for Bluebeard, though both were frequently invoked in nineteenth-century pantomimes and plays to assure audiences that there was a certain historical truth to the fairy-tale tyrant, and they continue to act as narrative magnets when the story is retold. With his ghoulish forbidden chamber and his magical key that betrays intruders, Bluebeard remains a figure constructed as a collective fantasy, even if some of his features are drawn from bits and pieces of historical realities that embed themselves in the folk narrative. Like the Russian Baba Yaga, the British giants, the glaestigs of the Scottish Highlands, or the rakshasas of India, he is firmly anchored in the domain of folkloric fright.

Perrault's "Bluebeard" recounts the story of a man's courtship and his marriage to a young woman whose desire for wealth conquers her feelings of revulsion for blue beards. After a month of married life, Bluebeard declares his intention to undertake a journey. In a seemingly magnanimous gesture, he gives his new bride keys that will open the rooms of the mansion and provide unlimited access to strongboxes holding gold and silver and to caskets filled with jewels. But he is not willing to share everything. Handing over the key to a small, remote chamber, he tells his wife: "Open anything you want. Go anywhere you wish. But I absolutely forbid you to enter that little room, and if you so much as open it a crack, there will be no limit to my anger."

"Plagued by curiosity," Bluebeard's wife does not wrestle long with her conscience: "The temptation was so great that she was unable to resist it." She opens the door to the forbidden chamber and finds a pool of clotted blood in which are reflected the bodies of Bluebeard's dead wives, hanging from the wall. Horrified, she drops the key and is unable to re-

Figure 1. Anonymous, *Bluebeard, or the Fatal Effects of Curiosity and Disobedience*, 1808. Bluebeard's wife is horrified by the sight of her five predecessors, whose well-preserved heads are posed on a table, each neatly labeled. Note that the wife wears Oriental dress, while the five wives, some with smiles on their faces, have Western hairstyles and hair ornaments. The spiderlike hands of the wife heighten the horrific effects.

move the telltale bloodstain left on it. Bluebeard returns home to discover the evidence of his wife's transgression and is about to execute her for her act of disobedience, when his wife's brothers, summoned by "Sister Anne" (who has evidently been in the mansion all along), come to the rescue and cut him down with their swords.

Perrault's "Bluebeard" frames the conflict between husband and wife as a conflict between the familiar and the strange, between the family (mother, sister, and two brothers) and a foreigner (one whose blue beard marks him as an exotic outsider). From the start, mother and sisters alike are resistant to the thought of marriage to a man "so ugly and terrifying that there was not a woman or girl who did not run away from him."

Figure 2. Harry Clarke, "Bluebeard," 1922. Bluebeard gazes intently at the viewer from his perch at the apex of a triangle formed by the faces and elaborate hairstyles of his wives and other aristocrats. Bluebeard's imposing qualities are further emphasized by the sinister flow of his beard, which reaches down to the floral decoration forming the lower border.

But seduced by Bluebeard's wealth and power, the younger of the two girls resolves to marry. It is also she who turns to her family for rescue, first to "Sister Anne," pleading with her to keep watch for the two brothers who were to visit her that very day. Sister Anne receives a reward for her services in the form of a dowry; the brothers are promoted to the rank of captain after their sister pays their commissions. This is a narrative that has less at stake in a successful resolution to the marriage plot than in a serene closure that installs the heroine's immediate family in comfortable material circumstances.

Perrault's title raises immediate questions. What is the significance of the blue beard to the husband, to the wife, and to their story? Although the color blue is encoded today with powerful cultural associations—it is often seen as the color of the marvelous, the distant, the dreamy, and the exotic—it no doubt resonated with earlier readers in a different way.

From Michel Pastoureau's magisterial study of the color blue, we know that, during the eleventh and twelfth centuries, the color blue experienced a stunning rise in its fortunes. No longer considered a "second-rate color" as it had been in antiquity, blue came to be considered both "aristocratic" and "fashionable." The French monarchy contributed in powerful ways to the developing taste for blue by using the color in its coat of arms, at coronation ceremonies, and at jousts and tournaments, and thereby turning it into what Pastoureau calls "the color of kings, princes, nobles, and patricians."[14] The "blue" beard of Charles Perrault's fairy-tale figure can be seen as a mark of aristocracy, a sign that this man of means is affiliated with royalty and aristocracy, with both the kings of fairy tales and the royalty of seventeenth-century France. Although Perrault's Bluebeard is not designated as an aristocrat, his literary progeny were, in many cases, elevated to the knighthood ("Ritter Blaubart" becomes a standard German designation for Bluebeard, with "Ritter" the equivalent of "Knight"). One critic has seen Bluebeard's elevation in social rank as symptomatic of a growing desire to politicize Perrault's story and to define Bluebeard's tyranny in class terms. The bluebearded tyrant becomes, in the course of the nineteenth century, an aristocratic blueblood.[15]

The beardedness of Perrault's celebrated autocrat is also revealing. As Marina Warner tells us, beards were "well out of fashion in the court of the Sun King," and Bluebeard's facial hair signals his status as "an outsider, a libertine, and a ruffian." *Barbe* itself seems related to *barbare*, or barbarian, even if etymological investigations do not bear out the connection. Beards, as Warner further notes, came increasingly "to define the male in a priapic mode," and for her, Bluebeard's name "stirs associations with sex, virility, male readiness and desire."[16]

"Bluebeard" deviates from fairy-tale norms by turning the groom into an agent of villainy. Most fairy tales that end in marriage begin with families in crisis, in homes that prove inhospitable, with hostile parents and siblings. Mothers, fathers, and same-sex siblings often seem more interested in stirring up trouble, creating conflicts, and standing in the way of a happy marriage than in facilitating a "happily ever after" ending. Whether we consider Snow White's mother (turned into a stepmother in the Grimms' version of the story), Cinderella's stepsisters, Donkeyskin's father, or Beauty's sisters, it becomes clear that the path to a happy marriage is paved with maternal envy, sibling rivalry, and paternal lust. "Bluebeard," unlike the fairy tales that form an acknowledged part of our cultural heritage, turns the groom into the source of danger and endorses fidelity to parents and siblings even as it writes large the theme of marital infidelity.

Folklorists have shown surprising interpretive confidence in reading Perrault's "Bluebeard" as a story about a woman's failure to respond to the trust invested in her. The homicidal history of the husband often takes a back seat to the disobedience of the wife. "Bloody key as sign of disobedience"—this is the motif that folklorists consistently single out as the defining moment of the tale. The bloodstained key points to a double transgression, one that is both moral and sexual. For one critic it becomes a sign of "marital infidelity"; for another it marks the heroine's "irreversible loss of her virginity"; for a third it stands as a sign of "defloration."[17] If we recall that the bloody chamber in Bluebeard's mansion is strewn with the corpses of previous wives, this reading of the bloodstained key as a marker of sexual infidelity becomes willfully wrong-headed in its effort to vilify Bluebeard's wife. Furthermore, as one shrewd reader points out, "Blue Beard wanted his new wife to find the corpses of his former wives. He *wanted* the new bride to discover their mutilated corpses; he *wanted* her disobedience. Otherwise he wouldn't have given her the key to the forbidden closet; he wouldn't have left on his so-called business trip; and he wouldn't have stashed the dead Mrs. Blue Beards in the closet in the first place. Transparently, it was a setup."[18]

And yet from the start, the finger of blame has unmistakably pointed in the direction of Bluebeard's wife. Perrault's "Bluebeard" highlights the curiosity of its female protagonist in a number of ways. First of all, the wife loses no time getting to the room forbidden to her. While her frivolous female neighbors are busy proving themselves to be true daughters of Eve by rummaging through closets, admiring themselves in full-length mirrors, and declaring their feelings of envy for so much wealth, Bluebeard's wife is "so overcome with curiosity" that she nearly breaks her neck running down the stairs to open the door prohibited to her. Although she does briefly reflect on the harm that could come to her "as a result of disobedience," she quickly succumbs to "temptation" and opens the door. Here is what she sees: "The floor was entirely covered with clotted blood, and . . . in it were reflected the dead bodies of several women that hung along the walls. These were all the wives of Bluebeard, whose throats he had cut, one after another."

Perrault devotes a good deal of space to judgmental asides about the envy, greed, curiosity, and disobedience of Bluebeard's wife and her intimates, but he remains diffident about framing any sort of indictment of a man who has cut the throats of his wives. To be sure, it may seem superfluous to comment on Bluebeard's character once the corpses of his wives come to light, but, unless we take the view that this is a story of "dangerous curiosity and justifiable homicide" (as does one nineteenth-

Figure 3. Anonymous, illustration for U.S. children's book, circa 1950. "The young wife turns the forbidden key / And, horror of horrors! what does she see? / The luckless victims of Bluebeard's crime, / But she herself is rescued in time." The youthful wife is about to enter the forbidden chamber. Her diminutive figure, which suggests a child rather than a young woman, tells us that the tale could be oriented toward children, reminding them of the perils of curiosity and disobedience.

century British playwright), the censorious attitude toward the curiosity of Bluebeard's wife seems more than odd.[19] What is at stake in this story, Perrault suggests, is the inquisitive instinct of the wife rather than the homicidal impulses of the husband.

In her short story "The Key," Luisa Valenzuela gives us the thoughts of Bluebeard's wife as she muses on how Perrault and others distorted her

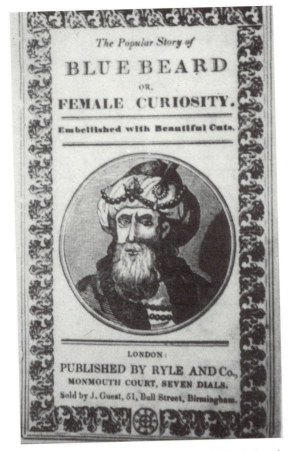

Figure 4. The Popular Story of Bluebeard or, Female Curiosity, circa 1850. The cover to this chapbook portrays a turbaned Bluebeard, whose story discloses his brush with female curiosity. Note how the "beautiful cuts" that "embellish" the book suggest the pleasures of the horror genre.

motives and turned her salutary inquisitiveness into a sin of indulgence: "Sacred curiosity, an ephemeral pleasure!" she declares with indignation. ". . . The curiosity that saved me forever when my lord went off on a journey, leaving me with a huge bunch of keys and forbidding me on pain of death to use the smallest of them, the curiosity that drove me to uncover the mystery of the locked room."[20] This is a heroine who recognizes that ignorance is not bliss, that it might not be wise to live in a castle "with a

Figure 5. French broadsheet, circa 1840. Traditionally used to broadcast the deeds of criminals, the broadsheet in this case takes up a fictional criminal, and illustrates his story with a scene that offers a panoramic view of Sister Anne up in the tower, the brothers coming to the rescue, and Bluebeard with raised sword, about to execute his wife. The right column offers an analysis of the tale that takes the form of advice to parents. It concludes by telling parents that the illustrated scene will leave a "profound impression" on children, warning them to resist the temptations of curiosity.

room full of dead women hanging from hooks on the walls, their throats slit, living with the man who had been the husband of those women." To those who insist that the wives were all "victims of their own curiosity," Bluebeard's last wife suggests that they consider the fate of the first wife: "What was the first one curious about, what could she have seen?"

While Anatole France tells us that Bluebeard was drawn as a "perfect model of cruelty," it was his wife who came to be positioned as a perfect model of disobedience and infidelity. Was Perrault's story, as the evidence suggests, complicit in vilifying the wife, or have critics of the story conspired to turn her into a figure who, looking for trouble, ends up creating it? Perrault, who recognized the entertainment value of the stories between the pages of *Tales of Mother Goose*, believed that the tales had a mission beyond mere diversion. In his preface to the collection, he made it clear that each tale had a "concealed lesson" embedded in it. To ensure that those lessons were not buried so deeply that readers might fail to unearth them, Perrault added "moralités" of his own—moral glosses cast in heavy-handed doggerel. "Bluebeard," as it turns out, was a tricky case, one so symptomatic of how fairy tales send mixed messages that Perrault, perhaps unwittingly, crafted what appear to be two very different readings of his own story.

The first of the two morals concerns the perils of curiosity and points out the high price of satisfying that urge. Curiosity is coded as a feminine trait, one that has its "attractions," not the least of which is the "pleasure" it provides. The moral encapsulates a concise cost/benefit analysis, pointing out that the high price for satisfying curiosity never compensates for the small dose of pleasure afforded by it. Restraint, constructed as the product of reason and logic, is consequently affiliated with the authority of the male narrator, who has marked its opposite as a supremely feminine trait.

The other moral appended to "Bluebeard" is less a moral than a disavowal of any lessons transmitted about husbands. If women's curiosity formed the subject of the first moral, men's behavior would logically serve as the subject of the second moral. One would hence expect a commentary on Bluebeard's vices to follow the meditation on the failings of his wife. While the wife's curiosity is seen as a quintessentially feminine trait, Bluebeard's behavior is framed as exceptional, deviating from the norm of masculine behavior. The second moral insists that no husband today has the "terrifying" qualities of a Bluebeard. It invalidates the notion that men could draw any lessons at all from his behavior. Quite to the contrary, men today are obliged to ingratiate themselves with their wives, and, these days, it is not hard to tell which of the two is "master."

Perrault's two morals are not only nearly mutually exclusive (the one prescribing correct conduct by endorsing a limit to women's "innate" desire for knowledge, the other proclaiming that women are free agents and reign supreme), they are also not at all congruent with the story's plot. But for Perrault, it was not unusual to preach about matters not practiced in the tales. We need only turn to his "Donkeyskin," a tale about a girl who has to ward off her father's incestuous advances, to get a clear sense of how the lessons attached to the tales of Mother Goose do not square with the facts of each plot. Here is the conclusion to the account of Donkeyskin's flight from her father and of her marriage to a prince:

> Evidently, the moral of this tale implies it is better for a child to expose oneself to hardships than to neglect one's duty.
>
> Indeed, virtue may sometimes seem ill fated, but it is always crowned with success. Of course, reason, even at its strongest, is a weak dike against mad love and ardent ecstasy, especially if a lover is not afraid to squander rich treasures.
>
> Finally, we must take into account that clear water and brown bread are sufficient nourishment for all young women provided that they have good habits, and that there is not a damsel under the skies who does not imagine herself beautiful.

What we have here can hardly be described as a clear sense of the moral drift to the tale. The narrator not only frantically disavows the issue of incest and the daughter's courage in deflecting her father's amorous advances, but also dismantles the notion that the story has any message at all by engaging in self-parody through the proliferation of irrelevant messages.

In "Bluebeard," Perrault uses a somewhat different strategy to undermine the possibility of deriving a lesson from Bluebeard's behavior. He alludes to the title of his collection when he emphasizes that the story is a "tale from times past" ("un conte du temps passé"). Located in the distant past, it is irrelevant for contemporary audiences, since the relationship between husbands and wives today is so completely different from the time in which the story was set. Perrault's double move of affirming the seductive pleasures of curiosity for all women and emphasizing the uniquely brutal nature of a husband who lived a long time ago set the stage for the tale's illustrators, who appear to have heeded, in different ways, the advice embedded in the two morals.

"Bluebeard" and Its Illustrators

In the long and distinguished line of artists who illustrated Perrault's "Bluebeard," virtually none focused on the carnage in the forbidden chamber. What would seem to be the most spectacular scene in the story, the very scene that has aroused curiosity, is occluded and denied representation. Rather than drawing attention to the moment when curiosity is satisfied, illustrators portray either the arousal of curiosity or the excitement and dread awakened by the anticipation of satisfaction. The curious woman becomes the real curiosity, the figure that cries out for representation, and that also becomes the source of our attentive fascination and wonder. A figure of excess in her own right, she may not be able to compete with the breathtakingly morbid tableau beyond the door, but she nonetheless becomes something of a curiosity, if not of a monstrosity.[21]

Gustave Doré, the prolific nineteenth-century French artist who illustrated *The Divine Comedy*, the Bible, Shakespeare, and Poe, presents Bluebeard's wife as a young woman seduced by the desire for the forbidden. Bluebeard dominates the compositional space in the first of a series of four engravings to accompany Perrault's "Bluebeard," with one hand raised in a cautionary gesture, the other tendering the key to the prohibited chamber. Transfixed by the key, his wife encircles it with her two hands, oblivious to her husband's warnings. Even as Bluebeard and his wife fill the visual space and are almost joined in compositional terms, it is clear that the wife is on more intimate terms with the key than with her admonishing husband, who in turn seems fascinated by and fixated on the curiosity that his wife has become.

Dwarfed by sumptuous surroundings that include oversized candelabra, plates, tables, and suits of armor, Bluebeard's wife and her female companions manifest their collective curiosity as they peer behind draperies and open chests in Doré's second illustration for Perrault's story. The drawn sword on the left prefigures the risks of curiosity, while the open book next to the serpentine candelabra base could allude to the biblical tale concerning the consequences of curiosity. Here again, Doré, like many illustrators of the Bluebeard story, is at pains to take his cue from Perrault's first moral and to emphasize that this story is about, more than anything else, the perils of curiosity and how easily its seductive power takes hold of all women.

In two additional scenes, Doré illustrated the scene of rescue, showing the brothers of Bluebeard's wife galloping in the direction of the castle, from whose turrets Sister Anne waves her handkerchief. In a typically vast

Figure 6. Kay Nielsen, "Bluebeard," 1930. Kay Nielsen's gauntly sinister Bluebeard offers the key to a coquettish wife, who appears unaware of the sights awaiting her in the forbidden chamber. The perpendiculars formed by the flowing blue beard, the cane, the tassels, and the swordlike decoration on the left contrast with the semi-ovals of the wife's dress, fan, hat, and of the draperies. The flat, decorative surface, perhaps because of its stark contrasts, produces an eerie effect.

Figure 7.   Gustave Doré, "Bluebeard," 1861. Bluebeard hands his wife the one key that is forbidden to her, admonishing her, with upraised hand, not to use it. The wife's attraction to the forbidden object is readily apparent, for her eyes are riveted to it as her hands reach out for it. Bluebeard, his eyes bulging with curiosity about his wife's reaction to the key, dominates the canvas with his robes and feathered hat.

Figure 8. Gustave Doré, "Bluebeard," 1861. Two women, presumably Blue-beard's wife and a companion, demonstrate the effects of female curiosity as they pry open a chest in search of treasure, while a third, nearly hidden from view behind them, peers behind draperies. The massive furnishings and clutter produce a claustrophobic atmosphere that turns ominous at the sight of the sword leaning against the table. The candelabra with its metallic snake and the open book held up to view by two sculpted figures suggests possible connec-tions to the biblical tale of Eve's transgressive curiosity.

and majestic landscape, the brothers penetrate the dark spaces of the forest surrounding Bluebeard's castle. At the castle, the brothers plunge their swords into Bluebeard's back, while their sister nearly expires with fear in the background. A gargoyle with breasts is positioned above a decorative sword penetrating a heart and encircled by a snake, which seems to signify the marriage of love, treachery, and violence in this tale. Doré's illustrations, with their technical sophistication and iconographic density, clearly address an adult audience, one that will be attuned to the marital issues at stake in the story and will recognize how curiosity and monstrosity are wedded in the figure of husband and wife.

Walter Crane published his illustrations to "Bluebeard" in the popular series *Walter Crane's Toy Books*, just sixteen years after Doré's *Tales of Mother Goose* had appeared in Paris in 1859. Crane's Bluebeard, like Doré's, is presented as an aristocrat, a nobleman who is both "rich and grand." The British illustrator seems to have been inspired by Doré's temptation scene, for he too shows husband and wife in an intimate moment, with the husband observing the wife's fascination with the keys offered to her. Again the raised finger, the warning, and the arousal of desire.

In Crane's next illustration, Bluebeard's wife is shown, key in hand, on her way to the forbidden chamber. She descends the stairs, her body framed by a tapestry depicting Eve face-to-face with the serpent while she is picking an apple from the Tree of Knowledge. In the background, six of the wife's companions, driven by the desire to penetrate the secrets of enclosed spaces, rummage through trunks, inspect the contents of cabinets, admire themselves in mirrors, and explore the deepest recesses of the mansion. "Succumbing to temptation" is the "sin of the fall, the sin of Eve," one representative critical voice asserts. A nineteenth-century Scottish version of the tale summarizes in its title what appears to be the collective critical wisdom on this tale: "The Story of Bluebeard, or, the effects of female curiosity."[22]

Although we never see the "horrid sight" that meets the eyes of Bluebeard's wife, we witness her reaction to what is described in the narrative accompanying the illustrations: "For there upon the floor was blood, and on the walls were wives, / For Bluebeard first had married them, then cut their throats with knives." Less expressive than most wives of Bluebeard, Crane's figure seems almost serene as she absorbs the horrifying spectacle of the dead wives.

In Crane's interpretation of the story, Bluebeard becomes increasingly demonic in visual terms. His first appearance marks him as a sophisticated, elegantly dressed nobleman, whose charming smile suggests benevolence rather than malice. But when he is seized by the brothers who rush

Figure 9. Gustave Doré, "Bluebeard," 1861. Summoned by Sister Anne, the brothers of Bluebeard's wife are seen charging toward the castle to rescue their sister. Undaunted by the rocky landscape and the seemingly impenetrable façade of Bluebeard's castle, the brothers raise clouds of dust.

31

Figure 10.   Gustave Doré, "Bluebeard," 1861. Bluebeard's wife is paralyzed by fear, while her two brothers plunge their swords into her husband's back. A gargoyle observes the murder with disapproval, while below him, a sword penetrating a heart and entwined by a serpent adds a macabre decorative touch.

in with their swords and are about to "cut the murderer down," he takes on the stereotypical features of the wicked Jew, bearded, robed, hook nosed, with satanic furrows in his brow. The sandy-haired assailants, despite their actions, stand in sharp physiognomic contrast to Bluebeard.

If there was any strategy at all to the efforts of nineteenth-century illustrators to align Bluebeard with aristocrats, devils, and Jews, it was no doubt to distance the "ordinary man" from the kind of behavior manifested by Perrault's villain.[23] Perrault, in assuring us that Bluebeard's behavior could only have happened "once upon a time," also created a link to what became in France the supreme trope for "once upon a time": *The Thousand and One Nights*, which had captured the imagination of the Continent beginning in 1704, when Antoine Galland published the first

BLUEBEARD.

ONCE on a time there lived a man
    hated by all he knew,
Both that his ways were very bad,
    and that his beard was blue;
But as he was so rich and grand, and
    led a merry life,
A lady he contrived at last to induce
    to be his wife.

Figure 11.   "Bluebeard." *Walter Crane's Toy Books*, 1875. Bluebeard, "a man hated by all he knew," hands his wife the keys to his mansion, pointing to the one for the forbidden chamber. Note that Crane's Bluebeard is represented as a European nobleman, rather than as an Oriental despot.

For a month after the wedding they
  lived and had good cheer,
And then said Bluebeard to his wife,
  "I'll say good-bye, my dear;
" Indeed, it is but for six weeks that I
  shall be away,
" I beg that you'll invite your friends,
  and feast and dance and play;
" And all my property I'll leave con-
  fided to your care:
" Here are the keys of all my chests,
  there's plenty and to spare.

Figure 12. "Bluebeard." *Walter Crane's Toy Books*, 1875. Bluebeard's wife, key in hand, rushes down the stairs, while her fellow sisters of Eve explore the contents of chests and cabinets, admire themselves in mirrors, and enter distant chambers. Behind Bluebeard's wife is a tapestry showing Eve being tempted by the serpent in the Garden of Eden.

"But this small key belongs to one small
    room on the ground-floor,—
"And this you must not open, or you
    will repent it sore."
And so he went; and all the friends
    came there from far and wide,
And in her wealth the lady took much
    happiness and pride;
But in a while this kind of joy grew
    nearly satisfied,

Figure 13. "Bluebeard." *Walter Crane's Toy Books*, 1875. Bluebeard's wife, whose joy "grew nearly satisfied" by her husband's wealth, peers into the forbidden chamber. She will see a "horrid sight": the women whose throats Bluebeard has cut and whom he has hung from the walls.

Figure 14. "Bluebeard." *Walter Crane's Toy Books*, 1875. Bluebeard's wife, confronted with the blood-stained key, begs her husband for mercy. Sister Anne can be seen, dressed in a flowing pink gown, about to summon the brothers of Bluebeard's wife.

volume of his French translation. Although it took nearly two centuries for the English translation to appear—Sir Richard Burton's translation did not appear until 1885—chapbook versions of tales from *The Thousand and One Nights* appeared in English within a year or so of Galland's translation. And so it is small wonder that Bluebeard—as he entered the twentieth century, though also even earlier—was resettled in the Orient, complete with robe, turban, and scimitar. As a serial murderer of wives, Bluebeard could be easily aligned with King Schahriyar, who plans to murder successive wives on his wedding night but is dissuaded from this practice by Scheherazade.

That Bluebeard was repeatedly associated with the Near and Far East becomes evident from Andrew Lang's insistence, in the introduction to *The Blue Fairy Book*, that "Monsieur de la Barbe Bleue was *not* a Turk!" "One of the ladies' brothers was a Dragoon, the other a Mousquetaire, of M. d'Artagnan's company perhaps," he added. "They were all French

Figure 15. "Bluebeard." *Walter Crane's Toy Books*, 1875. Sister Anne searches the horizon in vain for the brothers. Note that Bluebeard's crest contains a key, a keyhole, and a sword dripping with blood.

Figure 16. "Bluebeard." *Walter Crane's Toy Books*, 1875. Bluebeard, his wife, Sister Anne, and the brothers appear together in this scene, all except Bluebeard's wife with raised arm. Note that the coat-of-arms has changed to include a gallows rather than a keyhole.

And just as Bluebeard's cruel blade was
  descending on her head,
In rushed the brothers with their swords,—
  they cut the murderer down,
And saved their sister's life, and gained
  much glory and renown;
And then they all with gold and plate and
  jewels rare made free,
And ever after lived content on Bluebeard's property.

Figure 17. "Bluebeard." *Walter Crane's Toy Books,* 1875. Bluebeard's brothers "cut the murderer down," while Sister Anne comes to the aid of Bluebeard's wife behind the curtain. Note that Bluebeard's features have changed somewhat to become more diabolical and that he now appears as the stereotypical Jew.

folk and Christians; had he been a Turk, Blue Beard need not have wedded to but one wife at a time."[24] These remarks, published in 1889, fell on deaf ears, for illustrators found Bluebeard's connection to the Orient congenial to producing lavishly exotic costumes and settings.

Edmund Dulac, whose illustrations for "Bluebeard" in Arthur Quiller-Couch's *The Sleeping Beauty, and Other Fairy Tales from the Old French* (1910) cemented the connection between Bluebeard and the Orient, had built his reputation as an illustrator with images for the *Arabian Nights*. The first of his seven illustrations for Quiller-Couch's retelling of Perrault's story shows a turbaned Bluebeard assisting a wife with European features into a barque floating on his private canal. Fatima, who is finally given a name in Quiller-Couch's version, is depicted in haremlike surroundings.[25] One of four women in Bluebeard's mansion, she and her companions luxuriate in a posh setting that suggests a state of quiet languor.

Unlike Doré and Crane, Dulac does not take us to the threshold of the forbidden chamber. Instead he takes us inside the room containing the corpses of Bluebeard's previous wives. But Dulac does not let us view the scene through Fatima's eyes. We see Bluebeard's wife as witness to the grim spectacle behind the door, and the carnage is hidden from view. The keyhole view of Fatima, who is illuminated from behind by the light issuing from the door, produces a compelling visual effect in the beauty of its composition and colors. An alluring snapshot, it captures Bluebeard's wife with a look of dread written over her face and gives us the obverse of the grotesque scene of corpses hanging from the walls.

Dulac's remaining scenes show the Oriental tyrant in all his fury and his wife in a state of apprehension. Bluebeard towers over his dainty wife, determined to add Fatima to his chamber of horrors. She, in turn, summons Sister Anne, who has retained her European appellation, while Bluebeard, wielding his scimitar, orders his wife downstairs for her execution. In an architectural setting that is classical rather than Oriental, Bluebeard's brothers pursue the husband and slay him as he tumbles down a staircase.

When Arthur Rackham turned his hand to the Bluebeard story, he too moved its location from France to eastern regions. His famous silhouette of a turbaned Bluebeard shaking his fist at his wife who in turn beseeches Sister Anne to look out for her brothers gives us delicate latticework and eastern turrets that create the effect of a story from the *Arabian Nights* rather than from a French anthology. Rackham, more skillfully than any other artist, also depicted, in another illustration, the excitement, energy, and desire that draw Bluebeard's wife to the forbidden chamber. With a furtive look on her face showing that she is as anxious about transgression as she is eager to engage in it, Bluebeard's wife turns the key in the

Figure 18. Edmund Dulac, "Bluebeard," 1910. "They were rowed to the sound of music on the waters of their host's private canal." In this orientalized illustration for Charles Perrault's story, Bluebeard's wife, with her richly textured layers of clothing, enters a gondola filled with sumptuous cushions. Bluebeard's realm is marked by voluptuous beauty and sensual delights, but the apprehensive looks of the wife's attendants and the stern wooden carving on the gondola suggest that there may be trouble in paradise.

Figure 19. Edmund Dulac, "Bluebeard," 1910. "They overran the house without loss of time." Looking more like a harem than a party of young women at a French country manor, Bluebeard's wife and her guests savor the opulence provided by a wealthy husband. The sensual flow of the fabrics, the rounded shapes (the bowl of fruit, the parrot's perch, and the vast white oval on the wall), and the soft pastels suggest a state of quiet languor and aesthetic delight that contrasts sharply with the social energy described by Perrault in his version of the story.

Figure 20. Edmund Dulac, "Bluebeard," 1910. "And there, in a room, hung the bodies of seven dead women." Rooted to the spot, Bluebeard's wife contemplates the bodies of her husband's previous wives. The dimly lit room is illuminated by light from behind the door, and, despite the enchanted setting with white pillars, delicate curtains, and azure walls, the palace is the site of horrors. The floor of the room reveals the bloody deeds that have taken place.

Figure 21. Edmund Dulac, "Bluebeard," 1910. "You SHALL go in and take your place among the ladies you saw there." A frightened Bluebeard's wife has dropped the keys to the castle as she faces a death threat from her massively proportioned husband, who wears an oversized turban that inflates his height and power to intimidate. The Western-style architecture and landscape forms a sharp contrast to the orientalized dress of the two figures.

Figure 22. Edmund Dulac, "Bluebeard," 1910. "The unhappy FATIMA cried up to her:—'Anne, Sister Anne, do you see anyone coming?' " Although Bluebeard's wife is given an Arabic name in the version of the story illustrated by Dulac, Sister Anne retains her European Christian name. Leaning over the railing, Bluebeard's wife looks up in desperation to the tower, where the sister is searching the horizon for a glimpse of the brothers, who were planning a visit for that very day.

45

Figure 23. Edmund Dulac, "Bluebeard," 1910. "Then BLUEBEARD roared out so terribly that he made the whole house tremble." Wielding the scimitar with which he plans to execute his wife, Bluebeard summons her, ordering her to prepare for her death. The dry leaves on the branches repeat the color of Bluebeard's robes, and the gathering clouds intensify the sense of desolation at the site where the wife is to meet her doom.

Figure 24. Edmund Dulac, "Bluebeard," 1910. "They overtook him as he reached the steps of the main porch." With bloodied swords, the brothers of Bluebeard's wife pursue the villain and catch up with him as he desperately wards off their assaults.

lock and is about to push open the door that will reveal her husband's dark crimes.

The extravagant attention paid to the scene of temptation and to the scene of disobedience in "Bluebeard" seems to have exhausted the ability of illustrators to portray what might otherwise be considered a scene that invites visual representation. The German artist Hermann Vogel produced in 1887 one of the few scenes that disclosed what Bluebeard's wife finds in the bloody chamber. Capturing a moment of shock, he showed the key falling from her hand as she sets eyes on the corpses hung on the walls, as if on display. Vogel gives us six previous wives, the standard number once a French variant of Perrault's tale established the seventh wife as the tale's protagonist.[26] A chopping block and ax in the foreground reveal the scene of the crimes that reflect Bluebeard as a master in the art of murder.

Whose Story Is It?

"Bluebeard and His Seven Wives," the title of Anatole France's Bluebeard story, alerts us to the centrality of the bloodthirsty protagonist, whose nameless wives remain in his orbit, without real identities. Yet although most folktales and literary versions of "Bluebeard" identify only the villain by name, the story, as we know from Stephen King's *The Shining*, is intuitively seen as focusing on the wife. When Danny, the clairvoyant child in King's novel, reflects on the Bluebeard story, he notes: "Actually the story was about Bluebeard's wife, a pretty lady that had corn-colored hair like Mommy."[27] That view is supported by other commentators on the story, who point out that, even if the tale has two subjects, its "rightful protagonist" is the wife.[28] The ethical issues connected with Bluebeard's wife—disobedience, betrayal of trust, intrusiveness—have repeatedly preoccupied critics, who associate her disruptive behavior with the transgressive acts of Pandora, Eve, Psyche, and all those other mythical, biblical, and folkloric women who seem to be too curious for their own good or for the good of the human race.

While the wife may appear to occupy the "moral center" of Bluebeard tales, she is in some ways the story's protagonist only by default: "Any interest we have in the story lies with its villain," Lydia Millet tells us.[29] What arouses our curiosity, she insists, is both the character who has something to hide and the secret that he is harboring. The villain and his bloodthirsty deeds, in other words, have a narrative verve that exceeds that of the prospective victim and her act of defiance. Folktales never let us see inside the minds of their protagonists, but given the choice to read

Figure 25.   Arthur Rackham, "Bluebeard," 1919. A young woman with European features, Bluebeard's wife appears both wary and eager as she tests the key and is about to open the door forbidden to her. That door, made of wood and quite ordinary, contrasts with the other ornate openings in the architectural space. The illuminated background offers the promise of a revelation.

Figure 26. Arthur Rackham, "Bluebeard," 1919. Arthur Rackham's silhouette provides a fascinating cross section of Bluebeard's palace, with the husband demanding that the wife descend to her execution, the wife straining to learn if her brothers are on the way, and Sister Anne surveying the horizon for the brothers.

the mind of either Bluebeard or his wife, most readers would elect to enter the taboo regions of Bluebeard's thoughts.

"Don't you put the past in a room, in a cellar, and lock the door and just never go in there? Because that's what I do," Tom Ripley tells his friend Peter in the screenplay *The Talented Mr. Ripley.*[30] To survive, flourish, and thrive, Tom must somehow repress the two murders he has committed. That he uses the metaphor of the mind as a house, with the cellar as the space for what he wants to repress, is not at all unusual. As Mark Edmundson points out, Freud had suggested long ago "that the psyche was a house, specifically a haunted old Victorian manse," and in that metaphor, the basement becomes the perfect site for storing what is unwelcome in public spaces.[31]

When Tom embellishes the metaphor, it becomes evident how common it is to think of intimacy in terms of providing a key to a locked room containing repressed psychic material: "Then you meet someone special and all you want to do is toss them the key, say *open up, step inside,* but

50

Figure 27. Hermann Vogel, "Bluebeard," 1887. In a state of shock when she discovers her husband's wives, hanging from the wall as if on display, Bluebeard's wife drops the key to the forbidden chamber. The chopping block and ax in the foreground reveal the manner of the murders, and the blood on the floor will leave a tell-tale stain on the key that has fallen to the ground.

Figure 28. Otto Brausewetter, "Bluebeard," 1865. With keys dangling from her waist, Bluebeard's wife recoils in horror at the sight of the mutilated bodies of her husband's previous wives in a tub. An ax leaning against the tub reveals the murder weapon.

you can't because it's dark and there are demons and if anybody saw how ugly it was . . . ." Tom Ripley perfectly articulates the double-edged nature of Bluebeard's offer of a key to his wife. In making the gesture, Bluebeard establishes intimacy and trust at the same time that he presents an instrument that invites disobedience and betrayal. "I keep wanting to do that," Ripley insists. "Fling open the door—let the light in, clean everything out. If I could get a huge eraser and rub everything out . . . starting with myself." What Ripley realizes, of course, is that you can give someone the key, but that the room may need to be tidied up or cleaned out before its contents can be displayed to a partner. He concludes by grasping that the cleansing actually implies self-eradication, for the contents of that cellar represent the very foundations of his mental world.

The metaphor that Tom Ripley uses to characterize his inner life is literalized as a physical space in folkloric versions of Bluebeard. The importance of that space is underlined by the title of Béla Bartók's opera *Bluebeard's Castle*, a work in which the castle becomes a haunted third protagonist in the fairy-tale plot. Harboring the forbidden chamber storing Bluebeard's secrets and inspiring the wife to uncover those secrets, the dwelling becomes the site of mystery and morbid fascination. In Bartók's opera, it actually weeps and sighs under the weight of its horrifying secrets, becoming an architectural embodiment of its owner's mind, the outside of Bluebeard's inside. If fairy tales cannot take us inside the minds of their protagonists, they easily compensate for that expressive lack by externalizing feelings in actions, settings, and props. Just as Gothic plots literalize Freudian concepts of how the psyche operates, a fairy tale like "Bluebeard" can stage the intricate workings of the mind, making manifest what is usually hidden from view.

Just whose story, then, is it? Is "Bluebeard" a cautionary tale with a moral pointed toward the wife? Is it a story of suspense focusing on the husband's mysterious past? Is it a "double-plotted narrative" about two people who mirror each other in their use of duplicity?[32] Or is it a psychological thriller located in the mansion of the mind? As we shall see, that issue has been hotly contested and has divided readers and rewriters into several distinct camps, each with its own interpretive spin on the story. Yet "Bluebeard" can also be viewed, in a compromise solution, as a story with an impassioned social purpose, a mission to broadcast what can go wrong in marriage. Situating us squarely in the domestic arena, from the honeymoon to the first lovers' quarrel, it stands virtually alone among our canonical fairy tales in its negation of a "happily ever after" ending. It gives us an up-close-and-personal view of marriage, confirming everything we didn't want to know and were afraid to ask about it.

If most fairy tales do not take us beyond the words "happily ever after," it is in part because marriage is, in some ways, an institution haunted by the threat of boredom. When we say that a story ends with marriage, we imply that marriage offers closure, balancing out the highs and lows of the courtship plot and producing a state of narrative equilibrium, one destined to have tedium as its inevitable affective outcome. "Bluebeard" addresses the problematics of "happily ever after," challenging the notion of postmarital stability and interrogating issues that have unsettled the institution of marriage in a variety of times and places. Dismantling the myth of "happily ever after," it raises a multitude of specters haunting the institution of marriage.

The questions taken up by the story can be encapsulated in two phrases that define men as "having something to hide" and women as "wanting to know too much." The term "Bluebeard" has come to signify a roué, a rake, or a libertine, and Bluebeard's wife, as we shall see, is regularly associated with curiosity, nosiness, and prying. The friction that develops between experienced men and inquisitive women accounts for the sparks thrown by the story over the centuries.[33] If husbands in these marriage plots are threatened with discovery, the wives are equally imperiled by a sense of betrayal. These are the issues that, with all their rich figurative and literal variations and their sudden reversals, have kept the story alive as a vehicle for thinking about questions of trust and fidelity in marriage. Should a man's past be laid to rest or does it inform and color his present? When does curiosity shade into snooping and a form of prying that undermines trust? How do two people establish a relationship of which the touchstone is fidelity?

"Bluebeard" versus "Beauty and the Beast"

That Bluebeard takes a bow in virtually every one of the great national fairy-tale collections compiled in the nineteenth century offers evidence that the story's preoccupations had a powerful hold on the imagination of our ancestors. Whether we leaf through Perrault's *Tales of Mother Goose*, thumb the pages of the Grimms' *Children's Stories and Household Tales*, browse in Joseph Jacobs's *English Fairy Tales*, or pore over Alexander Afanasev's *Russian Fairy Tales*, Bluebeard is there with his forbidden chamber of horrors, as if to give the lie to the myth of romantic love broadcast by other tales in those collections.

Fairy-tale anthologies from the nineteenth century suggest that the story of Bluebeard was once at least as prominent a tale type as "Beauty and the Beast." While the one tale takes us beyond marriage, showing how a man can turn into a figurative beast, the other unfolds during the period of courtship, revealing how a real beast can have warm human qualities. "Beauty and the Beast," like "Cinderella," "Snow White," and other classic fairy tales, begins with an unhappy situation at home, centers on a romantic quest, and ends in visions of marital bliss.

"Bluebeard" represents a troubling flip side to "Beauty and the Beast," that quintessentially reassuring story that, according to the psychologist Bruno Bettelheim, relieves the "anxious sexual fantasies" to which children are prey. "While sex may at first seem beastlike," Bettelheim declares, "in reality love between woman and man is the most satisfying of all emotions, and the only one that makes for permanent happiness."[34] "Bluebeard," by contrast, confirms a child's "worst fears about sex," for it places the marriage partner in the functional position usually reserved for the villain, ogre, or monster of the tale and shows marriage as an institution charged with life-threatening perils.

The "permanent happiness" promised by the myth of perfect romantic love in "Beauty and the Beast" is clearly more appealing than the disturbing anxieties about love and marriage articulated in "Bluebeard." "Beauty and the Beast," with its messages about the transformative power of compassion, makes for better bedtime reading, and that fact alone may explain the apparent erosion of cultural interest in "Bluebeard" in the United States. But while "Bluebeard" may have disappeared from the nursery, it has retained its power as a narrative for adults, as a story that challenges the myth of romantic love and acknowledges the realities of marital life.

Gaston Leroux's *Phantom of the Opera*, the nineteenth-century French novel on which the hit Broadway musical was based, reveals under what conditions "Beauty and the Beast" can modulate into "Bluebeard" and does much to explain why we prefer the one fairy tale to the other. Erik, the "monster" and "beast" who rules the Paris opera house, is so frightfully ugly that his own mother required him to wear a mask. As the Angel of Music, he woos the singer Christine Daaé, telling her: "Love me and you shall see. . . . If you loved me I should be as gentle as a lamb; and you could do anything with me that you pleased."[35] In the end, Christine is unable to translate compassion into the kind of passion required for marriage. Refusing to play Beauty to the Phantom's Beast, she turns into an "inquisitive" woman who first rips off the Phantom's mask, then seeks to enter his forbidden chamber. "I want to look at this room which I have never seen and which you have always kept from me. . . . It's a woman's curiosity" (294–95), Christine says in a playful tone, hoping to cajole Erik into compliance so that she can end his murderous streak. But when Erik recognizes that his Beauty has turned into a wife of Bluebeard, he retorts: "I don't like curious women, and you had better remember the story of *Blue-Beard* and be careful." "Beauty and the Beast" gives us a story in which compassion breaks the spell of monstrosity to produce a happy couple; "Bluebeard" shows us a woman so determined to discover her husband's dark secrets that she risks becoming twin monster to her husband.

It may be tempting to favor stories that stage the joys of heterosexual unions over grisly stories about murderous husbands, but it is important to understand the ways in which we have preserved our cultural memory of "Bluebeard," despite its virtual effacement in popular consciousness by the competing myth of "Beauty and the Beast." Why do writers, artists, and filmmakers keep repeating a story that seems to have slipped out of our collective cultural consciousness?

The tale of Bluebeard, one could argue, has a social logic that was probably more compelling for earlier cultures than for our own. Anxious fantasies about sex and marriage would hardly have been surprising in seventeenth-century France (where the story had its literary origins) and in other times and places where a woman might be promised to a man on whom she had never set eyes. The words of Mary Granville, a young British woman, married in 1717 at age seventeen to a sixty-year-old suitor, speak volumes about the ordeal of arranged marriages: "As to his person he was excessively fat [and] negligent in his dress, and took a vast quantity of snuff, which gave him a dirty look." She finds the man to whom she is betrothed "disgusting" rather than "engaging," and bemoans the fact that he is "hardly ever sober."[36]

On one level, "Bluebeard" can be read as culturally specific, revealing the risks women run when they marry at a relatively young age and enter the household of a stranger, often an older man. Women were the principal victims of family violence in eighteenth- and nineteenth-century France, as the French historian Michelle Perrot reports, and "one staple of the crime reports of the period was the woman whose body was hacked to pieces."[37] But on another level, "Bluebeard" is a tale that addresses, in the form of a horror story, with all its grotesque exaggerations, perennial anxieties about what can happen once the honeymoon is over.

THE WOMAN IS MOBILE

Before looking at variants of "Bluebeard" to discover how the narrative has been reframed in other cultures, I want to speculate further about why this story has undergone a kind of collective cultural repression and how it came to be revived by filmmakers in the 1940s and then once again by writers, filmmakers, and artists in the 1960s and after. It is telling that authors like Margaret Atwood and Angela Carter turned to "Bluebeard" for narrative inspiration and that a photographer like

Cindy Sherman created a picture book of the Grimms' variant of "Blue-beard" (a story that goes by the name of "Fitcher's Bird"). This new cultural investment in an old tale about a bad marriage has, I believe, little to do with a rise in divorce rates or with renewed concerns about conjugal intimacy and marital fidelity. But it does have a great deal to do with the nature of the tale's heroine and with the story's inversion of the traditional relationship between the seeker figures of fairy tales and the goals of their searches.

The Soviet semiotician Jurij Lotman has made a strong case for identi-fying two contrasting figures operating in mythic plots: an active, no-madic hero who crosses borders and boundaries to explore an enclosed space and an immobile figure who inhabits that space and figures as the target of the hero's conquest.[38] That myths have traditionally gendered the one male and the other female seems obvious. But as the film critic Carol J. Clover has shown, the distribution of these roles is not graven in stone, for mainstream horror films (think of *Silence of the Lambs, Texas Chain Saw Massacre*, or *Halloween*) position women as heroic combat-ants, figures who are not at all passive and who succeed in outsmarting formidable male adversaries, many of whom operate out of dark, subter-ranean spaces. The gendered division of labor to which Lotman alludes was also not as rigorously enforced in folktales as in myths. If we look, for example, at some of the tales from the Brothers Grimm that did not make it into our fairy-tale canon, we find that there are many male Cinder-ellas who suffer in silence and many active women who undertake jour-neys and carry out tasks to disenchant bridegrooms.

Clover sees this unsettling of gender conventions as a legacy of woman's liberation, which has given horror the image of "an angry woman—a woman so angry that she can be imagined as a credible perpetrator of the kind of violence on which, in the low-mythic universe, the status of full protagonist rests."[39] To this persuasive analysis one could add that mod-ern horror may also be tapping into an earlier narrative tradition, one that included folktales such as "Bluebeard," "The Robber Bridegroom," or "Fitcher's Bird," in which women figure as investigative agents (uncov-ering crimes and outwitting villains), while men function as the criminal guardians of dark, secret places. Like the heroines of high opera described by the cultural critic Catherine Clément, these women cross over a "rigor-ous invisible line" that makes them "unbearable" and places them in a situation of desperate vulnerability.[40]

In Perrault's narrative, Bluebeard's wife may show a certain investiga-tive determination that links her to the heroines of modern horror, but she is decidedly less resolute than many of her folkloric cousins, who have receded from cultural memory. Folklorists have succeeded in reviving these brides of ogres and showing how they use craft to defeat treacherous bridegrooms.

BLUEBEARD'S WIFE AS TRICKSTER

The French folklorist Paul Delarue has mapped the evolution of "Bluebeard," documenting the liberties taken by Perrault in transforming an oral folktale into a literary text.[41] The folk heroines of "Bluebeard" delay their executions by insisting on donning bridal clothes for the event (thus buttressing the folkloric connection between marriage and death) and prolong the possibility for rescue by recounting each and every item of bridal clothing. One of Bluebeard's wives plays for time with words suggesting that she wishes to tart herself up for her execution: "I must get my prettiest blouse . . . I must get my prettiest stockings . . . I must get my prettiest hat."[42] Perrault's heroine, by contrast, who asks her husband for "a little time to say my prayers," becomes a model of repentant piety. Unlike many folk heroines, who become agents of their own rescue by dispatching letter-carrying pet dogs or talking birds to their families with urgent calls for help, Perrault's heroine sends her sister up to the castle tower to watch for the brothers who had planned a visit that very day. Most important, folk versions of the tale evidently did not fault the heroine for her curiosity. To the contrary, when the young women in those stories stand before the forbidden chamber, they feel duty-bound to open its door. "I have to know what is in there," one young woman reflects just before turning the key. The pangs of conscience that beset Perrault's heroine are absent. These folkloric figures are often described as courageous: curiosity and valor enable them to come to the rescue of Bluebeard's previous wives (often the heroine's older sisters) by putting their dismembered body parts back together again and by providing them with safe passage home.

Although the story of Bluebeard has been read by countless contemporary commentators as turning on the matter of sexual fidelity, what really seems to be at issue, if one considers the folkloric evidence, is the heroine's discovery of her husband's misdeeds, her craft in delaying the execution of his murderous plans, and her ability to engineer her own rescue. In its bold proclamation of the perils of some marriages, "Bluebeard" endorses a regressive move back to the household of the heroine's childhood. Bluebeard's wife becomes a double of the British Jack, who liquidates the ogre and climbs back down the beanstalk to live happily ever after with his mother. In fact, a Norwegian version of "Bluebeard," "The Hen Is Tripping in the Mountain," gives us a protagonist who is modeled on Molly Whuppie, the female counterpart to "Jack" of British folklore. The daughter of a widow whose sole possession is a hen, this girl succeeds in outwitting a "big, ugly mountain troll," rescuing her two sisters from his clutches, and living happily ever after with her family.[43]

When we consider the form in which "Bluebeard" circulated in an oral culture, it quickly becomes evident that the story must be closely related to two tales recorded by the Brothers Grimm. The first of these, "Fitcher's Bird," shows us the youngest of three sisters escaping the snares set by a sorcerer and rescuing her two sisters. "Clever" and "sly," she succeeds where her sisters failed. "Nobody raps her knuckles for being curious," Margaret Atwood points out, for she outsmarts the wizard, makes her escape "through the forest, alone, with the aid of nothing but wits and guts and a talent for improvised costumes."[44] The heroine of "The Robber Bridegroom," though not faced with a forbidden chamber and a test of obedience, rescues herself from a murderous suitor, mobilizing her wits and her narrative skills to escape the cannibalistic thieves with whom her betrothed consorts.

Embedded in a narrative tradition that positions the heroine as trickster, both these stories have counterparts in the folklore of other European cultures. The Italian "Silvernose," for example, features a "gentleman attired in black" who is "the height of courtesy."[45] Though the odd metallic facial feature is a tip-off for danger to a washerwoman, her three daughters successively insist on marrying Silvernose. Each is warned about the perils of opening a forbidden door, but all three succumb to their curiosity, with the third escaping death by adding craftiness to curiosity.[46] "Sly Lucia" succeeds in outwitting Silvernose, who has lured the girls to his house in order to fling them into the fires of Hell. Like "Fitcher's Bird" and "The Robber Bridegroom," "Silvernose" spotlights the investigative curiosity of its heroine and links it with other virtues such as cleverness and courage.[47]

That "Bluebeard" can be mobilized as a story empowering women to take control of their lives has been recently recognized by the psychologist Clarissa Pinkola Estés, who sees in the tale a celebration of the "Wild Woman." "Bluebeard," in her view, teaches something that moves directly against the grain of its interpretive history. "We must unlock or pry things open to see what is inside," Estés declares. "We must use our insight and our ability to understand what we see. We must speak our truth in a clear voice. And we must be able to use our wits to do what needs be about what we see." Relying on Eastern European and Slavic variants,

Estés was able to divine that the tale does not necessarily demonize feminine curiosity.[48]

"Bluebeard" has also been linked with other folkloric traditions, most notably "Rumpelstiltskin" (also known as "Tom Tit Tot"). There are many British and European variants of this story of a miller's daughter who gives her firstborn to a gnome capable of spinning straw into gold. One of these, a British story called "Perrifool," conflates "Bluebeard" with "Rumpelstiltskin" to produce a plot in which a princess saves her sisters (who have been captured by an ogre) even as she succeeds in harnessing the services of a "peerie yellow-headed boy" to discharge the tasks assigned by the ogre.[49] By discovering that the boy is named "Perrifool," the girl is freed of her obligation to him and then proceeds to liberate her sisters by tricking the ogre. The rescued girls and their mother murder the villain by pouring hot water over his head.

Like the Bluebeard story, "Perrifool" and other "Rumpelstiltskin" stories turn on the discovery of secret knowledge concerning masculine identity. In "Rumpelstiltskin," the heroine, by divining the name of the helper, acquires the means to defeat him. Knowledge, in this and in other fairy tales, is power. If the heroine of "Rumpelstiltskin" triumphs over adversity and redeems her firstborn child through knowledge, the heroine of "Bluebeard" succeeds in saving herself from marriage to a tyrant by exploring the hidden recesses of his castle. The story of "Bluebeard" can be read as part of a larger folkloric and mythological tradition enjoining women from pushing the limits of intimacy. Situated both at the upper reaches of high culture (think of Wagner's *Lohengrin*, whose heroine makes the mistake of trying to discover her husband's name and origins) and in the broad band of popular entertainments (think of Christine's impulsive curiosity in *Phantom of the Opera*), these plots point to the hazards of trying to learn more about a suitor or husband than he wishes to reveal. Sometimes cautioning against curiosity, sometimes endorsing it, they suggest that a woman with an inquiring mind can have fatal effects on a marriage but, with it, she can also avoid fatal effects for herself.

FEMININITY, CURIOSITY, AND DUPLICITY IN CULTURAL MYTHS

In Perrault's narrative, the curiosity of Bluebeard's wife is closely linked to what Laura Mulvey, in the context of an essay on Pandora, has called epistemophilia, or the desire to know.[50] This drive for knowledge turns the wife into an energetic investigator, determined to acquire knowledge of the secrets hidden behind the door of the mansion's forbidden chamber.

Oddly, this spontaneous curiosity is often perceived as delinquent and marks her as a transgressive figure courting danger. The interpretive history of Perrault's story, by underscoring the heroine's kinship with certain literary, biblical, and mythical figures (most notably Psyche, Eve, and Pandora), gives us a tale that undermines a robust folkloric tradition in which the heroine functioned as a resourceful agent of her own salvation. Rather than celebrating the courage and wisdom of Bluebeard's wife in discovering the dreadful truth about her husband's murderous deeds, Perrault and many other tellers of the tale often cast aspersions on her for engaging in an unruly act of insubordination.

Romer Wilson retold "Bluebeard" in 1930 with an introduction that spells out the treacherous appeal of curiosity. "If only Bluebeard's wife had not looked into the little room, they might both have lived happily ever after. But she did. Everybody knows how hard it is not to be terribly curious about things which are especially forbidden. It is just the same trouble that Eve had in the Garden of Eden, and the same trouble that made Pandora open that box of hers. There are a hundred tales about this kind of curiosity, but fortunately they nearly always come right in the end after the curious person has suffered severely in some way."[51]

Why this need to invalidate a trait that allows a woman to escape from marriage to a serial murderer? The answer, as Wilson suggests, can be traced in part to our most powerful cultural stories about the origins of the human race and about the genesis of marriage as the institution charged with reproducing the race. These stories have constructed a discourse linking femininity with evil, showing how the transition from nature to (agri)culture, from a state of innocence to a "fallen" condition, is motivated by the seductive duplicity of woman. As our foundational myths about the nature of the relations between the two sexes, these stories seep into other narrative traditions, shaping plots along with the interpretive history surrounding them.

Hesiod tells us the story of the first woman, a "manufactured maiden" given the name Pandora, a wonderfully ambiguous term that can mean "giver of all gifts" or "recipient of all gifts." Hesiod elects for the second meaning and emphasizes that "lies and crooked words and wily ways" figure prominently among the attributes with which she is endowed by the gods. After Zeus discovered Prometheus's theft of fire from the gods, he made plans to exact revenge by exchanging one deception for another. Commanding Hephaestos to fashion a "sweet and lovely maiden shape" from earth and water, he ordered Hermes to accompany Pandora to earth, where she was to seduce Prometheus's brother, Epimetheus. Naïve Epimetheus neglected to heed his brother's warning about gifts from Zeus:

"He took the gift and afterwards, when the evil thing was already his, he understood. Previously men lived on earth free from ills and hard toil and sickness. But the woman took off the great lid of the jar and scattered all these and caused sorrow and mischief to man."[52]

Pandora is more than a mere agent releasing evils on earth. She is also the beautiful work of art who is pure artifice. Combining the seductive allure of surface beauty with the intellectual traits of deception and treachery, she is the supreme incarnation of the femme fatale. Froma I. Zeitlin has articulated perfectly what is at stake in the story of Pandora: "Fashioned at the orders of Zeus as punishment for Prometheus' deceptive theft of celestial fire for men, the female is the first imitation and the counterpart to the first deception. She is endowed by the gods with the divine traits of beauty and adornment which conceal the bestial and thievish nature of her interior. Artefact and artifice herself, Pandora installs the woman as *eidolon* in the frame of human culture, equipped by her "unnatural" nature to seduce and enchant, to delight and deceive."[53]

Pandora, the first woman of classical mythology, becomes the incarnation of a seductive femininity that both conceals and releases all the evils menacing man. This figure of duplicity is further linked with curiosity, with an unruly need to explore enclosed spaces of secrecy. Pandora, as Laura Mulvey has pointed out, "is now better known for her curiosity than for her origin as artifact and lure. Although she was forbidden to open the box and warned of the danger it contained, she gave way to her curiosity and released all the evils into the world."[54] Her curiosity, like Eve's, has been linked with sexual curiosity. Even sober, scholarly accounts of Pandora's transgression leap to the conclusion that the wish to discover what is in a box must have something to do with sexual desire. The classicist Sarah B. Pomeroy concludes her analysis of Hesiod's account by stating: "Pandora is comparable to the temptress Eve, and the box she opened may be a metaphor for carnal knowledge of women, which was a source of evil to men."[55]

Like Pandora, Eve, the "mother of all the living," shoulders the blame for our loss of innocence and the accompanying curse of mortality.[56] Tertullian called women the "devil's gateway" and accused them of bringing death into the world. Interestingly, though the story of Eve's temptation is often framed as the sexually charged scene of a double seduction (the snake tempts Eve, and Eve in turn lures Adam into transgression), it is knowledge that Eve seems to crave more than anything else. "But the serpent said to the woman, 'You will not die; for God knows that when you eat of [the fruit] your eyes will be opened, and you will be like God, knowing good and evil' " (Gen. 3:4–5). Woman's intellectual curiosity, as we have seen from the story of Bluebeard, is easily translated into sexual curiosity and, from there, linked with deception, duplicity, and seductive sexuality. Yet it is also possible to read the story of the Fall in very different terms, as a story about the search for knowledge and about the collapse of a form of authority based on a willingness to be excluded from knowledge.

Greek retellings of the Bluebeard tale (which call Bluebeard the "Lord of the Underworld") disclose the story's kinship with one other cultural script that has powerfully shaped the connection between femininity and lack of restraint.[57] The Homeric hymn that relates the rape of Persephone and tells of Demeter's efforts to rescue her daughter from that monstrous bridegroom known as Pluto may not have the foundational power of the stories of Eve and Pandora, but it too positions woman as unable to contain her desires. Persephone, an unwilling bride, remains in the Underworld with her pitiless husband until he is ordered by Zeus to appease Demeter by returning her daughter. But Persephone, like Eve, is unable to resist partaking of forbidden fruit. After tasting the pomegranate given to her by Hades, she is condemned to spend a part of the year with him in the Underworld, and humanity must suffer the consequences of a barren season that brings death upon nature.

Bearing in mind that Bluebeard is often depicted as a saber-wielding tyrant dressed in Oriental robes and outfitted with a turban, we might want to consider the effect on "Bluebeard" and its interpretive history of one additional story linking women with a form of curiosity that is decidedly sexual in nature. Anyone who has read an unexpurgated version of *The Thousand and One Nights* will recall that King Schahriyar, after catching his first wife in flagrante, marries a succession of virgins, whom he beheads on the morning after each wedding. The arousal of desire, along with the satisfaction of sexual curiosity, is punished with death. By contrast, the woman, like Scheherazade, who is capable of arousing male curiosity (sexual and intellectual), rather than succumbing to it, lives happily ever after. Scheherazade both satisfies her husband and keeps him in a state of perpetual arousal by inventing a new story each night. That his curiosity is not merely intellectual becomes evident when Scheherazade bears her husband one son after another.

Whether the frame story to *The Thousand and One Nights* inspired "Bluebeard" or contaminated it, or whether it simply stands as an Oriental counterpart, is not clear. But the story of King Schahriyar and Scheherazade is revealing in its clear identification of a first wife as sexual transgressor and its insistence on woman's sexual duplicity ever after:

Friend, trust not at all in women, smile at their promising,
For they lower or they love at the caprice of their parts.
Filled to the mouth with deceit, they lavish a lying love
Even while the very floss fringing their silks is faithless.[58]

That "Bluebeard" was influenced in some way by *The Thousand and One Nights* seems even more plausible when we read the story told by Scheherazade's father in an effort to dissuade his daughter from marrying. That story turns on a secret that a wife tries to wrest from her husband. Although disclosing the secret means death for the husband, the wife still remains stubbornly determined to discover it. Her curiosity is cured by a "good beating."

The Corpses in the Closet

With so much attention lavished on the curiosity of Bluebeard's wife and on her transgressive desires, few critics have taken the trouble to investigate a scene in the story that signals a moment of real hermeneutic crisis for most readers. How do we explain the existence of those corpses in Bluebeard's castle? What is really at stake in the secret lodged behind the door to the forbidden chamber? Trying to understand the representational logic of this particular scene is a challenge that few critics have been willing to take on. What Bluebeard's wife sees when she opens the door are the bodies of the victims. Instead of eliciting visual delight and wonder at what is beyond the door, the corpses evoke horror and terror. Arranged as if on display, they are the visible signs of Bluebeard's murderous deeds.

Marina Warner, connecting the "Bluebeard" story with a Breton legend about the wife murderer Cunmar the Accursed, sees in that variant of the tale a sign that "Bluebeard" may be about nothing more than "a routine cause of mortality": "The seventeenth-century fairy tale can yield most interesting evidence when taken at face value: as stepmothers favoured their own children over the offspring of a previous marriage, or widowed mothers persecuted their sons' wives, as peasants starved but could advance through cunning, so, in the case of Bluebeard, widowers married many times in succession because wives died young, and died in childbirth, their infants with them."[59]

If one chooses to read "Bluebeard" on a symbolic level, it seems likely that those women in the forbidden chamber could also represent Bluebeard's discarded lovers, cast off once he discovered their insubordination. "He just loved a lot of women at the same time—was constitutionally unable to limit himself to one," the detective in Alistair Boyle's novel *Bluebeard's Last Stand* declares.[60] A Casanova who kills symbolically, Bluebeard is often recast as a serial seducer rather than as a serial killer. That the carnage in the forbidden chamber can be read as a literalization of the lady-killer metaphor suggests that Bluebeard's wives, captivated by romance, are willing victims.

From Françoise Gilot's memoir, *Life with Picasso*, we know that her famed husband may have read the story in this way, rescripting it so as to enlist sympathy for Bluebeard and then turning him into a cultural hero who commits his "murders" in the name of art. Bluebeard's wives are, after all, often put on display, with their heads on pedestals or with their bodies hanging from the walls, like portraits in a gallery.

Françoise Gilot herself used the Bluebeard story as a map for exploring the twists and turns taken by her own marriage to a man of celebrated genius. Over the course of the years, Gilot became aware of what she termed her husband's "Bluebeard complex": "Pablo's many stories and reminiscences about Olga and Marie-Thérèse and Dora Maar, as well as their continuing presence just off-stage in our own life together, gradually made me realize that he had a kind of Bluebeard complex that made him want to cut off the heads of all the women he had collected in his little private museum."[61] Although Picasso never allowed his past romantic interests to die out completely and continually played his past wives and lovers against his latest amorous interest, he was intrigued by the tactics of Bluebeard and recognized that new romances always "kill off" previous lovers: "To choose one person is always, in a measure, to kill someone else. And so one has to have the courage of the surgeon or the murderer, if you will, and to accept the share of guilt which that gives" (101).

At one point, Gilot reports, Picasso suggested that life would be much easier if he could just dispose of his previous wives in the manner of Henri Landru, a man known as the French Bluebeard: "Every time I change wives I should burn the last one. That way I'd be rid of them. They wouldn't be around now to complicate my existence. Maybe that would bring back my youth, too. You kill the woman and you wipe out the past she represents" (349). What Picasso fails to tell us is the way in which the burden of the past affects the new wife. Gilot writes poignantly about "the difficulty of trying to shake off that heavy load of his far-from-dead past, which was beginning to seem like an albatross around my neck" (212). She notes how she feels overcome by an uncanny sense of dread when she enters a house once occupied by her husband. The place appears to be a "house of Bluebeard": "I began to have the feeling that if I looked into a closet, I would find half a dozen ex-wives hanging by their necks" (152–53).

Gilot seems to understand "Bluebeard" as a metaphorical enactment of the issues that arise in marriages between men with a past and young women without much life experience. For her, the wives in the closet are the women who played a powerful role in her husband's past and who, additionally, have a real physical presence in the day-to-day routines of her own life (Dora Maar, Olga Khoklova Picasso, and Marie-Thérèse Walter were constantly making demands on Picasso's time). Much as Françoise Gilot wanted to avoid peering into the closet of her husband's past life, she perpetually came up against the ghosts, corpses, or skeletons from the past. By positioning her own marriage in relation to the Bluebeard story Gilot found a tool for thinking through and understanding the powerful emotions evoked by her husband's past.

"Bluebeard" is, then, not one story but many stories, multiple scripts competing with each other for the status of the best, truest, deepest, or most authentic version. In the chapters that follow, I will chart the dissemination of the story, showing how it has emerged in new cultural settings and how it came to be inflected by writers and artists who are often not even aware of the story's roots and its rich history. "Bluebeard" may not be a tale that we embrace as part of our cultural legacy, but it nonetheless repeatedly asserts its vigor as it migrates and takes up residence in the stories we tell and the pictures we see. Despite its countercultural drift, it has remained a narrative that shapes, in powerful if covert ways, the plots of the tales we tell.

2

CHAPTER

"Have you ever really been afraid? . . .
of a man? . . . of a house? . . . of yourself?":
Charlotte Brontë's *Jane Eyre*, Daphne du Maurier's
Rebecca, and Modern Gothics

> I saw thee mutable
> Of fancy, fear'd lest one day thou wouldst leave me
> As her at *Timna*, sought by all means therefore
> How to endear, and hold thee to me firmest:
> No better way I saw than by importuning
> To learn thy secrets, get into my power
> Thy key of strength and safety.
> —John Milton, *Samson Agonistes*

The traffic flow from folklore to fiction and film has always been heavy. "Cinderella" has been recycled many times, and its recent filmic incarnations—*Working Girl* with Melanie Griffith, *Pretty Woman* with Julia Roberts, *Ever After* with Drew Barrymore, and *Maid in Manhattan* with Jennifer Lopez—offer striking evidence that we are perpetually reinventing that story to manage new cultural desires and anxieties about courtship and romance. *Bluebeard*, on the face of things, does not appear to enjoy the rich cinematic afterlife of tales such as "Cinderella" or "Beauty and the Beast." Its seeming failure to invigorate cultural production in this country can be traced to its effacement by two British rescriptings of the story which have dominated our cultural imaginary, producing plots that have had a powerful popular appeal. Those rescriptings have focused on Bluebeard's wife, on how she succeeds in coping with her husband's troubled past and in healing the wounds left by the disruptive violence of a previous marriage.

Charlotte Brontë's *Jane Eyre* (1847) and Daphne du Maurier's *Rebecca* (1938), separated by almost a century, are both written from the point of view of women. Each of the two novels is narrated by a second wife, a woman who is presented as youthful, meek, and naïve—a Cinderella who has escaped a wicked "stepmother" (Mrs. Reed in *Jane Eyre* and Mrs. Van Hopper in *Rebecca*) and who becomes linked with a sinister Prince Charming, a man with a dark past. The similarities in the plot lines of the two novels can be attributed in part to the way in which both works recycle the stock characters and devices of the Gothic novel, borrowing freely from a genre that engages with the melodramatic effects of romance, mystery, and murder and that has been said to provide "an outlet for women's fears about fathers and husbands."[1]

Although the Gothic novel flourished at the end of the eighteenth century in the works of authors such as Horace Walpole, Ann Radcliffe, and Matthew Lewis, the genre is forever revived and continues to thrive in our own age in the form of the "Modern Gothic." Joanna Russ has characterized it in the following manner:

> To a large, lonely, usually brooding *House* (always named) comes a *Heroine* who is young, orphaned, unloved, and lonely. . . . After a short prologue, [the Heroine] forms a personal or professional connection with an older man, a dark, magnetic, powerful, brooding, sardonic *Super-Male*, who treats her brusquely, derogates her, scolds her, and otherwise shows anger or contempt for her. . . . In the tangle of oppressive family relationships going on in the House exists a *Buried Ominous Secret*, always connected with the Other Woman and the Super-Male. . . . The Super-Male is at the center of the Secret; when she unravels the mystery about him . . . she will simultaneously get to the bottom of the Secret.[2]

An anonymous critic writing at the end of the eighteenth century emphasized the importance of what Russ calls the "Buried Ominous Secret" and the way in which it is always connected with murder. "*Take*—an old castle, half of it ruinous. A long gallery, with a great many doors, some secret ones. Three murdered bodies, quite fresh. As many skeletons, in chests and presses. . . . Mix them together . . . to be taken at any of the watering-places before going to bed."[3] From Russ's inventory, it becomes evident that the Gothic conventions in *Jane Eyre* and *Rebecca* are the very plot elements basic to the Bluebeard story. Both Gothic novels and Bluebeard tales chart the vagaries of a whirlwind romance with a stranger or an impulsive marriage to an outsider—to a man whose house contains a room in which is buried a grim secret, connected with murder, about his past.

Unlike the Gothic novel, which delights in a proliferation of family secrets and intrigues, the Bluebeard story—like *Jane Eyre* and *Rebecca*—remains narrowly focused on one enigma and its effect on one couple. And rather than promoting the cult of the immortal outlaw, the noble villain, and the satanic hero, it is often tilted toward the wife, presenting the husband's criminal background as dreadful, horrific, and potentially threatening.[4] Pitting wife against husband, the Bluebeard plot confines the scene of action to the domestic arena and "enables us to see that the home *is* a prison, in which the helpless female is at the mercy of ominous patriarchal authorities."[5] It stages an oppressive reign of masculine tyranny and shows how the drive for knowledge can imperil the female protagonist, but ultimately proves liberating for her. In some ways a female counterpart to Oedipus, the heroine of "Bluebeard," like Jane Eyre and the narrator of *Rebecca*, secures the love of a father figure and struggles with maternal rival(s). In the end, however, she devotes her real energies to unraveling the mystery of the man to whom she is attached.

In the Bluebeard narrative, as in its literary descendants, the threat of violence always issues from the male partner, producing a plot that presents the institution of marriage as "haunted by murder" (to use the words of the film critic Mary Ann Doane).[6] That the wife feels threatened by the husband is not unusual, since she barely knows him and learns, shortly before or soon after her marriage, that he has a deep, dark secret. Drawing on the conventions of the Gothic novel in vogue at the end of the eighteenth century even as they revive the Bluebeard plot, *Jane Eyre* and *Rebecca* stage anxieties associated with sexuality, marriage, and mortality—anxieties so powerful that they seem to manifest themselves in a kind of cultural repetition (and variation) compulsion in our literary and cinematic fictions.

If Gothic plots seem mechanical, contrived, and predictable to us today, they nonetheless continue to flourish, drawing readers and viewers of all ages. Mary Shelley's words in the introduction to *Frankenstein*, "I bid my hideous progeny go forth and prosper," proved prophetic, for the Gothic emerged in the nineteenth century as a genre with a popular appeal so powerful that it continues to thrive in our own day and age.[7] What makes the Gothic plot so irresistible has something to do with the way in which it offers both surface and depth, giving us a plot-driven detective story that engages our investigative curiosity and a psychological thriller that draws us into the sinister secrets of the psyche. The Bluebeard thread in the fabric of Gothic narratives offers an exceptional opportunity for elaborating on the problematic issues arising as women leave childhood behind and move toward an alliance with adult males.

It was Charlotte Brontë who created a new master narrative of female desire and inaugurated with full force the critique of fairy-tale romance in fiction by women for women. In *Jane Eyre*, Brontë gives us a character who identifies with various fairy-tale figures but who also, in the end, resists conventional fairy-tale scripts to construct an identity of her own.

At Gateshead, where she lives with her cousins and aunt, Jane Eyre finds herself relegated to the role of a Cinderella figure, employed as "an under-nurserymaid, to tidy the rooms, dust the chairs."[8] On a daily basis, she is persecuted by two unpleasant "stepsisters" and by a "stepmother" who has an "insuperable and rooted aversion" to her (23).[9] Excluded from the "usual festive cheer" (23) of holiday parties, Jane, though initially compliant and self-pitying, takes a defiant stance and refuses to be framed and contained by the role of Cinderella. Rather than passively enduring her storybook role (which will keep her, as a "plain Jane," forever locked in the first phase of "Cinderella"), she rebels against the social reflexes taught by her world and writes herself out of the script when she stands up to her Aunt Reed and tells her that she "hates" her. Aware that even the second phase of the "Cinderella" story is something of a hoax, Jane voices her contempt for "tales . . . that promise to end in the same catastrophe: marriage" (201).

Just as Jane refuses to model her behavior on Cinderella, despite the seductive tug of that story, so too she refrains from accepting the role of child-bride in Rochester's fairy-tale fantasies. Fairy tales play a powerful role in Jane's childhood, especially through the nursery stories told to her by the maid Bessie, and continue to exercise a hold over her imagination through adulthood. Just before meeting Rochester ("a horse was coming"), Jane reflects on how her imagination is so fired by the stories of her youth that even the sound of hoofbeats evokes mythical figures, in this case a spirit called "Gytrash." "I was young," she reports, "and all sorts of fancies bright and dark tenanted my mind: the memories of nursery stories were there amongst other rubbish; and when they recurred, maturing youth added to them a vigor and vividness beyond what childhood could give" (98). If Jane has a tendency to let her imagination run wild with fairy-tale romance, Rochester too frames his encounter with Jane as a moment of supernatural intervention. "When you came on me in Hay Lane last night, I thought unaccountably of fairy tales," he declares, "and had half a mind to demand whether you had bewitched my horse" (107).

What begins as a romantic encounter quickly modulates into what was probably the best-known fairy tale in Brontë's day and age: the story of Beauty and the Beast. Though no Beauty, Jane is, however, at first enchanted by the prospect of domesticating a man who is described as "brown," "shaggy," and "metamorphosed into a lion." Rochester appears to her at times like "some wronged and fettered wild beast, dangerous to approach in his sullen woe." In a conscious reprise of a scene in Madame de Beaumont's "Beauty and the Beast," Rochester interrogates Jane about his looks: "You examine me Miss Eyre? Do you think me handsome?" (115) Like the French Beast who asks Beauty: "Do you think me ugly?" Rochester later asks: "Am I hideous?" to which Jane replies: "Very, sir, you always were, you know." Jane is prepared to undertake the task of transforming Rochester from a beast into human form. "It is time someone undertook to rehumanize you . . . for I see you are being metamorphosed into a lion, or something of that sort."

While Jane colludes in Rochester's fairy-tale romance, she is soon jolted into a recognition of what will happen if she plays along with the fantasy: "For a moment I am beyond my own mastery. What does it mean? I did not think I should tremble in this way when I saw him—or lose my voice or the power of motion in his presence" (214). Participating in the cult of suffering endorsed in fairy tales like "Cinderella" signifies for Jane the loss of identity, and indulging in self-effacing acts of compassion that are Beauty's trademark spells paralysis. What Jane experienced in the Reed household at the hands of her aunt is repeated when she moves to Thornfield (note the reference to the wall of thorns in "Sleeping Beauty") and meets Rochester, a man who has the same power to overwhelm and intimidate. If Mrs. Reed functioned like the wicked stepmother of fairy tales, who disabled the heroine by withholding love and affection, Rochester, who is "old enough to be [Jane's] father," immobilizes his child-bride through an excess of romantic love. In many ways Rochester only masquerades as a fairy-tale beast with a heart of gold. In fact he operates with cunning and calculation, engineering a bogus courtship with Blanche Ingram and "concealing deadly secrets by immuring them in third-story rooms."[10]

One critic who has looked at the novel through the lens of the "Cinderella" story points out that it is Rochester who "openly and insistently compares Jane to an 'imp' and a 'fairy' and evokes the spirit of a fairy tale . . . whereas Jane the grown-up woman tries desperately to break the charm of such illusions and 'sweet lies.' "[11] Jane may at first collude in the fairy-tale fantasy, but she makes a conscious effort to stop playing Beauty to Rochester's Beast, and she seems, from the start, ill at ease in the role of Bluebeard's wife. Early on, she recognizes that Rochester's mansion has "a corridor from some Bluebeard's castle," yet she never feels compelled to explore the dreaded forbidden chamber. Jane's citation of the Bluebeard story suggests that she has a clear premonition that

Rochester has something to hide, but she remains surprisingly indifferent to exploring the room in the castle that might shed some light on the mysteries at Thornfield.

"I don't understand enigmas," Jane declares. "I never could guess a riddle in my life" (173). Rochester's bride remains in the dark about the madwoman in the attic: "There was a mystery at Thornfield; and . . . from participation in that mystery, I was purposely excluded" (144). Jane is not only "purposely excluded," but she also appears to be willfully blind to the presence of the ferocious creature that threatens her own safety and that of others. Jane prefers Rochester's "sweet lies" to the truth. Even after coming face to face with Bertha Mason, who tears her rival's bridal veil in two, Jane seems remarkably unwilling to challenge Rochester's assertions about her febrile imagination or to take matters into her own hands and enter the spaces forbidden to her.

Jane does not have to hear Bertha Mason's shrieks and moans to know that something is wrong at Thornfield. Looking into Rochester's eyes, she senses that the man to whom she is betrothed has a deep, dark secret. Jane, an expert reader of faces, remains intrigued by the mysterious depths she perceives in Rochester's gaze. Yet in this case she does not dare explore what she has observed: "As for the vague something—was it sinister or sorrowful, a designing or a desponding expression?—that opened upon a careful observer, now and then, in his eye and closed again before one could fathom the strange depth partially disclosed; that something which used to make me fear and shrink . . . ; that something I at intervals beheld still . . . I longed to dare—to divine it; and I thought Miss Ingram happy, because one day she might look into the abyss at her leisure, explore its secrets, and analyze their nature." (165)

That Jane does not aspire to learn the depths of what Rochester himself comes to describe as a "disgusting secret" becomes evident during a conversation that takes place after the couple is engaged. When Jane asks to "gratify" her curiosity, Rochester realizes that Jane's blind faith in him may be crumbling and that he has courted a daughter of Eve. "You are welcome to all my confidence that is worth having, Jane: but for God's sake don't desire a useless burden! Don't long for poison—don't turn a downright Eve on my hands!" (230). What Rochester fails to realize is that Jane has made the mistake of staunchly resisting the role of Bluebeard's wife even though "Bluebeard" is the one fairy tale that could have offered her some guidance about the importance of entering forbidden territory. That Jane's question turns on nothing more than a trivial point—even after Rochester has hinted at a dread secret in his allusion to "a useless burden" and to "poison"—reveals just how powerfully invested she is in suppressing her real curiosity and avoiding the fate of Bluebeard's wife.

Once the secret of Rochester's marriage to Bertha Mason is broadcast, Jane is led into the forbidden chamber, where she encounters the "strange wild animal" that is the first wife of the man to whom she is affianced. Her confidence betrayed, Jane is devastated: "My hopes were all dead. . . . I looked on my cherished wishes, yesterday so blooming and glowing; they lay stark, chill, livid corpses that could never revive" (260). For Jane, the madwoman in the attic blights her hopes. If the forbidden chamber houses a previous wife who is still alive, the effect of her presence is to produce the metaphorical corpses of Jane's shattered dreams. What "destroys" Jane's confidence is Rochester's suppression of the truth: "Mr. Rochester was not to me what he had been; for he was not what I had thought him" (260).

Despite her own skepticism about fairy-tale endings, Jane manages to secure a "happily ever after" conclusion to her own story. "Human beings never enjoy complete happiness in this world," she observes. "I was not born for a different destiny to the rest of my species; to imagine such a lot befalling me is a fairy tale—a daydream." Responding to what she perceives to be a call from Rochester, she returns to Thornfield, then repairs to Ferndean to track down and marry the man she loves. Just as Jane refashioned "Cinderella" and "Beauty and the Beast," creating new endings for old stories, so too she rewrites "Bluebeard" to produce a happy ending that reunites her with Rochester. The endings to "Cinderella" and "Beauty and the Beast" ring false to Jane's ears and strike her as perversions rather than inspirations. These tales, as she declares, always end in the "catastrophe" of marriage. Ironically, the one fairy tale that charts a marriage plot ending in real catastrophe turns out to contain the model for her own happily-ever-after plot. By suppressing curiosity about the forbidden chamber, Jane appears to have saved herself from the disaster that nearly befalls Bluebeard's wife. Rochester's secret may be out in the open, but it is none of Jane's doing.

Jane remodels the fairy tales told to her in her youth and revises conventional notions of romance by producing a radically new cultural script, the one embodied in the written record that constitutes her autobiography. Making productive use of fairy tales by reacting to them, resisting them, and rewriting them rather than passively consuming them and internalizing their values, Brontë's *Jane Eyre* offers a map for reading our cultural stories and using them to reflect on individual identity, courtship and romance, and marriage. As Karen Rowe points out, stripping away "deluding fantasies" allows Jane to accede to a more mature and realistic vision of human nature.

Yet Jane Eyre is determined to preserve at least one delusion. When it comes to her husband's past, she seems to have a kind of moral blind spot. Just as she was unwilling to press her husband for knowledge about the forbidden chamber in the attic, so too she fails to interrogate and contest Rochester's treatment of Bertha Mason. Rochester describes Bertha as a woman with "a nature the most gross, impure, depraved." A woman of "excesses," she is seen as a polluting presence, a "filthy burden" whose "breath (faugh!)" mixes with the air Rochester breathes (270–71). If Jane later realizes that Rochester might feel contempt for her too were she to become "successor" to his previous mistresses ("these poor girls"), she is perhaps also aware that women who desire to know too much are destined to become successors to Bertha Mason.[12] Jane's happiness rests on a willingness to shut out the deeper knowledge of the ways in which her own social identity is built on the domination, suppression, and elimination of Rochester's first wife.

Nearly a century after Charlotte Brontë published her novel, *Jane Eyre* was all the rage in Hollywood. *Variety* reported in November 1940 that "*Jane Eyre* looks to be the screen's most popular gal. Right now eight producers are standing in line to woo her." David Selznick evidently won that competition, for it was he who financed Robert Stevenson's screen adaptation of Brontë's novel. The cinematic version of *Jane Eyre*, starring Orson Welles as Rochester and Joan Fontaine as Jane, had been inspired in part by the great success of Hitchcock's *Rebecca*, though Selznick was anxious to avoid "any resemblance to *Rebecca*." The rich cinematic culture of "paranoid woman's films" in the 1940s, which will be explored in the next chapter, included both *Jane Eyre* and *Rebecca*. The two films, in exploring the desire and dread aroused by marriage and the paranoid effects produced by domestic confinement, bore a strong resemblance to each other, despite Selznick's efforts to differentiate them.[13]

Stevenson's Jane Eyre is even more "poor, obscure, plain and little" than her literary antecedent, and she never really rises to the challenges of moving into a more dominant mode. The film opens with the young Jane Eyre at her most abject. The camera tracks a lighted candle making its way through the darkness to a bolted door. Ominous music sounds. Two resolute adult figures appear out of the darkness to take positions outside the door. "Careful, Bessie, she bites," are the words enunciated by the butler to the nursery maid as the door opens to reveal a slip of a girl, cowering in a closet, awaiting liberation.

This scene, linked with the film's later shot of the door to the forbidden chamber that houses Bertha Mason, establishes a kinship between the meek young girl at Gateshead with the rabid madwoman at Thornfield. At Thornfield, Rochester carries a lighted candle to the door of the chamber housing his wife, a woman who is also reputed to "bite." "Her excesses drove her into madness," Rochester informs Jane about Bertha, and it is hard not to associate to Jane's excesses as a child and to the way in which her lack of restraint led to confinement at the prisonlike Lowood. Bertha, as first wife, eventually comes to serve as cautionary example to Jane, and for the greater part of the film, Jane meekly obeys Rochester's imperatives to disregard the alarming signs that something is amiss at Thornfield.

"What you see may shock you," Rochester tells Jane just before she discovers the wounds inflicted by Bertha on her own brother. "Don't try to understand." He admonishes Jane to be "still as a mouse" and to "say nothing about this to anyone else," discouraging her also from asking for "explanations." Rochester's mastery of the situation proves illusory, but Jane's submissive attitude remains permanent, producing a heroine who has moved from childish insubordination to perpetual subservience. Stevenson's Jane Eyre seems perfectly content to renew alliances with the fables of old and to resurrect both Cinderella and Beauty as behavioral models.

From its opening shot to its final sequence in which the edifice of Thornfield is burned down, Stevenson's Jane Eyre indulges in a proliferation of doors, bolts, and locks, showing how the heroine is repeatedly faced with the unknown. Doors, which activate a tension between concealing and revealing and between repression and confession, heighten suspense by hinting at the forbidden and suggesting possible dangers. For Jane, doors function as barriers to freedom, confining her movements at Gateshead, imprisoning her at Lowood, and intimidating her at Thornfield. And as important, they turn the familiar, domestic space of home into the locus of secrets, creating an uncanny space in which the heroine is haunted by a monstrous presence that will not make itself visible.

Jane never takes the bold step of trying to open those doors to liberate herself. Excluded from knowledge and prohibited from access to the image of horror, Jane seems perpetually victimized by the mystery at Thornfield because Rochester keeps her in a state of ignorance. Stevenson's film emphasizes the irony of Brontë's ending, which positions Rochester as a blind man who depends on his sighted wife. The conflagration at Thornfield blights Rochester's vision in the way that Rochester once impaired Jane's power of perception. It also finally enables Jane to liberate herself from a prison dominated by a man who curbed her curiosity and thereby created the most oppressive of all her confinements.

Manderley, in Daphne du Maurier's *Rebecca*, is another one of the many haunted mansions in the house of Gothic fiction. Driving to it, the novel's narrator reflects on the seemingly endless stretch of road on the way to her husband's ancestral home: "It always reminds me of the path in the forest in a Grimms' fairy tale, where the prince gets lost, you know. It's always longer than one expects, and the trees are so dark, and close."[14] Manderley itself is widely renowned as "perfectly enchanting," a kind of magical "fairy-land" (15). Maxim de Winter's second wife, who narrates but remains nameless, is spirited away from a life of servitude to a domain in which she serves as mistress, though in name alone. A hybrid fairy-tale figure, she is both a wife of Bluebeard, curious about her husband's mysterious past, and a Gretel figure, a vulnerable young girl lost in the woods, looking for home.

Like Jane Eyre, the second Mrs. de Winter serves as a domestic for a woman who incarnates the evil stepmother of fairy tales. Vain, gossipy, withholding, and shallow, Mrs. Van Hopper manages to turn the narrator of *Rebecca* into a Cinderella figure whose prospects for rescue seem very remote indeed. This Cinderella is still very much a child ("I felt young and small and very much alone" [41]), and she moves from the cinders and the hearth to the domain of Bluebeard without ever really having the chance to grow up. At Manderley, the narrator, despite her status, is treated like a child, behaves like a child, and feels like a child. After breaking an expensive ornament, she is berated by Mrs. Danvers. "It was like being a child again," she reflects, acutely aware that her relationship to Maxim is more that of daughter than of a wife.[15]

Why does Maxim choose the narrator of *Rebecca* as the successor to his seductively beautiful and glamorous first wife? This is a question that both narrator and reader turn over many times in the course of the memoir. Maxim reveals that his initial attraction has something to do with a "certain expression": "I'm not going to define it. I don't know how to. But it was one of the reasons why I married you" (202). The "expression," appealing in part because of its innocent, childlike cast, is always threatened by the onset of knowledge and the prospect of maturity. "I don't want you to look like you did just now," Maxim grumbles. "You had a twist to your mouth and a flash of knowledge in your eyes. Not the right sort of knowledge" (201).

For the costume ball at Manderley, Maxim proposes that his wife do nothing more than put a ribbon in her hair and appear as Alice in Wonderland. "You look like it now," he adds, "with your finger in your mouth." Mrs. de Winter often feels as if she is like a pet dog, "rather spoilt, rather irresponsible, someone to be petted from time to time when the mood came upon him, but more often forgotten, more often patted on the shoulder and told to run away and play" (195). Maxim sums it up perfectly when he tells her, on the day he proposes marriage, "It's a pity you have to grow up" (153).

Like all children, the second Mrs. de Winter has a craving to learn the secrets shared by the adults in her world. Manderley becomes for her the site of mystery, of unanswered questions, and of veiled knowledge. It is a place visited, if not by a real ghost ("It's *not* a ghost story," du Maurier insisted), then by an unsettling presence that haunts wife number two "day and night," as the author put it.[16] If the narrator is not privy to Manderley's secrets, she is still acutely aware that the mansion is haunted by its past, and that like a child, she has been shielded from disturbing truths. "Somewhere, at the back of my mind, there was a frightened furtive seed of curiosity that grew slowly and stealthily, for all my denial of it, and I knew all the doubt and the anxiety of the child who has been told, 'these things are not discussed, they are forbidden' " (120). Throughout her account, the narrator exhibits a profoundly ambivalent attitude toward acquiring forbidden knowledge: she is enticed by secrets yet also repulsed by the notion that investigative curiosity positions her as a voyeur.[17]

Maxim seems powerfully invested in preserving a union that is more like that of father and child than of husband and wife. When he senses that his new wife is beginning to know too much, he explicitly plays father to her daughter, emphasizing that he prefers her in the role of child. "Listen, my sweet," he avows, "When you were a little girl, were you ever forbidden to read certain books, and did your father put those books under lock and key?" When Mrs. de Winter affirms that her father did indeed put a barrier between her and certain books, Maxim triumphantly declares: "Well, then. A husband is not so very different from a father after all. There is a certain type of knowledge I prefer you not to have. It's better kept under lock and key. So that's that. And now eat up your peaches, and don't ask me any more questions, or I shall put you in the corner" (202). While the reprimand to eat up the peaches and the threat to confine his wife to the corner is spoken tongue in cheek, the last sentence puts into clear profile the nature of the relationship between husband and wife.

Once the narrator becomes aware of Maxim's dread secret, she moves from a condition of morbid insecurity and awkward immaturity to one of authority, mastery, and even dominance. "I've grown up, Maxim, in twenty-four hours," she declares after Rebecca's body is discovered, "I'll never be a child again" (264). "I would never be a child again" (285), she later affirms, after learning that Maxim murdered his first wife. That the fields of power are gradually reversed, with the narrator maturing into adulthood while Maxim declines into a state of helpless dependence, becomes evident when the new Mrs. de Winter takes Maxim into her arms "like a child" and comforts him "as though he were Jasper," the family cocker spaniel. The narrator addresses these words to her depleted husband near the end of the novel: " 'Your lobster will be cold,' I said; 'eat it, darling. It will do you good, you want something inside you. You're tired.' I was using the words he had used to me. I felt better and stronger. It was I now who was taking care of him. He was tired, pale" (375). Like Jane Eyre, who mothers the wounded Rochester, Mrs. de Winter has grown into the role of wife and mother even as her husband has descended into a pitiable state of vulnerability. "I suppose it is his dependence on me that has made me bold at last" (9), she remarks as she reflects on her hard-won autonomy.

By unlocking her husband's secret, the second Mrs. de Winter not only penetrates the mysteries of her husband's past, but also moves from a state of childlike innocence, one that positioned her in opposition to Maxim's first wife, to a condition of knowing. What the narrator suffers from, again and again, is a sense of inferiority to Rebecca—"How different she is to Rebecca" (131) is the phrase that haunts her married life. Her first efforts to imitate Rebecca backfire and end by agitating Max, but her later efforts succeed, for they produce a woman who has lost her innocence and is finally in the know. This sudden collapsing of difference spells a quick end to matrimonial harmony.

If Maxim has a secret that is finally revealed to be the murder of Rebecca, Mrs. de Winter begins cultivating her own secret. For the costume ball to be held at Manderley, the narrator is determined to give Maxim the "surprise of [his] life." Behind locked doors, Mrs. de Winter and her maid Clarice feel "like conspirators" and keep the door "barred" against Maxim. "You can't come in," the narrator exhorts Maxim, as she insists on preserving the secret of her costumed identity. In assuming the identity of Maxim's ancestor Caroline de Winter, the narrator also resurrects Rebecca, the supreme imitator of the portrait on the wall. When she reveals what has been going on behind closed doors, the response is stunned silence. Maxim experiences a "shock" (217) that reveals the degree to which he has depended on maintaining differences between wife number one and wife number two.

Maxim's secret initially drives a wedge between him and his wife, but once it is revealed, it creates a powerful bond between the two. "I killed her. I shot Rebecca in the cottage in the cove," Maxim tells his wife. ". . . Will you look into my eyes and tell me you love me now?" (266). While the narrator experiences this news as a "great shock," she is also "shocked" at her lack of emotion and this "queer cold absence of distress" (267). Maxim's passionate embrace stirs her back to life, and she pleads for an end to the barriers between them: "We've got to be together always, with no secrets, no shadows" (268). Once the secrets are laid bare, the second Mrs. de Winter not only achieves the intimacy she so desires but also becomes the dominant partner, self-confident and bold at last. Unlike Bluebeard's wife, she finds that the marriage bond is cemented through the revelation of her husband's homicidal act.

What endows Maxim de Winter with charisma, charm, and glamorous allure is in large part his inscrutability. On first seeing him, the narrator thinks of "a portrait seen in a gallery I had forgotten where, of a certain Gentleman Unknown" (15). "Cloaked and secret," that figure exercised a certain fascination simply because he appeared remote and mysterious. If secrets generate rumors, gossip, and talk, they also give rise to desire and romance. Maxim, the talk of the town, becomes attractive precisely because he holds back. "You never know what is going on in that funny mind of his" (98), his sister Beatrice tellingly observes.

Secrets become a source of power in *Rebecca*. Throughout the novel, the narrator relies on discourses of knowledge and curiosity to construct the power dynamics of her world. Nearly every character with the exception of Maxim seems intent on spying, eavesdropping, meddling, peeping, and prying. There is Mrs. Van Hopper, whose lorgnette is an "enemy to other people's privacy" and whose curiosity is described as a disease. We learn of the "curious and prying" neighbors at Manderley, the servants who are "forever asking questions," the newspapers who "worry" the de Winters, the "story-tellers" who spread rumors, the policemen who "stare curiously." And the narrator herself is, of course, the quintessential inquisitive child, an Alice in Wonderland who is curious in the double sense of the term.

While Maxim as man of mystery stirs desire, he also arouses anxiety. More than once it crosses the narrator's mind that he is perhaps "not normal" or "not altogether sane" (29). Mrs. de Winter positions herself as a snooper, a younger version of Mrs. Van Hopper, who peers "through the keyhole of a locked door" (32). Not completely comfortable with transgressive activities, the narrator recalls that, as a child, she always had a "sick, unhealthy" feeling when "turning the pages of a forbidden book" (26). Yet for all the distress she feels as she investigates Manderley and her husband's past, she is also fiercely determined to fathom the secrets that create barriers to marital intimacy, unaware that the end of mystery may also spell the end of romance.

The Rebecca Notebooks, a twenty-five page synopsis of the novel, reveal that Daphne du Maurier had consciously planned an ending that is close to that of *Jane Eyre*, with a heroine who looks after an invalid husband. "We are shorn of our little earthly glory," Mrs. de Winter reports, "he a cripple and his home lost to him, and I, well, I suppose I am like all childless women, craving for echoes I shall never hear."[18] The transformation of the husband's past into a shared secret means a decisive shift in the balance of marital power. A "cripple" without the glamorous estate that made him a charismatic man of the world, Maxim's impotence is further underscored by his wife's childlessness.

If Maxim's secret endowed him with a certain aura and authority, it comes back to haunt him in a number of ways, not only empowering his second wife but endowing his first wife with power beyond the grave. Max's second marriage may survive Rebecca's devious plan to engineer her own murder, but it remains haunted by the spirit of the first wife. Riding in the car on the return trip to Manderley, the narrator dreams that Maxim is brushing Rebecca's hair: "As he brushed it he wound it slowly into a thick long rope. It twisted like a snake, and he took hold of it with both hands and smiled at Rebecca and put it round his neck" (379). Murders cry out for vengeance, and the ghost of Rebecca locks the couple into a condition of loss. In their morbid withdrawal from life, they enact a kind of symbolic double suicide that, like the conflagration at Manderley, signals Rebecca's triumph. It is "odd and ironic," Nina Auerbach tells us, that du Maurier's "brutal depictions of emptiness should be given the label 'romance.' " Sally Beauman adds that "a story that attempts to bury Rebecca, the 'unwomanly' woman, in fact resurrects her, while the voice that narrates this story is that of a ghost, a true dead woman."[19]

If Daphne du Maurier emphasized power over romance, showing how secrets secure domination yet also come back to haunt those who possess them, Alfred Hitchcock had other matters on his mind in his screen adaptation of *Rebecca*. His Mrs. de Winter also loses her childlike innocence once she begins to investigate matters at Manderley and to probe her husband's mind, but instead of getting the upper hand, she becomes a co-

conspirator, willing to repress what her investigative curiosity has uncovered for the sake of a happily-ever-after ending.

For Hitchcock's heroine, marriage to Maxim de Winter means growing up fast. Like the second Mrs. de Winter in du Maurier's novel, Hitchcock's wife is presented as artless, immature, and childlike. "You're a capable child in many ways," the hateful Mrs. Van Hopper tells the heroine. Maxim has different "maxims" for his child-bride: "Eat your supper like a good girl"; "Stop biting your nails"; "It's a pity you have to grow up"; "Promise me never to wear black satin or pearls and to be thirty-six years old"; "You can't be too careful with children"; "You ought to have married a boy, someone your own age." When Maxim finally tells his wife the truth about Rebecca, he notices a stark change in her appearance: "It's gone forever—that funny, young, lost look I loved. It will never come back. I killed that when I told you about Rebecca. It's gone. In a few hours you've grown so much older."

That the second Mrs. de Winter is something of a child becomes visible on screen when we find her opening doors whose knobs are shoulder height, see her miniaturized by enormous chairs, or witness her at one end of the massive dining room table smiling weakly at Maxim. "A characteristic camera movement," Tania Modleski notes, "begins with a closeup of the heroine receiving a bit of unwelcome news about Rebecca's superiority and then tracking out to a long shot in which she seems small, helpless, and alone."[20]

To be sure, the heroine of Hitchcock's film is like a child, but it is in part because her husband and housekeeper seem born to the manor. Maxim de Winter exhibits a graceful charm that contrasts sharply with the demeanor of his wife, who wanders awkwardly about the house, unsure of herself and her movements. Her bewildered look and hesitant movements stand in sharp contrast to the impassive manner and controlled movements of Mrs. Danvers. "Mrs. Danvers was almost never seen walking," Hitchcock observed, "and was rarely shown in motion. If she entered a room in which the heroine was, what happened is that the girl suddenly heard a sound and there was the ever-present Mrs. Danvers, standing perfectly still by her side. In this way, the whole situation was projected from the heroine's point of view; she never knew when Mrs. Danvers might turn up, and this, in itself, was terrifying."[21] Dwarfed by her surroundings and unsettled by the omnipresence of Mrs. Danvers, the heroine appears to be out of her depth in the role of mistress of Manderley and becomes powerfully vulnerable to the terrors of the mansion.

"I always believe in following the advice of the playwright Sardou," Hitchcock once remarked. "He said, 'Torture the women!' . . . The trouble today is that we don't torture women enough."[22] The heroine of *Rebecca* moves from a domestic situation in which she is perpetually mortified by her employer's behavior to a marital situation in which she is constantly haunted by her predecessor. Aware that her husband "adored" his first wife and finding that Rebecca has left her mark everywhere in ubiquitous monograms (her initials are embroidered on napkins, handkerchiefs, pillowcases, and embossed on her stationary and address book), the new Mrs. de Winter faces a serious identity crisis when she arrives at Manderley. "They're all comparing me with Rebecca," she protests to Crawley. In a clumsy effort to secure an identity as Maxim's wife, the protagonist looks through the pages of a beauty magazine and orders an outfit that conforms to her "black silk and pearls" fantasy of adulthood, only to find that Maxim dismisses the dress as silly. That her loss of identity presents real dangers becomes evident when she enters Rebecca's room and allows Mrs. Danvers to maneuver her into the role of dead wife. But the heroine recognizes the risks of overidentification and, in a moment of newfound self-assertion tinged with irony, declares: "I am Mrs. de Winter now."

Although Mrs. Danvers tries to force the heroine into one more moment of overidentification with Rebecca by tricking her into wearing the attire that Rebecca had once worn to the costume ball restaged at Manderley, she does not succeed in luring the heroine to a suicidal death. Still, in a scene that reverses the Cinderella story by making the fancy dress ball a calamity for the heroine rather than a triumph, Hitchcock reveals how the second wife's identification with the first wife brings her dangerously close to self-annihilation. If this Cinderella survives, it is by dint of her active curiosity: her desire to understand Rebecca and what she represented to Maxim prevails over her need to identify with her.

"The heroine [of *Rebecca*] is Cinderella," Hitchcock once asserted to François Truffaut, "and Mrs. Danvers is one of the ugly sisters."[23] It was Truffaut, rather than Hitchcock, who recognized that *Rebecca* alluded to a very different fairy tale. "It's the first one of your pictures that evokes a fairy tale," Truffaut remarked. "This fable-like quality is of interest," he added, "because it recurs in several of your works. It is suggested by the emphasis on the keys to the house, by a closet that no one has the right to open, or by a room that is sealed off."[24] In response, Hitchcock observed that "children's fairy tales are often terrifying." And in the context of *Rebecca*, the example that came to Hitchcock's mind was not, as might be expected, "Bluebeard," but "Hansel and Gretel"—a tale in which "two children shove an old lady into an oven."[25] The reference might not seem particularly pertinent to Rebecca, yet the conflagration in which Mrs. Danvers perishes seems to resonate powerfully with Hitchcock's shorthand version of "Hansel and Gretel."

Like Gretel, the heroine of *Rebecca* proves to have her wits about her and to rescue her male partner from near fatality—in the film Mrs. de Winter faints just as her husband is about to confess to Rebecca's murder and thereby derails the legal proceedings. But like Bluebeard's wife, she is also intent on investigating her husband's past and understanding what it is that stands between the two of them. Rather than shrink back from the sites forbidden to her, she crosses the threshold of the boathouse that was the scene of Rebecca's death (and that Max reprimands her for entering) and walks into Rebecca's bedroom (guarded by Mrs. Danvers). Doors figure prominently in this film, and Hitchcock uses tracking shots to lead his heroine to a door, and then he cuts to the shot of a colossal door filling the screen. The protagonist, despite the intimidation from both husband and housekeeper, forges ahead with her investigation, if not fearlessly (she does, after all, have to be tortured), then at least with determination.

The new Mrs. de Winter not only explores forbidden spaces but also asks questions that, at the least, are considered gauche. "Please don't think me morbidly curious," she tells the manager of her husband's estates, as she produces a barrage of questions about Rebecca's death, culminating in the final question: "What was Rebecca really like?" This scene of interrogation is repeated in the boathouse, when the heroine learns from Maxim the circumstances of Rebecca's death. In that scene, the camera creates a presence from Rebecca's absence. As Maxim tells the heroine what happened on that night ("She got up, came toward me . . ."), the camera is trained on Rebecca's movements, creating a ghost-like presence on screen. It is at the end of Maxim's narrative that the heroine "solves" the mystery by declaring: "But you didn't kill her—it was an accident."

In Daphne du Maurier's *Rebecca*, Maxim is so provoked by Rebecca's taunts that he murders his wife. Hollywood's Motion Picture Production Code (an outgrowth of the Hays Office) was averse to the idea of allowing a murderer to escape unpunished, and the scriptwriters were obliged to transform the murder into an accident. While the screenplay's revisions to the novel may have gotten Max off the hook with the Motion Picture Production Code, Hitchcock's filming of the confession scene reveals how powerfully the camera can speak to an audience, sending a message very different from the one enunciated in the soundtrack and revealing that Max is, after all, a Bluebeard rather than a Prince Charming.

As Max reenacts the murder of Rebecca, he gets up and moves toward a closed door. Ventriloquizing his first wife, he gives us what appears to be a precise account of the events that took place in the boathouse. "What are you going to do about it?" Rebecca jeered at him. "Aren't you going to kill me?" Max reconstructs his response, inserting the only tentative statement about what happened that night: "I *suppose* I went mad for a minute. I *must have* struck her" [emphasis added]. Although Max repeats Rebecca's words with dead certainty, he seems curiously unsure of his own response to her provocation. As he speculates on the violence of his reaction, he opens the door behind him to reveal the massive mound of rope and ship's tackle on which Rebecca fell and struck her head. Moving from the coils of rope to the heroine's horrified face, the camera seems to give the lie to Max's story.

The film's true forbidden knowledge seems to lie behind the closed door that Maxim opens as he speaks with his second wife. If Rebecca did indeed fall as she approached Max, she would have had to move behind Max, open the door to the adjacent room, and fall on the ropes. That she received a mortal wound from the mound of ropes we see on screen seems highly unlikely. What appears far more plausible is that Max, in his enraged state, took a rope from the equipment room and used it to strangle his wife. Recall that the heroine, when she first explored the boathouse, removed a piece of rope from it, in the characteristic ironic touch that is Hitchcock's signature, using what might have been the murder weapon for the innocent purpose of walking the dog. Hitchcock fans do not need to be reminded that "Rope" is also the title of a film by the master of horror cinema.

In the process of investigating the crime, the heroine of *Rebecca* comes up with the solution that allows her "to stay on at Manderley and live happily ever after" (to use the words of Rebecca's nefarious "cousin" Jack Favell). "Maxim, does anyone else know this?" she anxiously asks her husband as soon as he has told her about the "accident." And she scripts a way out for her husband, first by insisting that he lie about the identity of the body in the boat—"It's got to be the body of someone you've never seen before"—then, when Maxim tells her that the body is sure to be properly identified by others, urging that he lie about an earlier lie—"You must simply say that you made a mistake about the other body." Intent on excluding the words that might be spoken by the victim, she declares herself prepared to be both wife and partner in crime: "She can't speak. She can't bear witness. She can't harm you anymore. We're the only two people in the world that know, Maxim, you and I." As viewers, we never know for certain whether the death of Rebecca was an accident or an act of murder, but the second Mrs. de Winter's words betray her own intuition that the victim might have a story very different from that of her husband.

In *Jane Eyre* and *Rebecca*, the second wives work hard to repress the secret of conjugal violence once they become privy to knowledge about their husbands' first wives. Their complete knowledge enables a relationship of "perfect concord," as Jane Eyre puts it: "All my confidence is bestowed on him, all his confidence is devoted to me" (397). Jane's words are echoed in the second Mrs. de Winter's declaration that "we march in unison" and "have no secrets from one another" (6). That there is something sinister about these perfect unions becomes evident as we watch Jane Eyre ministering to the blind Rochester at Ferndean and observe the ennui of the de Winters at the various European watering spots that become their home.

The authors of *Jane Eyre* and *Rebecca* engage in a process of re-mythification, drawing on the folklore of domestic life to write new stories about love and romance. What is astonishing about the plots of these two novels, which were perceived in their time as breakthrough works about feminine desire, is their conservative turn in relation to their host narrative. Jane Eyre and the second Mrs. de Winter, rather than aligning themselves with discovery and disclosure, become partners in crime, eager to cover up anything—in one case even murder—that stands in the way of their own romantic attachments. Inspired by a radical critique of marriage for the sake of wealth and glamour, Charlotte Brontë and Daphne du Maurier reconfigure the folklore plot to create wives whose curiosity leads to collusion rather than detection. They nonetheless reinvigorate the genre, for the stories they produce cry out for de-mythification even as they continue to produce copies of themselves.

The Gothic form of the Bluebeard plot is revived not only in the nineteenth century with *Jane Eyre* and again in the twentieth century with *Rebecca*, but also in the contemporary Harlequin Romance. This genre, which professes to "explore today's love relationships" and "boldly face confusing choices," takes on the issues that matter to women today: "Career first? Love later?" to cite one example taken from a promotion at the end of each volume. More openly than virtually any other literary form, Harlequin Romances take the pulse of the marketplace and respond with lightning speed, producing fantasies and anxieties that correspond to the desires and fears of their audiences.

Sarah Holland's *Bluebeard's Bride*, number 2705 in the Harlequin Romance series, provides a breathtakingly transparent account of what is at stake in the modern Gothic version of the Bluebeard plot. Harlequins, as

Tania Modleski has pointed out, are an "easy read" in part because they play directly to the reader's fears and fantasies and do not employ devices for "distancing and transforming the anxieties and wishes of their readers." *Bluebeard's Bride* reveals how the Bluebeard story can be rewritten to represent a kind of wish fulfillment and to create a fairy tale that is a new, more powerful version of the Cinderella story.[26]

Elizabeth, the young woman who becomes Bluebeard's bride, has been raised on fairy tales, on "bedtime stories—all about princesses with long golden hair who lived in big castles."[27] Courted aggressively by the wealthy, glamorous Mark Blackthorne, she falls in love "beyond all reason," remaining with Mark even when it becomes evident that he may have murdered his previous wife. "Elizabeth's capacity to love him had become limitless—and frightening—especially when she realized how vulnerable she'd allowed herself to become," the dust jacket tells us. Drawn to the Cinderella fantasy of romantic surrender to a complete stranger, Elizabeth finds herself the protagonist of a Bluebeard story, in which she is anxiously vigilant about her husband's every move. For this reason, her husband's mansion appears sometimes as "fairytale castle," sometimes as "haunted mansion" (112).

Elizabeth becomes the quintessential paranoid woman, deeply divided and ambivalent, continually observing herself and her surroundings. The paranoia manifests itself textually in the barrage of questions she addresses to herself: "How could she justify marrying a man who she thought might be a murderer?"; "What was in the West Wing?"; "What secret lay hidden beyond the locked door?"; "Who were all the others?"; "Is she spying on me . . . or am I just going paranoid?" (88). "You talk as though I'm Bluebeard," Mark observes when he is subjected to Elizabeth's interrogations about his past. "Do you really think I have a room full of dead women in the house?" he adds. Elizabeth's response is given to us in the form of an interior monologue: "Mark Blackthorne, a man with power and wealth at his fingertips . . . a man who kept secrets locked behind the doors of the West Wing" (93).

Gothic romances may have a formulaic quality to them, but that quality derives from a loose set of conventions that came to be codified after the fact. Harlequin Romances, by contrast, follow guidelines prescribed by the publisher. The formula, as one critic puts it, "rarely varies": "A young, inexperienced, poor to moderately-well-to-do woman encounters and becomes involved with a handsome, strong, experienced, wealthy man, older than herself by ten to fifteen years. The heroine is confused by the hero's behavior since, though he is obviously interested in her, he is mocking, cynical, contemptuous, often hostile, and even somewhat brutal."[28]

From Joanna Russ's inventory of the generic features of the Gothic plot, it becomes evident that the only real difference between the Gothic mode and the Harlequin Romance is that the Gothic requires a more robust elaboration of the plot's setting (the haunted mansion) and of the secret embedded in it (within the mansion and its inhabitant's mind).

In *Bluebeard's Bride*, Mark's hostile, secretive manner and his often brutal treatment of Elizabeth come to be markers of masculine charisma. Mark's mysterious past, in the form of the women he has loved and abandoned, is a sign of his sexual attractiveness. What makes this romance so compelling for its female audience is Elizabeth's perpetual state of uncertainty, the "gripping suspense" that has so powerful a hold on her. *Bluebeard's Bride* gives us our culture's version of the Cinderella fantasy. In it, the female protagonist is still young, naïve, and humble, but Prince Charming has morphed into Bluebeard, a magnetic man of wealth with a brutal manner and a mysterious past. That the cruelty and contempt of the latter-day Bluebeard in the Harlequin Romance are nothing more than a mask for deep devotion to the heroine makes this new story nearly as disturbing as the fairy tale from which it derives. For it seems that masculine brutality is a prerequisite for the "gripping suspense"—or what might also be called masochistic yearning—that is the dominant affect of the Harlequin heroine, the affect that keeps her hooked on the man of mystery in her life. Once Elizabeth has entered the West Wing and discovered that there is no real mystery in Mark's mansion, she is unlikely to be able to sustain the "limitless" love generated by the anxiety and desire she felt as Bluebeard's bride. Like Jane Eyre and Rebecca before her, Elizabeth is destined to move from romantic rapture to the boredom of domestic life.

"Terror and romance await Nancy in this town filled with horrible secrets!" The cover for *The Bluebeard Room*, Carolyn Keene's seventy-seventh installment in the Nancy Drew series, proclaims the attractions of what we ordinarily think of as antithetical affects. The young detective courts danger even as she keeps romantic entanglements at bay, producing a heroine who is forever pursuing mystery and eluding the arms of those who want her to settle down. Nancy Drew, unlike Jane Eyre and the second Mrs. de Winter, solves the mystery of the Bluebeard Room, then moves on to the next criminal case, conveniently escaping the fate of her more mature literary predecessors. Her serial detective work turns her into something of a female Bluebeard, always moving on to new adventures and new romantic challenges.

For Jane Eyre as for Mrs. de Winter, once mysteries are solved, enigmas are unlocked, and secrets revealed, there is little left but boredom. This is the conclusion reached by Mrs. de Winter herself, after she has finally fathomed the mystery of her husband's past. "We have no secrets now from one another," she proclaims with some pride just before she begins her retrospective narrative. "All things are shared. Granted that our little hotel is dull, and the food indifferent, and that day after day dawns very much the same, yet we would not have it otherwise. . . . We both appreciate simplicity, and if we are sometimes bored—well, boredom is a pleasing antidote to fear." It is difficult not to recoil in horror at the prospect of reading a novel equal in length to *Rebecca* about life after the conflagration at Manderley. "Dull," "indifferent," and "bored": these attributes rarely make for absorbing reading. What drives the plot of "Bluebeard" and of melodramatic literature in general is precisely the mix of terror and romance, a mix produced by the "horrible secrets" which the heroine must explore.

3

C H A P T E R

Investigative Pleasures:
Bluebeard's Wife in Hollywood

A love-smitten analyst playing a dream detective . . .
—Alfred Hitchcock, *Spellbound*

I am marrying a stranger, a man I don't know at all," Celia announces in the opening scene of Fritz Lang's *Secret beyond the Door* (1948). The words, spoken in a brooding voice-over, capture the strange mix of dread and desire felt at the prospect of yielding to the unknown. In George Cukor's *Gaslight* (1944), Paula also thrills to the notion of marriage to a stranger. "But I don't know you," she protests with a seductive smile that betrays the passionate nature of her desire when Gregory proposes marriage.

"Some women give birth to murderers, some go to bed with them, and some marry them," Francis Iles wrote in *Before the Fact*, the novel on which Hitchcock's film *Suspicion* was based.[1] This chapter will investigate cinematic women who marry murderers, or, better, women who marry men who have a past and who seem determined on murdering them.

It is not surprising that the cinematic culture of Hollywood in the 1940s would be invested in staging dramas that enacted both the anxiety and the excitement attending marriage to a stranger. This was, after all, a time of crisis, when women in great numbers were marrying men who were real strangers—soldiers going off to war who were taking vows out of a frantic need to establish intimacy and affection. "Hurried, lonely people made frightful mistakes in choosing mates," one cultural historian has observed, "and in 1945 and 1946 discovered they really didn't care that much about their spouses." It was also a time when women were realizing that the men to whom they had been married were becoming strangers.

After experiencing the dark horrors of combat, veterans returned home disaffected and alienated, estranged from the familiar realities of prewar life. Physically disabled or mentally unhinged, these men found themselves unable to go on from where they had left off. Near the end of the war, Coleman R. Griffiths of the National Conference on Family Relations warned: "The strand of continuity between the boy or girl who left home and the warrior who returns will be broken. As warriors they will have practiced deceit, treachery, and killing—evil means to the good that ought to lie at the end of the road."[2]

Soldiers returning from the war experience were often *not* themselves. Headlines in the newspapers ("Veteran Beheads Wife with Jungle Machete" and "Ex-Marine Held in Rape Murder") suggested that the violence of combat could spill over into civilian life.[3] To be sure, newspapers were invested in sensationalizing the notion of war-crazed veterans and were inclined to exaggerate the danger from returning combatants, who may or may not have been any more likely to engage in domestic violence than their civilian counterparts. But there was still a way in which men who had seen combat returned to the home front traumatized, sometimes in a belligerent frame of mind, and often needing to undergo a period of adjustment before returning to "normal" routines. In the postwar period, the *Reader's Digest* and *Ladies' Home Journal* regularly contained articles with suggestions for helping veterans make the transition back to civilian life.

As Andrea Walsh has pointed out, films from the 1940s featuring a wife in distress flourished in a "culture of distrust" and were "a powerful indictment of romantic love." "In this wedding and divorce boom era," she adds, "when many lonely and desperate women married men they hardly knew, these films possessed a great cautionary power . . . [they warn] against 'love at first sight' and cautioned women against domestic isolation."[4] The Bluebeard story, with its heroine who lives with a sinister stranger in a remote castle, provided the perfect plot apparatus for working through the marital crises experienced by men and women whose lives had been unsettled by the war experience. Like *Beauty and the Beast* (filmed in the immediate post–World War II period by Jean Cocteau), *Bluebeard* became a kind of foundational story, a point of departure for thinking about courtship and romance for a generation healing itself from the wounds of war. As we shall see, it was explicitly framed as an alternative to "Cinderella" and "Sleeping Beauty," which were discarded as dated narrative models for reflecting on love and marriage.

Bluebeard films of the 1940s form an extraordinarily intricate cinematic network, taking cues from each other in such obvious ways that they sometimes appear more closely related to each other than to any primal originating narrative. Like the tales in the folkloric sea of stories, they do not really refer to a foundational narrative but participate in what Roland Barthes has called "a serial movement of disconnections, overlappings, variation," revising, adapting, and reimagining the story embedded in previous films.[5] To be sure, some of the films nod in the direction of Charles Perrault's "Bluebeard," but most of them seem to be paying homage to a narrative tradition that is in the air, that has circulated in Anglo-American and European cultures as folktale, folk wisdom, children's story, adult melodrama, and song, and that settled into film as a natural resting place.

Still, that Perrault's folktale was on the minds of some filmmakers becomes evident in George Cukor's *Gaslight*, a movie that not only borrows from the French story to stage its marital drama but also explicitly reflects on the tale's enduring psychological appeal. Shortly after falling in love with Gregory, Paula (played by Ingrid Bergman) has second thoughts about marrying a stranger and plans a solitary journey "just to know what I'm doing, just to be sure." Her instincts are correct, but despite her reservations she ends by marrying Gregory, a jewel thief who murdered her aunt some years back and now plans to find the jewels that he missed on the first try. On a train ride, Paula meets Miss Thwaites, the quintessential old biddy with an expert's passion for gossip, horror, and vicarious pleasure. "It's so exciting," Miss Thwaites reports, squealing with delight about her reading matter for the train ride. "It's all about a girl who marries a man, and what do you think, he's got *six* wives buried in the cellar."

What delights Miss Thwaites is, again, the special blend of romance and horror that characterizes the story of Bluebeard. As the older woman waxes increasingly enthusiastic about the homicidal maniac in the book she is reading, confessing that she "enjoys a good murder now and then," Paula, who has had firsthand experience of a real murder, begins to shut down emotionally. But only momentarily, for she soon thrills to the touch of a hand mysteriously emerging from offscreen. It is Gregory, who embraces Paula with a passion that leaves Miss Thwaites aghast. "Well!" she gasps in consternation, slumping down into her seat. A moment later, she recovers and repositions herself to get a better view of the transgressive encounter enacted before her eyes. The desire to see, tinged earlier with dread and now with relieved voyeuristic pleasure, is doubled in the sensation-seeking spectator on screen and off.

Like Miss Thwaites, we are positioned as fascinated voyeurs, riveted by a spectacle that blends erotic intrigue with criminal mystery. Our attraction to whirlwind romance, our passionate fascination with violence, and our love of "good" murder stories lure us into what Paula calls a "house of horror," which contains in its deepest recesses the enigma of Gregory's murderous desires. Miss Thwaites's renewed shrieks of delight on seeing Paula enter that house are a signal to the cinematic spectator: Paula is about to stage for us the plot of the novel that so agitated Miss Thwaites on the train. To Gregory's Bluebeard, she will play the role of Bluebeard's wife.

In the 1940s Hollywood produced more than a dozen films modeled on the Bluebeard plot. The titles, ranging from *Suspicion* and *Caught* to *Experiment Perilous* and *Undercurrent*, imply risk, describing a menace that has been captured by one critic in the sentence "Somebody's trying to kill me, and I think it's my husband." Critics have searched in vain for just the right phrase to characterize these films. Mary Ann Doane refers to the "paranoid woman's film" and locates the paranoia in the "formulaic repetition of a scenario in which the wife invariably fears that her husband is planning to kill her—the institution of marriage is haunted by murder." Andrea S. Walsh follows suit by using the term "woman's film of suspicion and distrust." Thomas Elsaesser writes of "Freudian feminist melodrama," while Marjorie Rosen writes of "anti-female thrillers" and "masochistic stories." Other critics emphasize the importance of the haunted house, mansion, or castle and the dark secret it contains. Norman Holland and Lenore Sherman define the films as a special genre featuring "woman-plus-habitation." Still others stress the vulnerability of the female protagonist, who becomes the target of violent aggression: Michael Walker, for example, adopts the term "wife-in-distress cycle."[6]

These critics have sharpened our understanding of the genre, yet none of them makes more than passing reference to the Bluebeard plot that informs the cinematic narratives and their Gothic antecedents. In each of these films, it is the opening of a man's secret drawer, cabinet, or chamber that brings down the threat of death, turning each of these films into what Michael Walker has described as a "psychological reworking of the Bluebeard fairy tale."[7] Walker does not pursue the allusion, but the Bluebeard story is so fundamental to the shape of the plot, the network of symbols, and the construction of characters in these films that I will henceforth refer to the genre as the Bluebeard cycle.

Films like *Gaslight* and *Secret beyond the Door* give us the flip side to the male *film noir*, a cinematic genre that positions a hard-boiled detective as the investigator of a woman. In the *noir* genre, we have what Richard Maltby calls a "less than perfect, frequently neurotic, sometimes paranoid" investigator who nonetheless consolidates his masculine identity by undertaking a crime-related quest that involves a seductive, duplicitous woman.[8] In the female counterpart to these melodramatic thrillers, it is a man—not just any man but usually a husband or a fiancé—who becomes the target of both a woman's romantic interest and her investigative curiosity. The man's pathology seems to be the main obstacle to happiness, though the woman, drawn to a disturbed partner, is also not unproblematic and seems to suffer from a paranoia that places her in a symmetrical position with her male *noir* counterpart. The female *film noir* blends psychological mystery with Gothic melodrama to produce a powerful hybrid form that plots the complexities of romantic liaisons.

Hollywood cinema had prepared the way for the role of woman as investigator in a remarkable cycle of 1930s films that showed marriages haunted by the threat, not of murder, but of divorce. In *Pursuits of Happiness*, Stanley Cavell analyzes seven of those films—among others, *The Philadelphia Story* and *Bringing Up Baby*—which he designates as Hollywood comedies of remarriage. In them, the status of the heroine as *married* woman transgresses the norms of classical comedy and produces a plot invested in getting the central pair, not together, but *back* together. Thirties comedy, driven by a heroine "who may hold the key to the successful conclusion of the plot" (as Cavell puts it), gives way to 1940s melodrama, a genre in which the marital estrangement implied by the threat of divorce is so intensified that it takes the form of a powerful rupture imperiling the wife's safety.[9] This heroine must also find a key (in many cases one that is both metaphorical and real) to the mystery of her husband's behavior—without it she remains menaced by murder. In films from the 1940s, women are given roles that, in the words of one critic, allow them to be "active, adventurous, and driven by sexual desire," even as they are terrorized, terrified, and driven to a state of near paralysis in the claustrophobic atmosphere of the marital home.[10]

If cinematic women of the 1930s are actively in "pursuit" of happiness, women of the 1940s play a higher-stakes game in which the goal is above all survival. To be sure, the wives in Bluebeard films are also intent on restoring trust and preserving a marital union, but they take risks unimagined by their 1930s counterparts. At times they appear downright reckless in their willingness to remain at all costs with a husband who, to the cinematic spectator, appears to be a homicidal maniac. But the magnitude of the danger can also reflect well on the heroine, who is, in many cases, fearless, indomitable, and prepared to go to war for the marital cause.

In the cinematic tradition inaugurated by Hitchcock's *Rebecca* (1940) and stretching from Robert Stevenson's *Jane Eyre* (1944) to Max Ophul's *Caught* (1949), the heroine takes the initiative in resolving the marital crisis. Films belonging to the Bluebeard cycle explicitly disavow fairy tales such as "Cinderella" and "Sleeping Beauty" as paradigms for romance. In *Caught*, Leonora's wedding to Smith Ohlrig may be billed by the press as a fabulous fairy tale come true (we see multiple headlines alluding to the bride as a Cinderella figure), but it quickly degenerates into marriage to a real ogre. Mark may call Celia a twentieth-century Sleeping Beauty in Fritz Lang's *Secret beyond the Door*, but his kisses quickly turn cold, and his wife does not take that change of heart lying down. *Undercurrent* may show the wife Ann on display as a Sleeping Beauty and her husband may kiss her with a dramatic passion that hints at his qualities as Prince Charming, but the astute viewer will read this as a sinister moment in which Alan is deceiving Ann into thinking that she has a fairy-tale marriage. Only in Hitchcock's *Notorious*, the brilliant exception that proves the rule, does the heroine turn into a sleeping beauty, and, in that case, she succumbs to narcotics administered by those seeking to obstruct her undercover work. "Cinderella" and "Sleeping Beauty," the quintessential stories of women waiting to be rescued by men, are systematically discredited as stories that bear false promises and mask the real state of affairs in contemporary marriages.

Before considering three representative films from the Bluebeard cycle (*Gaslight, Secret beyond the Door*, and *Notorious*), I must note that critics are deeply divided in their view of what is at stake in these films. Andrea Walsh, who first drew our attention to the family resemblances among 1940s films featuring women threatened by their husbands, focuses on films like *Gaslight* and *Suspicion* and rightly entitles her analysis "Suspicion Confirmed." By contrast, Mary Ann Doane, writing three years later, referred to these two films and others as belonging to a "paranoid cycle." If we turn to the films themselves, we discover that the notion of persecution, whether real or imagined, is a powerful component in the narrative logic of every plot, yet a single-minded focus on it has a way of effacing other issues critical to the construction of female subjectivity. Suspicion and its pathological cousin paranoia produce a variety of affects ranging from terror to desire, from fear of the unknown to a wish to investigate and understand that unknown. In all of the films in the Bluebeard cycle, the heroine walks a treacherous tightrope between terror and desire (both cognitive and erotic), and it is in her guarded balancing act that we can discover something about the complexities of wartime and postwar engagements with the terrors of desire in marital matters.

"Gaslight genre"—this is the term often used to designate films in which a man seems to be trying to kill his wife. In many ways, George Cukor's *Gaslight* is a foundational text, giving us the consummate persecuted wife, paralyzed by her husband's campaign to drive her mad so that he can rummage in the attic for the jewels that escaped him when he killed the house's occupant years earlier. Paula, as befits an onscreen heroine, is haunted by light and sound, driven to distraction by the visual and acoustic effects engineered by Gregory. The gaslight that he periodically dims and brightens to disorient Paula is a substance that combines the notion of something toxic with something that ordinarily brings enlightenment. It works as a powerful technological poison with near fatal effects. A "helpless victim," as the advertising campaign informs us, Paula is so terrorized by Gregory and the light that becomes his weapon that her critical faculties are disabled, leaving no energy for investigative purposes.

Gregory's mischief turns the domestic arena into a space permeated by unsettling sounds and visual effects. Paula can never be at ease, for she has been enclosed and contained, the prisoner of a husband who has turned home into an uncanny domain that offers no secure ground. Small wonder that, whenever the beleaguered Paula appears on screen, her eyes dart around, looking into corners, taking in larger vistas, and examining her own bodily movements. Contrary to one critic's claim, films in the Bluebeard cycle do not just give us "strange fantasies of persecution, rape and death—masochistic reveries and nightmares, which cast the husband into the role of the sadistic murderer," but real imperilment.[11]

While paranoia may be a useful term for describing the cinematic space and style of *Gaslight*, it is the wrong clinical term for Paula's condition. Gregory really is trying to drive Paula mad, and Paula is right to be wary and suspicious. If we fault her at all, it is for her misplaced confidence in Gregory and for failing to train her suspicions on him. In many ways, however, the film leads us to pathologize Paula rather than Gregory. Its introductory flashback, for example, focuses on Paula's traumatic childhood, leaving us completely in the dark about what drives Gregory to kill. Even when we learn that an obsession with jewels motivated Gregory's murder of Paula's aunt, we are never given any clues at all about what inspired the obsession. Psychoanalytic critics will be quick to point out the phallic connection and to read Gregory's quest for jewels as the search for a missing fetish object that will turn him into a real man at last. But just as many versions of the Bluebeard folktale pathologize the wife, focusing on her disobedience and curiosity, cinematic rescriptings of the Bluebeard plot draw us into the orbit of the wife's anxieties and desires.

Paranoia may not capture what is amiss with Paula, but, like suspicion, it has a certain structural logic that helps us determine what matters in the cinematic Bluebeard plot. Possessing a curious double face, paranoia on the one hand promotes a form of hypersensitivity that leads to exaggerated fears and abject terror, but, on the other, fosters a drive for greater awareness, for knowledge, power, and mastery of reality (one not unrelated to the curiosity of Bluebeard's wife in the folkloric tradition). As the science fiction critic Carl Freedman has pointed out, paranoia is "no mere aberration" but instead is "structurally crucial to the way that we . . . represent ourselves to ourselves and embark on the Cartesian project of acquiring empiricist knowledge."[12] Like any mental state acutely sensitive to its surroundings, paranoia promotes a kind of investigative energy that struggles to make sense of the world, even if that sense appears as nonsense to everyone else.

This desire to identify the forces threatening the self has a flip side, one that emerges with relentless logic in the midst of efforts to gain psychological mastery. As those efforts pay off and as investigative desire yields or seems to yield results, fear can quickly mount, for the disclosure of secret knowledge always produces risk. Thus the search for knowledge inevitably turns back on itself to produce terror rather than certainty and to create an investigator subjected to that terror, one who must submit to a masochistic position if the search is to continue. George Cukor, as director of *Gaslight*, was acutely aware of the way in which the character of Paula was divided against itself, with one part of her succumbing to terror, the other fighting for survival. He was enamored of the idea of casting a "powerful woman" like Ingrid Bergman in the role of Paula: "It will be twice as interesting to see whether she will be able to fight back, whether he will be able to really ruin her, or break her."[13] Bergman rises to the challenge, producing a Bluebeard's wife who serves as model to those who follow her in the role.

Bluebeard films are propelled into action by a crisis of interpretation, by the need to get to the bottom of a life history. "What does it all mean?" Celia asks herself in Fritz Lang's *Secret beyond the Door*. But that vibrant investigative energy is always also tainted by and sometimes dominated or nearly defeated by the heroine's submission to masochistic desires and by her dark passion for psychological disturbances. "Maybe I should have run away," Celia notes about her first meeting with Mark, revealing that she is not at all in the dark about the morbid nature of her fixation on the stranger who becomes her husband. For the greater part of Cukor's film, what we have before our eyes is a woman unable to run away—a woman so vulnerable and tormented that she is driven insidiously to the brink of madness. Terrorized by light and sound, the distraught Paula becomes so powerful a symbol for a person being driven mad that the term "gaslight," used as a verb, has entered common parlance to signify deluding a person into thinking he or she is insane.

Although *Gaslight* shows Paula's gradual descent into a state where her interpretive powers are so disabled that she becomes utterly disoriented, she is also positioned, near the film's end, as one member of an investigative couple. If only as the minority partner, she collaborates with a detective from Scotland Yard named Cameron to solve the mystery of her husband's nocturnal activities and to reveal the criminal depth of his passion for jewels. Gregory has two forbidden chambers: the dusty attic containing furniture and paintings (along with the costume in which are sewn the missing jewels) and his desk (a repository of secret knowledge about his double identity). Paula helps to break into the latter, and she takes control of matters in the final scene by tormenting Gregory with feigned madness. In Patrick Hamilton's *Angel Street* (1939), the play on which the film was based, Mrs. Mannigham (the Paula of Cukor's screen adaptation) takes an even more active role in her rescue. "You should have been a policeman," Detective Rough tells her, praising the "keenness" of her powers of observation.[14]

In Bluebeard films, the search for knowledge is conducted in physical and psychic spaces that are figured as mansions and minds, both containing secrets locked from view. "What goes on in his mind?" Celia asks in *Secret beyond the Door* as she watches her husband, Mark. "He keeps it locked like this door." Vincent Minnelli's *Undercurrent* perfectly captures the reciprocal relation between mind and mansion, which are conjoined in their capacity to conceal a traumatic kernel. Ann's growing sense of discomfort at her husband's house and her cozy sense of belonging at the ranch of his brother Mike reflect her intuitive understanding that physical spaces are symptomatic of mental states. "I think this is one of the most charming houses I've ever seen," she tells Mike (whom she assumes to be the caretaker). "It has dignity. It doesn't look as though it's been shut up at all. It looks, well, as though it was waiting for someone. . . . Haven't you ever had a feeling of complete peace and contentment? That's what I felt when I came in here. There's nothing to fear or think about. . . . It's a home." The obvious contrasting space, the marital mansion, becomes a forbidding space, an uncanny domain permeated with evidence of her husband's treachery. Hence Alan's emphatic admonition ("Faith and trust."), so perfectly in keeping with the spirit of the folkloric Bluebeard who tests for blind obedience even as he keeps a roomful of evidence revealing that he is not to be trusted.

Only two years later, when Hitchcock made *Notorious*, he took up the Bluebeard plot, but reversed the developmental trajectory found in *Gaslight*. *Notorious* begins by positioning its heroine as a professional investigator, a spy hired by American agents to infiltrate a Nazi ring operating out of Rio de Janeiro. Alicia's mission is to marry a stranger—a friend of her father's, to be sure, but a man about whom she knows only that he keeps vital (military) secrets in a locked wine cellar. But once Alicia succeeds in stealing the fabled key, opening the door to the wine cellar, and penetrating its secrets, she lapses into a completely passive role, transformed from a confident, resourceful Bluebeard's wife into a sleeping beauty carried off in the arms of her fellow agent, Devlin, and played to tormented perfection by, once again, Ingrid Bergman.

How do we account for the strange conflation of desire and death in these films? How is the relationship between the drive for knowledge and the yearning for submission figured in them? Note that Paula's evolution from victim to sleuth ends with the dissolution of her marriage, while Alicia's reverse move from sleuth to victim will be marked as the romantic climax to *Notorious*. In the one film, the institution of marriage becomes problematic precisely when it ceases to be haunted by the threat of murder; in the other, a relationship is represented as supremely stable when one partner is in a state of abject passivity.

Let us begin by thinking about Alicia, the woman to whom the attribute "notorious" is meant to be attached. From the start, Alicia is framed as the target of the male gaze. As she leaves the courtroom where her father has been sentenced to prison, she is engulfed by reporters and photographers seeking to capture her response. "Notorious" both for her own loose ways and for her father's politics, Alicia is persuaded to redeem herself and prove her patriotism by assisting in a spying operation. Through the activity of surveillance, Alicia reverses the gaze, turning her eyes on a circle of men who are unaware of her double role.

Alicia becomes an arch-investigator, rising to every challenge assigned her, including the securing of a marriage proposal from one of the Nazi ringleaders. Once in the marital home, she succeeds in procuring the keys to the rooms and closets of her husband's house. But like Bluebeard's wife, she is denied access to one critical space. We see Alicia, accompanied by the butler, opening one door after another until she is finally stopped at the door to the wine cellar, the forbidden space she must enter in order to accomplish the mission of fathoming her husband's scientific secrets. Alicia becomes the consummate dissimulator, so adept at deceit, duplicity, and disguise that she fools her husband, Alex Sebastian, completely, leading him to believe that she harbors tender feelings for him. In Alicia's moment of supreme triumph, when she succeeds in purloining the key to the wine cellar, she passionately embraces the man who has given her his full trust, doubling her political betrayal of him with sexual betrayal.[15]

Alicia has become everything that the interpreters of "Bluebeard" broadcast: the woman who, like all women, is untrustworthy, treacherous, and traitorous. "She has stolen Sebastian's love and his secrets, indeed his life, and she has feigned her love 'with those clinging kisses' while lusting for another," Michael Renov avers. "It is every man's suspicion that his mother is right—that she is the only woman he can trust—that suspicion is borne out by Alicia and by the film."[16] Alex, by contrast, becomes a model husband, with a love for his wife that is both ardent and heartfelt. Consider the moment at which Alicia steals the key to the wine cellar. In a dazzling display of cunning duplicity, Alicia manages to remove the key from Alex's desk while he is toweling himself off in the bathroom and telling his wife, "I can't blame anyone for being in love with you." When Alex emerges, he tenderly takes Alicia's hands to reassure her. "Darling," he tells her apologetically, "it's not that I don't trust you, but when you're in love at my age, every man who looks at you is a menace. Will you forgive me for even talking about it? I'm very contrite." Alex is so smitten with Alicia that he succeeds in creating a character who could be described as Hollywood's only charming Nazi.

A curious hybrid, *Notorious* combines a spy story complete with Nazis and cold war political intrigue with a romantic love story. In the political plot, Alicia begins as a spy, victorious in her every effort to penetrate, explore, and discover. But as her espionage star rises, her romantic star falls, and the American agent Devlin torments her with his icy demeanor. A scene at the door to the wine cellar marks a sharp shift in Alicia's trajectory as investigator. As Alicia and Devlin close the door to the wine cellar, they stand at the site of her double duplicity, the scene of her sexual and political betrayal of Alex. It is at this point that the register of the political collapses into the register of the personal and the spy story becomes one with the romantic plot.[17] And it is at this point that Alicia, who has been so serenely in control of her investigative faculties, falters and moves to a state of almost complete paralysis.

Soon after the scene made by Alicia and Devlin at the entrance to the wine cellar (they embrace in front of Alex in order to put him on the wrong track), Alicia's exuberant confidence in her investigative powers wanes, and even before she is slowly poisoned by Alex's mother, we see her fall prey to very real anxieties about being caught. As she takes one dose after another of the coffee that turns out to be far more toxic than the alcohol in which she had earlier indulged, she yields the role of investigator entirely to Devlin. Her vision disabled, she begins to fail in her mission and desperately needs Devlin's intervention in order to survive. Aching for Devlin, she writhes and agonizes before the camera until she is reduced to pure passivity, waiting for a rescue that pantomimes the conclusion to "Sleeping Beauty." Depleted of investigative energy, Alicia has become a virtually inert figure, moved from Alex's mysterious mansion into the dark, claustrophobic interior of a car that carries off the new couple.

If *Gaslight* put Ingrid Bergman on display as devoted wife who descends into a state of abject terror but finds her way back by engaging her powers of detection, *Notorious* shows Bergman as duplicitous sleuth who degenerates into pure victim. In the cinematic culture of the 1940s, it seemed impossible to steer a course between the extremes of mortified passivity and confident mastery. To the contrary, it seemed of critical importance to represent both ends of this emotional spectrum, perhaps as a message about the ease with which self-assurance can slip into utter vulnerability and how only utter vulnerability guarantees romantic fulfillment. For Hitchcock, the uranium stored in the cellar's wine bottles worked as a perfect metaphor for what was at stake in the film. Highly unstable and potentially lethal, the radioactive substance captures the volatile complexities of human emotions, which can be explosive even when they appear inert.

Fritz Lang's *Secret beyond the Door* takes us a step beyond *Gaslight* and *Notorious* by introducing a heroine who, for a time at least, negotiates something of a truce between nervous vulnerability and intellectual strength. Celia, unlike Paula and Alicia (whose names resonate powerfully with her own), manages to produce a heavy dose of anxious affect even as she shrewdly plots a course that will secure a happy ending for her and the stranger she met and married in Mexico.

Celia begins as a "twentieth-century Sleeping Beauty" (the term is her husband's) and is galvanized into investigative action by the enigmatic behavior of her spouse. On first meeting Celia, Mark describes her as "a wealthy American girl who's lived her life wrapped in cotton and wool. But she wants to wake up. Maybe she can." Mark's words point not only to his wife's passivity but also to the sheltered quality of her existence. "Wrapped in cotton and wool," she is protected against physical harm as well as emotional turmoil. It is Mark who will gradually remove those protective layers, exposing Celia to perils but also inciting her to awaken from delicate passivity to discover the pleasures of intellectual and emotional engagement.

Secret beyond the Door works far more self-consciously than either *Gaslight* or *Notorious* with its folkloric subtext, developing constant explicit points of contact with the Bluebeard narrative and positioning the heroine as a canny investigator of both the murderous secret locked in a physical space (room number seven in the marital home) and the traumatic secret locked in her husband's mind. As Celia does her Freudian detective work, she is ever more aware of the risks to which she is exposing herself, yet she perseveres. Like Dr. Petersen, the "love-smitten analyst playing a dream detective" in Hitchcock's *Spellbound*, Celia must unlock the door to a childhood memory and show how it is the source of the hero's psychosis. The epigraph to *Spellbound* reveals how the knowledge system of psychoanalysis is linked to a mythic discourse connected with both *Bluebeard* and the story of Pandora. It is cast both as the key to a forbidden chamber and as a process resembling Pandora's transgressive opening of a box containing evils (though in the case of psychoanalysis releasing evils has a benign effect): "Our story deals with psychoanalysis, the method by which modern science treats the problems of the sane. The analyst seeks only to induce the patient to talk about his hidden problems, to open the locked doors of his mind. Once the complexes that have been disturbing the patient are uncovered and interpreted, the illness and confusion disappear, and the devils of unreason are driven from the human soul."

Secret beyond the Door initially puts Celia in charge of the narrative and the events that unfold in it. Her voice-over ensures that we see events from her point of view, from the flashback giving us the particulars of her family history to the moment when we hear an offscreen scream that seems to signal her death. Once Celia opens the door to room number seven, she possesses knowledge of her husband's murderous intent and lives in perpetual danger that Mark will turn on her. When it appears that Mark has made his homicidal move, his voice takes over, relating the events that lead to the avoidance of tragedy and to the installation of a postnuptial happily-ever-after ending.

Lang's title calls attention to the centrality of the forbidden chamber and to the secret encased in it. In *Secret beyond the Door*, that chamber refers on the one hand to a physical space, a room designed by Mark, who, in his role as architect, specializes in reconstructing rooms in which notorious historical murders have been committed. On the other hand it refers to a mental space, the mind that Mark, according to Celia, "keeps locked" and that she has to "open . . . for *his* sake." While Mark offers tours of six of his historical rooms, he refuses to show the seventh to his assembled guests, claiming that "a man must have some secrets."

Operating as an expert detective, Celia, like Alicia, takes advantage of her husband's momentary absence in the shower. Savvier than her counterpart in *Notorious*, she makes a wax imprint of the key to the room, orders a copy made up for her, and, armed with a flashlight and key, enters

101

the forbidden chamber. Through her voice-over, Celia had dominated the narrative in acoustic terms. Now she takes full charge of the cinematic apparatus through her control of light and of the path it takes through the house, a path that will lead directly to the forbidden door to which Celia possesses the key. Unlike Paula, who is subjected to the terrors of gaslight, she uses light to dispel her fears, though not before finding that knowledge can produce uncanny effects.

When Celia opens that door, she remains unruffled, believing this "felicitous room" (the term is Mark's) to be a reproduction of the bedroom of Mark's first wife (who died under mysterious circumstances). Yet a look at the two candles on the dresser—of different sizes, just as in her own room—makes her freeze with horror. These candles are what Slavoj Žižek has referred to as a "phallic detail," less because of their shape than because they constitute a detail that "does not fit," that "sticks out" from the idyllic surface scene to denaturalize it and render it uncanny. Like the punctum in Roland Barthes's meditation on photography, the phallic detail unsettles, startling us and obliging us to rethink everything that lies on the surface. Žižek reads the "phallic element" as a meaningless stain that renders all constituent elements of a scene "suspicious" and opens up an abyss that requires a search for meaning. Nothing is what it seems to be. Everything has to be rethought, renegotiated, and reinterpreted. It is at precisely this point that the film produces a rupture, liquidating Celia as investigating subject and appearing to shift to Mark as the agent who will solve the enigma of the troubled marriage.[18]

Without Celia's tenacity, her faith in Mark, and her determination to make the marriage work, that enigma would never yield to investigative pressure. It is Celia who first divines the presence of Mark's skeletons, which "come rattling out of every closet." "I'm just curious," she tells Mark. "I don't want to pry. I want to understand you." Driven by more than the desire to know, she asks herself, "What can it mean?" *Secret beyond the Door* doubles the secret of its title, for there are two enigmas to be solved. There is the case of Mark's first wife, from whom he became estranged after his return from the war. Was she murdered or did she die of natural causes? Then there is the strange behavior Mark exhibits after being locked out of Celia's bedroom. That behavior is linked to a traumatic childhood memory that haunts the adult Mark. Celia will help Mark to remember how, as a ten-year-old boy, he had raged against his mother when he believed that she had locked him in his room to keep him from interfering with her plans to spend the evening with a gentleman caller. Pounding and clawing at his bedroom door until his hands were bloody, the young Mark seized the lilacs he had gathered with his mother: "I crushed them, strangled them, killed them—I wanted to kill her."

While Mark's troubled relationship with his first wife is little more than symptom of the deeper childhood trauma, it is telling that that relationship unraveled after Mark's return from the war. Although the film works hard to attribute Mark's trauma to oedipal rather than cultural causes, its casual allusion to the effect of war on Mark's marriage should not go unheeded. It is almost as if the film were reluctant to meditate on the estranging effects of war experience while it freely indulges in an intricately contrived oedipal explanation for Mark's pathology. "All my life I've been hemmed in by women," Mark sneers at one point, underscoring the notion that men are threatened by women who, like Celia, take charge. It is here, rather than in the shift from Celia's voice-over to Mark's, that we can locate the film's real gender trouble, for it is here that the film's implied endorsement of the intelligent, energetic, shrewd, and loyal woman is undermined.

For Mark to live happily ever after, he must eliminate the maternal superegos that have been "hemming" him in and controlling his every move, from the widower mother to whom he had a strong oedipal attachment to the sister who arranged his first marriage. And Celia must not only solve the mystery of Mark's mysterious mood swings, but must also transform herself, as she dutifully does, from detective, psychoanalyst, master interpreter (the controlling woman par excellence) to the adoring, self-effacing wife of the film's final scene.

Reading the film as a successful investigative project that begins with a dark, oedipal secret and ends with its disclosure and effacement has a certain seductive appeal, particularly since this reading would buttress the view that the Bluebeard plot can serve as a gendered master narrative of the psychoanalytic process, with the husband as analysand and the wife as analyst. Yet this reading misses the problematic aspects of Celia's character and becomes possible only by eliding key moments in the flashbacks that precede Celia's marriage to Mark. Recall Maltby's words about the protagonists of *film noir*: "less than perfect, frequently neurotic, sometimes paranoid." In the female *noir*, the protagonists, like their male counterparts, are strangely immobilized, despite their detective work. Žižek observes that the "*noir* narrative reduces the hero to a passive observer transfixed by the succession of fantasy scenes, to a gaze powerlessly gaping at them: even when the hero seems 'active,' one cannot avoid the impression that he simultaneously occupies the position of a disengaged observer, witnessing with incredulity the strange, almost submarine, succession of events in which he remains trapped."[19]

In *Secret beyond the Door*, the doubling of the investigative process leads to Celia's discovery of what has been troubling Mark and to the viewer's discovery of disturbances in Celia's psyche. (The same doubling can be found in Ann's detective work in *Undercurrent*, for by "borrowing" the key to Mike's ranch she may ostensibly be planning to solve her marital troubles, but she really betrays a passionate fascination with her husband's brother.) It is this second plot that prevents the film from flattening out into a vulgarized version of Freudian melodrama that predictably takes Mark from a condition of neurotic misery to normal human unhappiness. Celia seems so invested in solving her marital problems that it is easy to miss the nature of her own desires. But the scream that marks the shift from Celia's point of view to Mark's sends a clear signal that Celia has not effaced herself in the drive to heal Mark. The scream is symptomatic of the passionate mix of death and desire haunting her. It echoes the scream heard at the very beginning of the film, when a Mexican woman's shriek is heard off-screen in a tableau that brings Mark and Celia together for the first time. Chatting with a friend in a busy market square, Celia hears that scream and reports the events that follow hard upon it: "A woman, and two men . . . fighting over her with naked knives. Death was in that street. And I felt how proud she must be." A poster for *Caught* reveals the degree to which female desire is affiliated with danger and violence: "Dazzling Romance, Dream of Every Girl, Turned into Nightmare of Terror!"[20]

Celia's scream may lead to a silencing of her voice, but it also signals her need and desire for Mark's intervention as murderer/rescuer. For Celia, death and desire are emphatically conjoined. It is under the sign of the two that she falls in love with Mark, and it is the mingling of the two in her relation to Mark that holds her "spellbound" (as a friend puts it). Mark represents the fulfillment of erotic desires in large part because he also represents the threat of death. While the erotic triangle in Mexico positioned the woman safely outside the deadly conflict between two men, the romantic triangle of Mark, Celia, and her earlier suitor Bob or the pre-oedipal triangle of Mark, Celia, and Mark's mother positions Celia as target of Mark's murderous impulses. It is only after enacting her own version of the love triangle in Mexico that Celia seems able to free herself from a state of terrorized hysteria and to move in the mode of calm determination. Purged of her need to intensify desire through the threat of death, Celia is able to free Mark from the tyranny of his past. "For both, the fantasy of the dangerous sexual other who will either kill or be killed is successfully overturned."[21]

Central to *film noir*, Elizabeth Cowie tells us, is "the connection of desire with death." In the *noir* genre, American cinema finds for the first time "a form in which to represent desire as something that not only renders the desiring subject helpless, but also propels him or her to destruction."[22] Lang rewrites the story of Bluebeard in such a way as to explore the psyches of both husband and wife. Under the cover of a plot that investigates the murderous reach of oedipal disturbances in the adult male psyche, Lang constructs a second plot that explores female desire in its darkest narcissistic and masochistic recesses. That Celia finally wants to heal Mark by identifying the traumatic memory that gave rise to his murderous impulses is testimony to her own healing, to her success in letting go of the seductive power of a husband who keeps her in a state of perpetual terror and obliges her to keep her wits about her at all times.

What has held Celia in thrall has something to do with what Žižek calls "the horrifying, lethal and at the same time fascinating borderline that we approach when the reversal into bliss is imminent."[23] It is almost as if the film leads us along the surface of a Möbius strip, guiding us through a *noir* psychodrama and allowing us to witness its morbid phases until we find ourselves on the reverse side of the strip, in the film's idyllic final scene, with Mark and Celia as a happy couple engaged in casual banter. The image of the harmonious couple can be vouchsafed only by working through scenes of bitter antagonism, conflicted feelings, and hostile emotions.

The profusion of films in the 1940s with a Bluebeard subtext betrays the presence of extraordinary cultural anxieties about marriage. Like the folktale on which their plots are based, the films challenge the myth of love at first sight and reveal that hastily made marriages can be fraught with danger. But unlike the marriage in the folktale, many of the cinematic marriages work, and the films themselves, while staging the hazards of marriage, also provide a blueprint for it. By showing that marital intimacy, trust, and commitment are developed through elaborate negotiations and renegotiations, they provide a realistic, almost pragmatic, guide for producing marital accord.

Combining cerebral investigative powers with passionate romantic devotion, the women in these films use their brains to penetrate the secret inhibitions of masculinity and to dismantle sophisticated defenses against intimacy. Their aim is to shift the site of affective investment from jewels (as in *Gaslight*), from wealth (as in *Caught*), from espionage (as in *Notorious*), from gambling (as in *Suspicion*), from hatred of a brother (as in *Undercurrent*), from an obsession with childhood trauma (as in *Secret beyond the Door*) to the marriage partner of the opposite sex.

Bluebeard films from the 1940s give us stories of domestic life, transforming an ordinary marriage plot into an adventure story, a murder mystery, or a detective story. Classic detective fiction, as Walter Benjamin has pointed out, invests the objects of everyday life with the promise of adventure, with a tantalizing invitation to follow a track and to explore a mystery.[24] The commodity-filled bourgeois home, ordinarily the site of unnerving tedium, becomes a place of nervous anxiety, each item marked with the promise of yielding a clue to the tense central enigma. It comes as no surprise that virtually all Bluebeards (folkloric and cinematic) are wealthy men living in mansions cluttered with commodities. *Gaslight* is particularly symptomatic in this regard, for there, household clutter is also used to create a claustrophobic atmosphere and to intensify the challenge of finding Alice Alquist's lost jewels. From Perrault's castle, with its treasure-filled caskets, cabinets, and strongholds, to the mansion in *Caught*, whose Bluebeard-like inhabitant proclaims "I'm rich, I have everything," the marital abode becomes a site where domestic serenity is subverted through menacing danger. Rather than dusting the furniture and keeping it in a polished state, the heroine must explore it, trying to discover the secrets it harbors about her husband.

Yet while these films highlight the heroine's spirit of adventure, curiosity, and desire for knowledge, they also freely indulge in spotlighting her terrorization and victimization. "The woman's exercise of an active, investigative gaze can only be simultaneous with her own victimization." For Linda Williams, the woman's investigative gaze is punished by representational practices that turn curiosity and desire into masochistic fixations.[25] Nowhere is this more evident than in Iles's *Before the Fact*, which, unlike Hitchcock's *Suspicion* (the film it inspired), ends with Lina's death. In its last chapter, Lina lies in bed, indulging in self-pity, yet at the same time submitting to her own murder by swallowing the poisoned draught Johnnie gives her.

> Lina flung herself down among the pillows. Let him then! Quickly! If Johnnie could do that, Lina no longer wanted to live.
>
> She burst into a torrent of sobbing.
>
> No, it was impossible. Johnnie could not be going to kill her. Not Johnnie. . . .
>
> At any moment Johnnie might come in—break the door down and kill her in her own bedroom: throw her out of the window on to the flagstones below and say she had fallen—anything. At any moment Johnnie might come and kill her; and what was she going to do?[26]

Bluebeard films stage a double movement between agency and victimization, between a sense of adventure and timidity, between investigative curiosity and masochism, always within the confines of marriage. The institution of marriage functions as a kind of trap in which the heroine is "caught," to use the title of another wife-in-distress film from the 1940s.

Although Bluebeard films present women as active bearers of the gaze and as detectives, analysts, and interpreters, they simultaneously ensure that those investigative powers, analytic skills, and interpretive talents are confined to the site of domesticity, restricted to problem solving within the context of a marriage. For this reason, the happy endings are, once again, a letdown. When the secrets beyond the door to marriage are solved, there is real closure. The woman who has passed beyond the door is now permanently encased behind it, with nothing left to investigate, analyze, and interpret once she has figured out what is behind her husband's threatening behavior. No more secrets, no more mysteries, no more adventure. And this, above all else, becomes the real curse of living happily ever after.

4

CHAPTER

Rewriting "Bluebeard": Resisting the Cult of Death

> All my life I'd been hooked on plots.
> —Margaret Atwood, *Lady Oracle*

Some stories are not meant for mixed company. With conspiratorial pleasure, the narrator of Margaret Atwood's "Significant Moments in the Life of My Mother" reports that there are always "some stories which my mother does not tell when there are men present: never at dinner, never at parties." These stories, we learn, are told in domestic settings: "usually in the kitchen, when they or we are helping with the dishes or shelling peas, or taking the tops and tails off the string beans, or husking corn." They are melodramatic tales, charting the consequences of "romantic betrayals, unwanted pregnancies, illnesses of various horrible kinds, marital infidelities, mental breakdowns, tragic suicides, unpleasant lingering deaths." Unlike the charmingly spirited, deftly nuanced tales spun around the fireside, these stories are "not rich in detail or embroidered with incident: they are stark and factual." They encapsulate collective truths—the wisdom of the ages—about romance, courtship, marriage, divorce, and death, and they are passed on from one generation of women to the next. Gossip and gospel truth, gossip as gospel truth, these stories are received with reverent attention: "The women, their own hands moving among the dirty dishes or the husks of vegetables, nod solemnly."[1]

The old wives' tales to which Atwood is referring represent a buried narrative tradition, one that flowed largely through oral tributaries as women's speech until it was appropriated by male editors and collectors who channeled it into a print culture. Beginning with the tales from the

Arabian Nights told on a successive thousand and one nights by Scheherazade on through *The Tale of Tales* recited by old crones and recorded by the Italian storyteller Giambattista Basile to the *Children's Stories and Household Tales* collected by the Brothers Grimm, men have produced the literary conduits for disseminating stories once recited by women and attributed to them. Atwood's observations about her own childhood suggest that the oral tradition remains very much alive today, drawing its strength from the lived experience of women and existing side by side with a literary tradition that records tales from an oral storytelling culture. Atwood, as her mother's daughter and as a woman, has access to stories that never made it into print. Appropriating those tales, she produces new literary stories that are a hybrid of gossip and fairy tale.

The tales told by Atwood's mother and by her friends have a vital social function, conveying experience in the form of a story, a narrative that shares the power of Bluebeard's chamber to arouse curiosity.[2] That power is trained not only on adult listeners but also on small children, who, like Margaret Atwood in her youth, are positioned on the margins of the storyteller's circle. Conveying social attitudes and expectations, the tellers of tales, in Marina Warner's words, "pass on vital information about the values and beliefs of the community in which they are growing up, will instruct them in who is trusted and who is not, about what is considered praiseworthy and what is condemned, about alliances and enmities, hopes and dangers." The stories told propose different developmental trajectories: "They chart the terrain. Some directions are urged, but the signposts are not entirely coercive. Gossip and narrative are sisters, both ways of keeping the mind alive when ordinary tasks call; the fictions of gossip—as well as the facts—act as compass roses, pointing to many possibilities."[3]

And the possibilities are indeed legion. In *The Robber Bride*, Atwood inverts the gender terms of the Grimms' "Robber Bridegroom" and includes a scene of storytelling that demonstrates how tales between the covers of books take on new narrative energy and shift their shape when they become the subject of "talk."

> "*The Robber Bridegroom*," reads Tony, long ago, a twin at each elbow. The beautiful maiden, the search for a husband, the arrival of the rich and handsome stranger who lures innocent girls to his stronghold in the woods and then chops them up and eats them. "One day a suitor appeared. He was . . ."
>
> "She! She!" clamour the twins. . . .
>
> "All right, Tony, let's see you get out of this one," says Roz, standing in the doorway.

"We could change it to *The Robber Bride*," says Tony. "Would that be adequate?"

The twins give it some thought, and say it will do. They are fond of bridal costumes, and dress their Barbie dolls up in them; then they hurl the brides over the stair railings or drown them in the bathtub.[4]

The rising generation demands not just role reversals but also seems to delight in inflicting the violence of the old tales onto Barbie dolls, the embodiments of another generation's idea of femininity.

From the 1960s through the 1990s, the Bluebeard story captured the imagination of many women writers, artists, and filmmakers. Serving as a vehicle for addressing anxieties about romance, marriage, and marital fidelity, it offered an opportunity to use the optics of another time and place to envision the ways in which women cope in marriages imperiled by sexual betrayal or domestic violence. From the sparks thrown by the friction between traditional tale and real-life melodramas, the stories, films, and photographs produced by these women generated new debates about the dark side of passion and revealed the unholy aspects of matrimony. Margaret Atwood's "Bluebeard's Egg," Angela Carter's "Bloody Chamber," Cindy Sherman's *Fitcher's Bird*, and Jane Campion's *The Piano* work through the problematics of courtship and marriage in very different cultural contexts, exposing the risks of mismatches and the ways women manage when passion goes wrong. Each of these works draws on the Bluebeard story to deepen and enrich our understanding of what happens when trust is broken and domestic tranquility is unsettled by sinister events.

Margaret Atwood's short story "Bluebeard's Egg" is one of those gossipy narratives about romantic betrayal and marital infidelity that is given shape by the fairy tales circulating in our culture. Much of it is presented as the bits and pieces of information that pass from woman to woman, in the girl talk shared by Sally, the story's protagonist, with Marylynn, the woman in whom she confides. But the narrative also takes us inside the mind of Sally and moves us through the private paces of her marital routines. We learn that, despite Sally's sense of security about her marriage, there is a "dread" that seeps into things. As the tale unfolds, we discover that Ed, a heart physician who seems utterly solid and steady, may in fact be a Bluebeard figure who is in the process of moving on from Sally, his third wife, to a new romance with Marylynn.

While readers become privy to Sally's every anxiety and desire, they are blocked access to the mind and thoughts of Sally's somewhat cagey husband. Ed, as Sally muses, may be much like the egg stained by the heroine of the Grimms' "Fitcher's Bird" when she crosses the forbidden threshold. Assigned to rewrite that story in a course called *Forms of Narrative Fiction*, Sally ponders Ed's inscrutable behavior and likens him to an opaque object: "Ed Egg, blank and pristine and lovely."[5] Sheer surface, this heart surgeon seems impervious to efforts to enter his mind, and for precisely that reason retains a kind of primal purity and innocence. Yet there is also something ominous about his nickname of Ed Bear, which is one letter in excess of a perfect anagram for "Beard." Atwood's title is an immediate tip-off to the reader that there is some kind of trouble in the marriage between Sally and Ed.

As Sally reads him, Ed is a far cry from a Bluebeard figure. Unlike the shrewdly savage Bluebeard of folkloric tradition, Ed's most characteristic feature is his stupidity, "his monumental and almost energetic stupidity" (145). "Nowhere near sinister enough" to play the role of Bluebeard, he is aligned with a different type of fairy-tale hero. Ed is the hapless dimwit, the "third son who, armed with nothing but a certain feeble-minded amiability, manages to make it through the forest with all its witches and traps and pitfalls and end up with the princess, who is Sally, of course" (146). "Of course": that phrase, with its overtones of smug confidence, makes it more clear than almost any other textual clue that there is a chink in the armor of Sally's marital security.

Subliminally aware that "Ed's colossal and endearing thickness" may have an element of calculation to it, Sally betrays her own suspicions when she reflects on how Ed is "no mere blockhead." "You'd have to be working at it to be that stupid," she marvels. On "bad days," Sally begins to suspect that Ed's stupidity is a strategy "to shut things out" and to leave Sally "locked outside," playing the prince hacking "through the brambles to Ed's Sleeping Beauty" (147). Ed's resistance to allowing Sally to enter the chamber of his inner world becomes evident in his refusal to discuss his earlier marriages: he protests "ignorance" of what went wrong and thwarts her desire to understand the "finer points" of the marital breakdowns. Reduced to making a joke of Ed's past, Sally accepts his explanation, shrugs off the failed marriages, and authorizes Ed's "stupidity" by reporting to her friend Marylynn that Ed just "doesn't know" (145).

Sally's miscalculation of Ed, her fatal underestimation of what goes on in the mind of this heart surgeon, becomes evident in her efforts to rewrite the story of "Fitcher's Bird." In *Forms of Narrative Fiction*, the course Sally takes in order to divert herself from the obsession with solving the puzzle known as Ed, the instructor includes a unit on "Folk Tales and the Oral Tradition." She reads to her students what is described as a variant of

Bluebeard and what turns out to be an abbreviated version of the Grimms' "Fitcher's Bird."[6] Sally's assignment, to rewrite the tale from the point of view of anyone or anything in the story, becomes especially problematic, for the rescripting challenges her not only to rethink the personal dynamics in the folktale but also to interrogate a fable that reflects on the circumstances of her own life.

Rewriting a story from a new point of view means more than changing the narrative perspective. In adapting the story, Sally must rethink its terms and reshape it in the context of her own wisdom and experience. And so it is not by chance that her first thought is to produce a story in which the forbidden chamber contains nothing at all, thus suggesting that her Fitcher figure will be an open book, a man with no secrets whatsoever to guard. Yet Sally is too bright not to realize that her effort at cleverness has produced a delusion: why would the wizard have "a forbidden room in which he kept nothing?" (175).

What finally proves intriguing to Sally is a version of the story in which she is cast as "cunning heroine." Yet the effort to write about a clever heroine also misfires in the end, for it fails to ring true to her own experience, which is what she can bring to the effort to transform "Fitcher's Bird" into her own tale. Sally would like to think that she plays the trickster to Ed's simpleton, but she clearly has not done all her homework in the night course on forms of fiction. For as every seasoned folklorist knows, the simpleton, numbskull, and ne'er-do-well usually ends up duping nearly everyone else in the story. It is Ed who proves to be the sly trickster, turning the tables on Sally and leaving her in the role of simpleton wife.

Sally's engagement with "Fitcher's Bird" reveals exactly what it is about fairy tales that makes them up close and personal. The exercise assigned to Sally in class is the exercise that most readers implicitly perform when reading these stories. Not only do we adopt a point of view, identifying with one of the characters in the story, we also adapt the story, producing a new text that conflates the words on the page with the experience of real life. "Fitcher's Bird" becomes a text that challenges Sally to consider the role that she plays in her marriage and to reflect on how her own story conforms to or deviates from the terms of the old tale. Once Sally is absorbed in the exercise, there is no turning back. "Fitcher's Bird" becomes the text that goads her into knowledge and that obliges her to confront anxieties that manifest themselves as the "dread that seeps into things." Domestic ritual, the myth of Ed's monumental stupidity, mindless jobs, along with the jokes and deflating humor that spice her gossip sessions with Marylynn are all powerful, if futile, defenses against that dread.

Once she is in the know, Sally lies awake at night, reflecting on the enigma of Ed and trying to fit together the pieces of the puzzle beside her. "Breathing deeply as if asleep" (184), Ed remains consummately inscrutable, either a simpleton in a truly profound sleep or a trickster cleverly feigning slumber. Yet for once, Sally is poised on the brink of understanding. She may not know for certain whether Ed has been conducting an affair with her best friend Marylynn, but once on the track to the truth, she can no longer shut out knowledge. What will come of Sally's new awareness? Atwood leaves us in suspense, ending her narrative with Sally's nightmarish vision of an egg, "glowing softly as though there's something red and hot inside it" (184).[7] Whether the egg signals a kind of rebirth and new beginning or whether it will hatch to produce a monster is unclear. But its presence at the end of the narrative signals the triumph of birth and beginnings over endings and death. Once the egg cracks and comes to be spattered with blood, as in the story "Fitcher's Bird," Sally will have succeeded in entering her husband's forbidden chamber and in discovering the truth about his past.

While the egg, charged with symbolic power, is positioned as a kind of sacred, self-contained object harboring secret knowledge, it is only one in a series of containers and chambers that harbors mysteries and resonates powerfully with the forbidden chamber in folktales. As in most re-scriptings of the Bluebeard tale, the forbidden chamber in "Bluebeard's Egg" manifests itself in both physical and psychic terms. A new "keyhole desk," purchased by Sally to satisfy her fantasies about domestic perfection ("She needs it to sit at, in something flowing, backlit by the morning sunlight, gracefully dashing off notes"), turns out to be the site at which Sally becomes privy to secret knowledge about her husband. The keyhole desk has powerful allusive qualities, bringing to mind the many recycled versions of "Bluebeard" that replace the forbidden chamber with a locked desk containing secret knowledge.

The first paragraph of "Bluebeard's Egg" describes another space that hints at the possibility of sexual betrayal: a playhouse at the bottom of a ravine adjacent to Sally's house. That Sally longs to clear it away, while Ed "likes it the way it is" (144), suggests that the structure may serve as the site for romantic trysts. There is also Ed's "new facility," a site of medical diagnosis and healing that Sally intuitively associates with infidelity. As a "heart man," Ed routinely examines a multichambered organ that comes to be implicated in the story's discourse on forbidden chambers. Allowed into the facility and examined by Ed, Sally begins to understand that her husband operates in a powerfully seductive manner when he scrutinizes other women's hearts in this seemingly clinical space:

Ed unwired her and she put on her clothes again, neutrally, as if he were actually a doctor. Nevertheless this transaction, this whole room, was sexual in a way she didn't quite understand; it was clearly a dangerous place. It was like a massage parlor, only for women. Put a batch of women in there with Ed and they would never want to come out. They'd want to stay in there while he ran his probe over their wet skins and pointed out to them the defects of their beating hearts. (161)

The story "Bluebeard's Egg," positioned as the central narrative in a collection of Atwood's stories, also comes to function as a secret and sacred center, self-contained yet also radiating its truths outward to other tales in the collection. Nested within other narratives, it also contains an embedded story ("Fitcher's Bird") that comments on and broadens our understanding of the marital trouble fueling the plot. As one critic puts it, Atwood's story "enters into dialogue with itself and represents the apparatus of its own interpretation."[8] "Bluebeard's Egg" challenges us to compare Sally's narrative, as it is related to Marylynn and as it emerges from her own silent thoughts, with a folkloric text that Sally struggles to decode and then re-encode as her own story. As readers, we enter into this self-reflexive process, producing our own versions of "Bluebeard" as we work through Sally's rescripting of a story that has challenged its readers to reflect not only on the deep enigmas of marital life but also on the profound mysteries of the stories that we tell to each other and to ourselves.

Sally appropriates the story of Bluebeard, using it as a key to open the door to realities that—however painful, disruptive, and disturbing—have an emancipatory potential. As a reader of "Fitcher's Bird," she knows that the clever, cunning heroine—especially the third in a series of wives—can rescue herself rather than await rescue from distant brothers. And if she does not yet know for certain how her life will play itself out against the folktale, she knows that she does not have to repeat the old story. In rewriting "Fitcher's Bird," she becomes aware of the way in which the old stories can be redesigned to produce new endings that will lead to fresh beginnings. "If we make stories for each other / about what is in the room / we will never have to go in," Atwood writes in the poem "Hesitations outside the Door."[9]

 The first-person narrator of Angela Carter's "Bloody Chamber" is only dimly aware of the cultural story that she seems destined to repeat in her marriage. Unlike Sally, she has never studied "Bluebeard" and its cultural variants and seems unaware that her husband's "bloody chamber" is prefigured in the British folktale "Mr. Fox." In that tale, Lady Mary weds the "gallant" Mr. Fox, who keeps the "bodies and skeletons of young ladies all stained with blood" behind the door of a roo castle that is described as a "bloody chamber."[10] A "brave one, Mary confronts Mr. Fox by recounting her discovery as a dream aṇu producing evidence for his crimes. As in the Grimms' "Robber Bridegroom," Lady Mary's brothers and friends draw their swords and cut the sinister bridegroom "into a thousand pieces."

Carter's title, "The Bloody Chamber," reveals that she is planning neither to proceed down the well-worn paths of folkloric invention nor to yield to the influence of conventional interpretations developed by folklorists. Generations of taletellers and legions of experts on folklore have focused on the bloody *key* or the *forbidden* chamber in the story of Bluebeard. With one stroke, Carter demolishes the myth that "Bluebeard" hinges on the wife's disobedience in staining the key entrusted to her by her husband or that the story turns on the wife's curiosity about taboo matters. Instead she enunciates in the title exactly what is at stake in this Bluebeard tale: a bloody chamber that houses the corpses of a husband who has murdered one wife after another.

Angela Carter once described herself as a writer who traffics in the "demythologizing business," seeking to interrogate stories that are a part of our collective cultural archive.[11] With "The Bloody Chamber" (1979), she launches a project framed as an effort to provide "a critique of current relations between the sexes." Positioning herself as a "moral pornographer," she reworks the familiar scripts of fairy tales, aiming to "penetrate to the heart of the contempt for women that distorts our culture."[12] "Beauty and the Beast," "Little Red Riding Hood," "Puss in Boots," and "Bluebeard": these stories all have, according to Carter, a "violently sexual" side to them, a "latent content" that becomes manifest in her rewritings for adult audiences.[13] Carter aims above all to demystify, debunk, and deconstruct these sacred cultural texts, showing how they are implicated in perpetuating stereotypes and reproducing social ideologies as they are fiercely repeated in different times and places. Initiating social change means breaking the magic hold of these stories.

Like Atwood, Carter does not give us a seamless reinterpretation of "Bluebeard." Instead she borrows bits and pieces from the repository of our collective literary and folkloric imagination to construct a story that challenges our understanding of characters and plots that have stood the test of time: "ideas, images, stories that we tend to take on trust without thinking what they really mean."[14] Carter's male protagonist is a decadent connoisseur who seduces with his wealth and power, and he bears a resemblance to both the mythical Hades and the Bluebeard of folklore. His piano-playing wife, in her beguiling innocence, is as much Little Red Riding Hood as Bluebeard's wife. And the wife's mother, a fearless warrior who defeats Bluebeard single-handedly, seems part Demeter, part Medusa, and part feminist fantasy. Yet "The Bloody Chamber," with its forbidden space, its slain wives, and its disobedient wife, also bears all the telltale signs of a Bluebeard story.

If "The Bloody Chamber" sends any message at all, it is enunciated in the words of Jean-Yves, the blind piano tuner whom the heroine marries after her husband's death: "Though it must be so, yet it might not be so."[15] Echoing and modulating the protest of the folkloric Mr. Fox, who insists on his innocence ("It is not so, nor it was not so. And God forbid it should be so."), Jean-Yves suggests that the conventional marriage plot of Western civilization, though seemingly written in granite, might still yield to change. The stories may dictate a certain ending, but there is still the possibility of an unexpected intervention, a new twist to the old plot.

Carter's bloodthirsty husband is constructed as a figure who is more a collection of cultural citations than a man of flesh and blood. The Marquis, a consummate sadist, clearly gets his title from the Marquis de Sade; his native land of Brittany is shared with Gilles de Rais and Cunmar the Cursed (historical models for Bluebeard); his aestheticism is linked with that of the hero of Huysmans's novel *Là-bas* (1891); and his robust sensuality can be affiliated with that of Rochester in Charlotte Brontë's *Jane Eyre* (note that Carter's Bluebeard is succeeded by a piano tuner, who, like Rochester after the conflagration at Thornfield, is blind). In demythologizing the story of Bluebeard, Carter first of all resurrects the figure of Bluebeard in all his literary and folkloric glory, creating a figure of excess whose violence is at once more complex but also more transparent than that of his literary predecessors.

The Marquis, whose voluptuous sensuality and fierce aestheticism are anything but life affirming, can be seen as the incarnation of a principle of deadly corruption, of sensual pleasure turned lethal. In his affiliation with darkness and death, he becomes a Hades figure, linked with aggression, violence, and unreproductive sexuality. When the narrator decides to set out in search of her husband's "true nature," his "heart," his "real life," and his "real self," she is drawn to the chamber forbidden to her: "It was imperative that I should find him, should know him" (26). What she finds is an "ill-lit" chamber, lacking electricity, containing the corpses—fresh, embalmed, and decayed—of her husband's previous wives. Fleeing the room, she slams the door behind her and hears it crash with a reverberation so powerful that it appears as the "door of hell." What the narrator reenters is a castle of gloom enveloped in darkness so "thick" that it appears like a "permeable substance" lit by a "black sun" (30). Surrounded by the scent and smell of ubiquitous funereal lilies, the narrator has entered what, in a transparent reference to Dickens's recasting of "Bluebeard," is designated as a "castle of murder."

Linked to a regime of death, art, and sensual corruption, the Marquis is figured as a "connoisseur" who uses his wealth and power to collect women and/as works of art. Laboring under a repetition compulsion, he constantly acquires new additions to his "gallery" and surrounds them with mirrors that duplicate their images in such a way as to produce an entire "harem" of wives. Supremely visual in his desires, he inspects his latest purchase with an expert eye. "I saw him watching me in the gilded mirrors with the assessing eye of a connoisseur inspecting horseflesh, or even of a housewife in the market, inspecting cuts on the slab," the narrator reports. "I'd never seen, or else had never acknowledged, that regard of his before, the sheer carnal avarice of it; and it was strangely magnified by the monocle lodged in his left eye" (11).

As an authority on aesthetics, the Marquis has committed himself to what one critic calls "the education of one person in the sexual fantasy of another through complex role playing cued to works of art and imagination."[16] His wife becomes the heroine of a "black, inverted fairy tale," as Carter puts it, in which woman is linked with aesthetic display and death:

To be the *object* of desire is to be defined in the passive case.
To exist in the passive case is to die in the passive case—that is, to be killed.
This is the moral of the fairy tale about the perfect woman.[17]

The Marquis's cult of death is firmly anchored in Western myths that celebrate voluptuous self-annihilation through romantic passion. The *Liebestod* in Richard Wagner's opera *Tristan and Isolde* is a prime example of one of those myths, and it is no accident that one of the Marquis's previous wives was a diva who burned with "white-hot passion" in the role of Isolde. While the narrator yields to the sensual appeal of the Marquis's moral corruption and becomes complicit in her own seduction by giving in to her masochistic desires, her mother, who incarnates the principles of life, vitality, and spirited resistance, comes to her rescue.[18] Womb/tomb: these are the two bloody chambers between which the heroine must negotiate her own path. From the opening paragraph, with its image of a "burning cheek" pressed against the "impeccable linen" of a pillow, the narrator sets up a contrast between the "white, enclosed quietude of my mother's apartment" and the "unguessable country of marriage."

117

Carter's pistol-toting, horseback-riding mother seems to be the ingenious invention of a feminist author. Yet a closer look at the mythical underpinnings of the Bluebeard tale reveals its kinship with a story that positions a mother as savior of a distraught daughter. The Greek folktale known by the title "The Lord of the Underworld" reveals a link between the Bluebeard story and the myth of Demeter and Persephone. As in the Italian "Silvernose," the husband in the Greek tales is in some cases a diabolical figure who traps the heroine in the world below. "The Lord of the Underworld" shares many features with "Cupid and Psyche" and "Beauty and the Beast" (two tale types that also conflate marriage with death), but it also reveals how the ghoulish Bluebeard can be seen as the double for a satanic creature who lures young women into a marriage that spells desolation and death. Whether we think of Bluebeard as a secularized Satan or imagine the Lord of the Underworld as a demonic incarnation of Bluebeard, it becomes clear that both stories emphatically connect marriage with the domain of death.

In the myth of Demeter and Persephone, it is the mother, giver of life, who reclaims her daughter from Hades. The Homeric hymn that relates the rape of Persephone and Demeter's efforts to rescue her daughter from that monster bridegroom known as Hades shares so many features with the story of Bluebeard that it is not surprising to find the two stories occasionally conflated to produce a hybrid text. Like Bluebeard's wife, Persephone marries a sinister figure associated with death, succumbs to temptation when she partakes of forbidden fruit, and is liberated from a barbarian grip by a member of her immediate family. The mother in "The Bloody Chamber" is not only a Medusa figure (as she is described in the text) but also a double of Demeter in her affiliation with life and liberation.

In the coda to Carter's story, we learn that the heroine marries the piano tuner hired by her husband and that "the three of us" (mother, daughter, and piano tuner) lead a serene life, running a music school. While Carter's critique of romantic love and her demystification of self-destructive sexual passion are presented in compelling fashion, her vision of an alternative ideology appears flat and unappealing. The restrained austerity of the aural culture that prevails once the heroine sets up house with a piano tuner has trouble competing with the voluptuous sensuality of the Marquis's regime of visual pleasures. The contents of the bloody chamber may have been buried or burned and its door may have been sealed, but its Gothic horrors stubbornly remain the real source of narrative pleasure.

With the death of the Marquis, the narrative moves from the excesses of melodrama to the sprightliness of the pastoral mode. What is left to the heroine is a life of philanthropy, education, and familial solidarity. Despite a clear intention to break the spell of narratives that glamorize self-immolating passion, Carter's text makes it clear that the quiet delights of domestic life are no match for the seductive fascination and theatrical verve of the Gothic imagination.

"I am all for putting new wine into old bottles," Angela Carter tells us, "especially if the pressure of the new wine makes the old bottles explode."[19] With "The Bloody Chamber," Carter unsettles a narrative tradition, showing its tragic consequences as well as its perverse attractiveness. She perceives the writing of fiction to be part of a "slow process of decolonialising our language and our basic habits of thought."[20] Working within a tradition that has shaped our way of thinking about romance, sexuality, and marriage, Carter creates a new story that challenges us to reclaim our past, to understand the appeal of stories once told, and to create cultural agendas that truly belong to us.

Like Angela Carter, Cindy Sherman has been seen as a "de-myth-ifier," an artist who challenges the symbolic constructs that, according to George Steiner, are "imprinted, almost in the manner of genetic information, on our sensibility."[21] Sherman encourages us to explore images and associations from every possible angle, to turn them inside out and set them topsy-turvy in order to undo their powerful cultural hold. A photographer who launched her career by interrogating and exaggerating female stereotypes in classic Hollywood cinema, in *film noir*, and in foreign films, Sherman shoots to kill. Her black-and-white photographs offer copies, re-presentations, and restagings of cinematic moments for which there is no original, but which both stir and disturb cultural memories of how women are figured in films of the 1940s and 1950s. Laura Mulvey has emphasized how the film stills produce the effect of woman as fetishized object to be looked at: "The camera looks; it 'captures' the female character in a parody of different voyeurisms. It intrudes into moments in which she is unguarded, sometimes undressed, absorbed into her own world in the privacy of her own environment. Or it witnesses a moment in which her guard drops as she is suddenly startled by a presence, unseen and off-screen, watching her."[22]

In her film stills, Sherman aims to disrupt a representational regime that reproduces and proliferates endless copies of itself. In replicating and parodying the images of women in our cultural imaginary, she not only produces a repulsively deformed image that demystifies the "original" (which may or may not have ever existed as empirical reality), but also exposes the hidden grotesque deformations of that "original." Sherman never represents herself as an idealized figure that produces aesthetic pleasure, instead distorting her appearance through make-up, costumes, and accessories. What we see is not the seductive, fetishized body created by Hollywood cinema, but an image that exercises the fascination of the grotesque. "The world is so drawn toward beauty that I became interested in things that are normally considered grotesque or ugly, seeing them as more fascinating than beautiful."[23]

In her photographic illustrations for "Fitcher's Bird" by the Brothers Grimm, Sherman unsettles the folktale by supplementing it with hideous images and producing a sense of discomfort so powerful that the bedtime story transforms itself into a Gothic nightmare. For Sherman, what is at stake in this story is not the seduction of the bride and the girl's betrayal of the husband, but something far more important. "The shock (or terror)," she tells us, "should come from what the sexual elements are really standing for—death, power, aggression, beauty, sadness, etc."[24] Sherman trains readers in the art of facing violence and death. "I love horror films," she reported once to an interviewer. "But I like them because they function in the same way fairy tales do in allowing society to see something very gruesome and hard to deal with, which somehow physically prepares us for our own death. Or prepares us for the potential of violence in our lives."[25]

Like Atwood, Sherman is drawn to "Fitcher's Bird," the variant of the Bluebeard story recorded by the Brothers Grimm. The German heroine, unlike her French counterpart, has her wits about her and proves so resourceful that she engineers her own rescue. By endorsing confidence, daring, and fortitude, this fairy tale holds out the promise of victory over even the most daunting powers, teaching its readers, as Walter Benjamin reminds us, "to meet the forces of the mythical world with cunning and high spirits."[26] In a sense, Cindy Sherman could be said to take on the role of the third sister in "Fitcher's Bird." She has the courage to look into the wizard's cauldron, to contemplate the consequences of his magic, and to survive the encounter with the dismembered bodies of her sisters. And she also has the "cunning"—the power of artifice and of art—to reconstitute those bodies and to refashion her own fictive self in a way that leads to the triumph of life over death.

Sherman's *Fitcher's Bird* begins with a caveat to the reader:

Now this is a story for people who are not squeamish, for it is a story about a wizard who likes to cut people up. This wicked wizard's name was Fitcher, and he used to disguise himself as a poor man with a basket and go begging from house to house to catch beautiful girls. His power was so great that all he had to do was catch someone, and the person could not move away from

120

him and had to do what he wanted. The spell could only be broken by a woman who proved to be obedient to his will and agreed to marry him, because then, of course, no spell would be needed.[27]

The text of Sherman's *Fitcher's Bird* is only the loosest translation of the Grimms' tale. The warning to the squeamish, the open declaration about the wizard's evil proclivities, and the ironic meditation on the husband's lack of need for spells once he has married are all absent from the Grimms' version of the tale. From the start, Sherman tips the reader off to the story's violence, making it clear that her version will not fall into the trap of blaming the wife for the grisly acts of violence practiced by the husband and will also resolutely refuse to implicate the wife in the tale's troubled courtship.

In her photographic transformation of "Fitcher's Bird," Sherman does not appear as model. Instead the tale's protagonist appears on the title page in the form of a doll, an immobile and passive figure whose beautiful face can do little more than register shock. Like Anne Sexton's Snow White, she can roll her "china-blue doll eyes open and shut," but appears deprived of any agency. Fitcher too is an inanimate figure, though his gnarled hands and bearded visage endow him with a more lifelike quality and with the possibility of some agency. And indeed, in the triple focus on his hand in three consecutive photographs, the viewer gets the sense that it is he who controls events, guiding them masterfully with a visible hand, while the maiden who is to marry him, represented as a head in one shot and as all eyes in a second, can do no more than observe and recoil in horror.

Despite her state of evident paralysis, the third in the trio of sisters lured into the basket of the wizard succeeds in moving from passive victim to clever rescuer. Sherman's Fitcher is figured as a master of dismemberment—"a wizard who likes to cut people up." Using his ax and his chopping block, he is an expert in the art of division, separating into pieces what was meant to be whole. The third sister must reverse this process, rejoining the dismembered parts of her sisters and bringing them back to life. The "cleverest" of the trio, she claims the magician's power for herself by producing a form of body art that does not separate and divide but mixes, combines, and commingles to produce hybrid forms.

The third sister becomes the preserver of life. Not only does she defy the powers of the wizard by making her sisters whole again, she also preserves the egg, protecting it from bloodied defilement by placing it in a bed of goose down. She transforms herself into a hybrid creature, half human, half animal, by dipping her body in honey and rolling in feathers.

121

And to entice her bridegroom to his death, she fashions what is to function as her own double: a skull decorated with flowers and jewels, which Fitcher will believe, at least from a distance, to be his bride. The display created through the decorated skull produces a symbolic nexus linking the bride with beauty and death. The sly sister creates a second self that corresponds precisely to the desires of her groom, while she herself escapes his fatal touch by transforming herself into a thing with feathers, a creature affiliated with lightness, safety, life, and hope.

The heroine claims the powers of the magician, but she uses them to restore life rather than to produce death. Although it is true that the object she exhibits to dupe the wizard can be seen as an aesthetic display, one that seeks to create beauty from death, that object is more artifice than art. Her real art emerges in performance, in the living body, seen only from waist to knee, that she dips in honey and feathers in order to ensure her survival. Art needs bodies, and Sherman's photographs for *Fitcher's Bird* show us how art uses dead bodies and dead body parts to create beauty. Defying the aestheticization of death in the wizard's art and refusing to concede that death is the mother of beauty (to borrow a phrase from Wallace Stevens), Sherman makes a mockery of efforts to dress up death in the photograph of a skull embellished with flowers and jewels by Fitcher's bride. In the grotesque final image, which shows the horrorstruck wizard, we see the real face of death: disfigured, misshapen, and revolting, producing a sense of dread in every spectator.

The filmmaker Jane Campion, like Angela Carter and Cindy Sherman, appears to be an expert at making the old mythical bottles explode. Although Campion and her collaborator Kate Pullinger may not have planned to update the story of Bluebeard in their novel *The Piano*, one of the initial inspirations for their work was a scene from a pantomime version of Bluebeard—a scene that was later incorporated into the 1993 cinematic version of *The Piano*.[28] What Campion shows us is a tableau with Bluebeard, sword in hand, preparing to decapitate his seventh wife, as he stands next to a bloody display of the heads of his previous wives. The play within the film mirrors the violence in the marriage between Ada McGrath, who has traveled to New Zealand with her daughter as a mail-order bride, and Alisdair Stewart, a strait-laced settler who regards Ada as his property. But it also encourages us to meditate on the richly nuanced relationship between the folktale and the cinematic context in which it is embedded.

The Piano gives us a stark deviation from the narrative norm of Bluebeard stories by turning the wife in both novel and film into the repository of a secret. As Barbara Johnson has noted in an incisive critique of *The Piano*, the film can be read as a meditation on "sex and power and sexual power reversals," as a work that overturns our conventional understanding of gender roles.[29] And so, in *The Piano*, it is Ada who carries the burden of a troubled past and who possesses a dark secret that makes her the center of the film's narrative energy. "Have you a secret my small one, a big secret, something frightening you saw," is the question put to the young Ada by a piano tuner. "There is more to her silence than will ever be spoken," he tells the kitchen maids.[30] In reflecting on the enigma that was Emily Dickinson, Jane Campion noted that Ada leads a life that is similarly "secretive" (115). What fascinates George Baines, the settler with whom Ada makes a strange pact in which he barters piano keys for sexual contact, is the mystery of a woman who will not speak but whose music is profoundly expressive.

In another stunning reversal of roles, the Bluebeard of *The Piano* is a completely transparent character, a man who epitomizes the colonial mentality, overcoming brute natural forces to assert his domination over nature, women, and other races. Everything about Stewart, from the ax that he habitually carries with him to clear out the bush to the mirror in which he narcissistically examines his image, is in character with this mentality.[31] It is his wife who stirs our curiosity, filling us with a sense of wonder about her story and her history.

In a prologue to the narrative version of *The Piano*, we learn that Ada's story has captured attention in at least two corners of the world:

The story of Ada and her piano has been told and retold by those in the small New Zealand settlement of ——, and by those back in Scotland who knew Ada and her daughter, and her daughter's daughters. It was not only women who spoke of the story; men talked about it in public houses and fine houses, some shuddering, others wondering at the lengths some would go for love or passion. There was something irresistible in the story that made it popular to all. (1)

The Piano is, in short, a story for mixed company. The film begins by proclaiming the mystery of Ada's "dark talent," her ability to silence herself, to impose her will in an act that defies patriarchal authority (the novel reveals that Ada stopped talking after being reprimanded by her father). It charts how a regime of tactile and auditory pleasure, represented by Ada and the music she makes in touching her piano, is pitted against the disciplined and disciplining visual culture of Stewart, who is repeatedly shown at keyholes, behind the lens of a camera, or looking into mirrors. Wherever he goes, Stewart seeks to dominate and exploit, creating an identity that is driven by the self-destructive logic of all efforts to achieve perfect mastery.

In his desire to produce a compliant wife who will subordinate herself to his desires, Stewart bears a close resemblance to traditional Bluebeard figures. As in Perrault's seventeenth-century tale, he travels on business shortly after welcoming a wife into his household. While Stewart issues no injunctions about forbidden chambers to his mail-order bride, he has laid down the law about his wife's piano, forbidding her to take possession of it. Taking advantage of her husband's absence to disobey his order about the instrument she has inherited from her mother, Ada hopes to persuade George Baines to recover the piano for her. Ada succeeds, but her triumph over Baines leads to a sexual seduction that was not part of her original calculation. When Baines can no longer bear the constraints of the liaison ("The arrangement is making you a whore and me wretched"), Ada sends him a piano key into which are carved the words: "Dear George, you have my heart, Ada McGrath." Handing the wrapped-up key to her daughter, who is to serve as messenger, Ada unwittingly mimes the role of Bluebeard's wife in the pantomime, for her body stands as a shadow against white sheets hanging outdoors to dry.

In Campion's version of Bluebeard, it is a piano key rather than a door key that stirs up trouble. Ada's daughter Flora disobeys her mother's instructions, taking the key to Stewart, who is so enraged that, like the robber bridegroom in the German tale of that title, he uses his ax to chop off one of Ada's fingers. Stewart then instructs Flora to take the severed appendage to Baines. The substitution of piano key for door key is thus doubled in the substitution of finger for piano key, with the severed finger as an associative cue for thinking about keys, secrets, touch, passion, and violence. The rich symbolic nexus created by Campion's film and Pullinger's novel produces a psychological depth and emotional complexity lacking in the pantomime version of the folktale staged within the film.

The Bluebeard folktale, as enacted in the shadow pantomime, is so palpably real to the Maori tribesmen who witness it that they storm the stage to disrupt the performance, bent on rescuing the hapless wife from an ax-wielding tyrant. At first blush, this episode seems designed to highlight the naiveté of the natives, revealing that they are unable to distinguish representation from reality.[32] Yet it also serves as an interesting parallel to the way in which Campion herself disrupts the folkloric tradition of Bluebeard narratives through her cinematic intervention. And as subsequent events make clear, the play staged in the film foreshadows in a strangely literal sense the violence that follows in the wake of its performance. It can be seen as the original of the counterfeit version played out in reality by Stewart, and it thereby carries an authenticity that makes it a natural target of disruption by the natives.

In a sense, one of the fatal effects of the Bluebeard story has to do with its habit of inspiring admiration and imitation rather than intervention and restaging. At the performance of the folktale, Stewart is transfixed, gazing with more pleasure than dread at the tableau enacted before his eyes. This visual curiosity is exactly what comes to be marked as a fatal flaw in Pullinger's novelistic treatment. Standing at a peephole at Baines's hut, Stewart is transfixed by the sight of his wife and Baines making love: "Crushed and inflated with anger, not thinking clearly, he stepped up to look again instead of bursting through the door and throwing them apart. That fatal second look, the look for curiosity, was his undoing: He was transfixed, fettered, alone" (152). "A prisoner of his curiosity," he loses himself in the lascivious pleasures of desire expressed.

Just how profoundly Stewart turns into his own jailer becomes evident from a comment of his relative Aunt Morag, who—unaware that Ada is being kept prisoner—is shocked that Stewart has barricaded the house by boarding the windows and putting a latch on the outside. "I have to say you have done wrong here," she declares. "You see you have put the latch on the outside. When you close the door it will be the Maoris that lock you in, you see? With the latch on that side you are quite trapped."

The passionate curiosity that afflicts Bluebeard's wives turns out to be shared by Ada as well as by Stewart. As the canoe carrying Baines, Ada, Flora, and the piano is making its way to Nelson, Ada orders the piano to be thrown overboard: "The loose ropes sped their way after it. Ada watched them snake past her feet and then, out of that fatal curiosity that had always been her way, odd and undisciplined, she placed her foot among the loops. Should she not share the same fate as the piano?" (213). Yet while Stewart's curiosity is visual and voyeuristic by nature, Ada's, tending to the tactile and auditory, proves strong enough to allow her to resist the "darkness all around" and "great stillness" of the oceanic depths into which she is pulled by the piano (214).

Campion's rescripting of "Bluebeard" pits Stewart, whose dependence on the visual dictates the creation of distance, against Ada, for whom touch becomes the dominant sense. As one critic puts it, the film turns on the conflict between "Stewart, the archetypal nineteenth-century colonial husband bound by a burdensome sense of his position within patriarchal history, and Ada, the transgressive wife who creates alternative discursive strategies to counter such intended subjugation."[33] Stewart, the detached voyeuristic male who perpetually imposes distance, ultimately loses Ada, who makes the connection with Baines by progressing from expressive playing to the intimacy of physical touch. Is it any wonder that the accusation Stewart hurls at Ada, shortly before he chops off her finger, expresses exactly what is impossible for a man invested in visual mastery to achieve: "I trusted you, do you hear?" (185).

The Piano unsettles the conventional gender roles delegated to husband and wife in the Bluebeard story. Campion, like Atwood, Carter, and Sherman, does not take the kind of partisan stands usually associated with feminist writing, instead retelling the Bluebeard story in ways that complicate the psychological dynamics of the marriage plot. To be sure, her Bluebeard figure is unattractive, but the woman who marries him is also not a model of heroic behavior.

What all these stories tell us—the folktales, the novellas, the novels, the picture books, and the films—is that the tale of Bluebeard remains alive in cultures the world over. What keeps it pulsing with vitality is exactly what keeps life pulsing: romance, passion, and love. Like the settlers in New Zealand and the natives of Scotland, we remain transfixed by stories about marriages in which couples fail to live happily ever after, by accounts of the conflict and turmoil in alliances that, for one reason or another, fail to succeed. For us, too, the stories are irresistible, for they offer opportunities to talk, to gossip, to chatter, and to prattle on endlessly. And from the tangle of that chitchat, we begin to define our own values, desires, appetites, and aspirations, creating an identity that will allow us to produce marriage plots with resolutions different from the ones in tales from olden times.

The Bluebeard story, as we shall see, presents itself as a map for thinking about issues broader than romance, power, and marriage. In the last two decades of the twentieth century, Bluebeard was a tale to which a number of German writers resorted in their efforts to come to terms with a past that could not be worked through or mastered. Faced with crimes so heinous that they defied representation, some writers found that the only way to write about Germany's past was to return to the "simple form" of the fairy tale, to begin with "once upon a time," as did Günter Grass in *The Tin Drum*. It did not take long for Bluebeard's chamber of horrors to emerge as an apt metaphor for the gas chambers and other atrocities of World War II. At the same time, the German variant of "Bluebeard," the Grimms' "Robber Bridegroom," was a powerful reminder that storytelling could become a weapon for defeating tyrants. By broadcasting the deeds of those who murder in secret, there was the hope of rescue and redemption.

In the film *Germany, Pale Mother* (*Deutschland, bleiche Mutter*, 1980), Helma Sanders-Brahms shows us mother and daughter wandering through the Pomeranian forest in search of shelter. Lene and Anna enter a deserted building with a tall chimney and ovens. While the scene is encoded with all kinds of allusions to fairy tales—the woods, the brick tower, and the ovens stir associations with "Rapunzel" and "Hansel and Gretel"—it is also anchored in a historically specific situation that points unmistakably to the crematoria of the Holocaust. "You are in a house of murderers," as the mother puts it in the story she begins to tell her daughter. The Grimms' "Robber Bridegroom" becomes Anna's bedtime reading, and it is told to her as her mother tucks her in under a blanket and then is continued after Lene is raped by two U.S. soldiers. It concludes in a voice-over to documentary footage showing the wartime destruction of German cities.

Although Lene's recitation is not taken word for word from the Grimms' *Children's Stories and Household Tales*, it adheres closely to both the letter and the spirit of the old tale, telling how the robber's fiancé is a silent witness to murder, unwilling to intervene until her own life is at stake. Only later, on the day of her wedding feast, does the heroine deploy her narrative skills to indict her criminal bridegroom. Sanders-Brahms has called the fairy tale in her film a "mad, monstrous presence." But "The Robber Bridegroom" story accomplishes a great deal in symbolic terms. It captures the violent core of the film's time and place, showing Germany itself as a "Mörderhaus" in which the shameful secret of mass murder was hidden and in which women are oppressed yet also complicit in the destruction of life.[34]

Lene's bedtime story drives a wedge between mother and child. Instead of witnessing the nurturing and healing power of story, we see its harmful effects—Anna loses her appetite and spurns the crust of bread offered by her mother. Sanders-Brahms recalls her own experience with the damaging power of storytelling: "My mother liked it when she told me fairy tales and I cried. Over time I became less sensitive and stopped crying. Then she raised the stakes by intensifying the feelings and fears." In other words, those stories were less therapeutic than threatening, using images of horror to terrorize and silence rather than to create dialogue and provide comfort.

But *Germany, Pale Mother* contains within it both a critique and a recuperation of storytelling. On the one hand, Lene, like many of the war generation, tells her daughter *Märchen*, falsehoods that perpetuate the deadly lessons of the past. She recites and repeats what she knows by heart, thereby missing the opportunity to fashion the bedtime story for her daughter in a way that will make it *their* story, not a story that was told two centuries ago under very different cultural circumstances. Were she to do more than merely appropriate the story—to challenge its premises and to rethink it—she might build a bond that would not only restore her daughter's appetite, but also strengthen her own resistance to violence ("That is the right of those who conquer," she tells her daughter after the rape). Missing the opportunity that Scheherazade seized when she used her entertainments to heal King Schahriyar of his murderous aggression, she fails to recognize that the telling of a story can alter reality.

Even as the mother's storytelling disempowers her and has a chilling effect on the child, it also invokes the trope of storytelling as a form of disclosure ensuring survival. When the child—who is now an adult film-maker—reconstructs the memory of her mother's storytelling, the truth of her past emerges in the form of chimneys and ovens, in the damaging domestic life of her parents, evocations of the Holocaust that reflect the reality of Germany as a "house of murder." In the truth that comes out as the story is told and then restaged by the daughter in cinematic terms, there is the promise of healing.

In *Bluebeard's Shadow* (*Blaubarts Schatten*, 1991), Lily Bitter also finds her salvation in storytelling. Like the heroine of the Grimms' fairy tale "Robber Bridegroom," she moves from a state of victimization and abject despair to agency and liberation through storytelling. "One day she will be Scheherazade. She will have to narrate, she will have to tell her story her whole life long. There's no other way."[35] But unlike Scheherazade, whose entertainments lead King Schahriyar from madness to reason, Lily recognizes that her narrative gifts are lost on her husband and that they can be used only to rescue herself.

Lily is a writer by profession, but her narrative (told in the third person) is marked less by a search for artistic accomplishment or commercial success than by a struggle for survival. And that struggle requires the formation of a new identity, one based on the demystification of stories that permeate our culture. For Lily, "Bluebeard" is the master narrative of her culture, a story that holds the key to understanding the sexual politics of Germany, both east and west. To be sure, her reflections draw on countless narratives—"Sleeping Beauty," "Cinderella," and "The Frog King," to name just a few titles—to map her anxieties and desires, but they insistently return to "Bluebeard" as the paradigm for understanding the conflicts that produce gender trouble so disturbing that men and women come to be enmeshed in a perpetual battle of the sexes (*Geschlechterkampf*) whose real casualties are children.

Bluebeard's Shadow: the title of Lily Bitter's story is powerfully evocative. The shadow suggests the "stony darkness" that is Bluebeard's element, but it also emphasizes the commanding presence of the figure, the way in which Bluebeard engulfs everything that surrounds him. And yet it can also be seen as a cipher for Bluebeard's wife. Much as Lily reviles Bluebeard, seeing him as the source of sadistic cruelty, she understands her own complicity in his deadly regime. Like the bluestockings (*Blaustrümpfe*) who team up with Bluebeards to advocate abortion and thereby avoid commitment to life, she is Bluebeard's partner in crime, a shadow who subordinates herself to the moves he has choreographed for her.

But why "Bluebeard"? What is it about this story that provides Lily with a key for working through the powerful sense of loss and guilt she experienced after undergoing an abortion? Pregnancy, abortion, birth, and children are conspicuously absent from the thematic concerns of the Bluebeard tale. And yet as Lily herself notes, the story of Cunmar the Accursed, which has often been adduced as an inspiration for "Bluebeard," identifies the source of marital trouble as the wife's pregnancy. Cunmar was said to have murdered his wives as soon as they were with child, and when Triphine, his latest wife, becomes pregnant, she tries unsuccessfully to flee the tyrant. For Lily, the bloody chamber represents Bluebeard's dread of maternity and all its overpowering biological implications—swollen bodies, bloody placentas, and wailing babies. Ultimately Bluebeard's need to destroy his wives is driven by the desire to eliminate the children who threaten his authority, autonomy, and dominion.

Although Karin Struck's novel presents itself as a polemic against abortion, it addresses more than the sexual politics of reproduction. The domestic tyranny to which Lily is subjected is repeated on a grand scale in the political practices of states, both socialist and fascist. As Adorno and Horkheimer put it in *Dialectic of Enlightenment*, "the private vices of one era become the public virtues of the next," and the figure of Bluebeard, who enacts his murderous aggression in secret, becomes the model for state-sanctioned violence on a large scale: "A big Bluebeard will not be satisfied with a little war against a wife and child within the four walls of his house where no one can see him. A big Bluebeard . . . will start a war against an entire nation, against the world."[36] Hence the importance of working through Bluebeard's story, perpetually critiquing it and rescripting it, in order to avoid falling into a silent complicity that promotes the elevation of the petty tyrant into a totalitarian leader.

In Elisabeth Reichart's "The Chamber" (*Die Kammer*, 1992), the Bluebeard story becomes a map for navigating the repressed depths of the psyche and for recovering from personal trauma.[37] As a child, Andrea Weidenbach was locked in a chamber by her father and forced to impersonate seven different women by putting on their spectacles and imitating their voices. The paraphernalia of the father's pathology, along with references to war and to Poland, make it clear that the chamber of the title refers not only to the daughter's site of incarceration but also to the gas chambers of World War II. Personal trauma and the horrors of history merge in an image that also resonates powerfully with a story that is part children's story, part collective myth. As one critic points out, the story of Bluebeard is central to the "nexus of associations" linking the incarceration of the child, the murders in the gas chambers, and repressed memories.

The narrative begins when Andrea Weidenbach, leaving her ophthalmologist's office, prescription in hand, looks with horror at the image of her smiling face in the mirror. The appearance of vision, spectacles, and mirrors in this first scene reveals the importance of perception, observation, and reflection in her story. Haunted by the darkness of the chamber in which she was imprisoned as a child and beleaguered by the attendant repressed memories as an adult, Andrea must find a way, beyond the medical intervention of spectacles, to overcome her intermittent blindness and to develop visual acuity. Her divided condition, literalized by the look in the mirror, is underscored by the proliferation of moments of watching, witnessing, and observing that immediately follow—a woman peers over her spectacles at Andrea while Andrea herself observes her own gestures. As a professional actress, Andrea is the quintessential observed person, always on stage, performing and reciting the lines she has been given.

Andrea's story is, tellingly, narrated in the third person, but by the concluding paragraphs, it modulates into the first person mode, turning into a flood of words that document her effort to overcome stony silence and to find a voice that will memorialize her suffering and reveal "the sign under which the corpses in the chamber died." If she herself is unaware of the way in which the Bluebeard story shapes her recovery, it is in part because she must liberate herself from more than a single site or figure. The source of her oppression is located in cultural forces more powerful than a husband or a father. As Mererid Puw Davies points out, this means "that the traditional 'Märchen' solution to oppression, the simple overthrow of an individual villain, accompanied by reassuring textual closure, is no longer an option."[38] And yet the story itself remains key to Andrea's recovery, for it is by emerging from the shadows and assuming a voice that she overcomes fading vision and self-division. Becoming her own witness and producing her own testimony, she tells her story in the first person, abandoning the third-person stance that was a sign of her psychic disintegration. Storytelling, once again, is linked with survival, survival in a culture that had experienced a collective trauma which repeated itself in serial fashion at home and across generations. To be sure, storytelling does not always work for all characters—Ingeborg Bachmann's Franza becomes silenced and suicidal in *The Case of Franza*—but, by drawing on the wisdom of old wives' tales, it produces new narratives that can guide readers through the gender politics of contemporary domestic relationships and social issues.[39]

5

CHAPTER

Monstrous Wives:
Bluebeard as Criminal and Cultural Hero

> Look how he suffers. . . . He is no longer so monstrous.
> —Paul Dukas, *Ariane et Barbe-bleue*

"T hat little Frenchman beats them all," declares an avid follower of
crime fiction in Alfred Hitchcock's *Shadow of a Doubt* (1943).
Today most viewers are unlikely to divine the identity of "that
little Frenchman," but Hitchcock could count on audiences to recognize
in that reference an allusion to Henri Landru, the short, bald, bearded
con artist who came to be known to readers of the *New York Times* as
the French Bluebeard, or as *Landru, dit Barbe-Bleue*, for readers of *Le
Figaro*. Executed in 1922 at Versailles for murdering ten women and one
boy and disposing of their bodies by incinerating them in a stove, Landru
gained notoriety both in France and abroad during his trial and after his
sentence to death by the guillotine. The appellation of Bluebeard did
much to enhance his reputation, erasing the sordid facts of his crimes and
charging the man himself, despite his unattractive appearance and lack
of charm, with the charisma of a mythic figure. "An entire legend stands
between the awful little hovel at Gambais and Bluebeard's castle," as *Le
Figaro* put it.

Henri Landru's powerful cultural effect can be divined from his trial,
which was attended by literary notables such as Colette, along with press
from all over the world. Ranked +2.27 on a scale of −25 to +25 for creative merit in a literary review put out by the French wing of the Dada
movement, the Bluebeard of Gambais (as he came to be known in the
popular press) received a rating higher than Nobel Prize–winning author
Anatole France and the poet Henri de Régnier, two men who had made

the mistake of rewriting Bluebeard's story instead of re-enacting his crimes.[1] Chaplin's *Monsieur Verdoux* (1947), whose title figure, like the historical Landru, cultivates roses and cremates corpses, and Hitchcock's Uncle Charlie in *Shadow of a Doubt* were inspired in part by Landru's notoriety. What became evident at his trial was how his rather unexceptional physical presence was transformed by his criminal charisma. Here was a completely unremarkable man who managed to fashion himself into a figure of real public attention, whose crimes attracted unprecedented attention from the public and from the media and who himself gave rise to endless amounts of chatter.

Landru's association with the folkloric Bluebeard has a certain logic to it, for Bluebeard had figured prominently not only in fairy tales but also in ballads and broadsheets, where his crimes were seen as sensational abominations, deeds that inspired awe as well as horror. Like many illustrious lawbreakers whose criminal offenses were broadcast by balladeers and showmen of an earlier age and whose stories circulated in pamphlets and almanacs, Bluebeard had become an important part of a culture of distraction that featured figures designed to entertain and provide diversions on long winter evenings. Arousing the kind of curiosity and suspense to which Bluebeard's wife succumbs, the sadistic deeds of Landru and his folkloric predecessor produced untold pleasures for listeners and readers. It is no accident that Landru, like Bluebeard, has not faded from cultural memory, with Claude Chabrol's 1963 film *Landru* keeping the name of the French Bluebeard alive as a code word for a dangerous womanizer.

By the beginning of the eighteenth century, a "new literature of crime" had emerged from ballads and broadsheets, one that positioned criminals as legendary figures, both infamous and admirable. Michel Foucault tells us that "there were those for whom glory and abomination were not dissociated, but coexisted in a reversible figure." What distinguished the criminal was not only the "beauty and greatness" of his crime but also his "cunning" and "tricks." If ballads and broadsheets had once focused on the sensational side of crime, on the acts' clever execution and cultural effects, the literature on crime emerging in the eighteenth century turned to the more intellectual side of the matter, investigating perpetrators and focusing on the struggle between the lawbreaker and law.[2]

Bluebeard, once an iniquitous brute who had excited the popular imagination with his bloody deeds, developed an intellectual side that aligned him with reason and cunning rather than with passion and wrath. He was to emerge as the champion of antibourgeois ideologies that are fully justified by the pathologies of modern marriage. What drove Bluebeard to a life of crime in the twentieth century is clearly established in the nineteenth century as the unbearable state of matrimony. As we shall see, the logic of Bluebeard as the victim of marriage produces a Bluebeard who becomes something of a cultural hero in his effort to combat social evils (as in Chaplin's *Monsieur Verdoux*), to thwart the boredom of every-day life (as in Hitchock's *Shadow of a Doubt*), and to struggle against existential isolation (as in Béla Bartók's *Bluebeard's Castle*).

"Mythical heroes, even infamous villains," one commentator on the Bluebeard story writes, "are part of our heritage; we can learn from them our basic aspirations and motivations." That critic mourned the fact that Anatole France, in his "Seven Wives of Bluebeard," turned the title figure into a "sheepish hero, robbed of all his prestige."[3] These observations are a compelling reminder that old myths die hard and that we treasure our villains, perhaps in part because they mirror, if not our aspirations, then at least our motivations. More important, Bluebeard, in all his mythical glory, helps us get to the bottom of the pathologies that lead him, from one century to the next, to a life of crime.

In a surge of sympathy with Bluebeard, Sam Weller of Charles Dickens's *Pickwick Papers* explains just why the fairy-tale villain deserves pity rather than censure: "I think he's the wictim of connubiality."[4] Wedlock does Bluebeard in, and Weller is moved to tears. Bluebeard has had many other defenders, both fictional and real, as becomes evident from the titles of countless nineteenth-century theatrical scripts that reworked the fairy tale. *Bluebeard; or, Dangerous curiosity & justifiable homicide*, published in London in 1841, is symptomatic of a trend that perceived the domestic tyrant as a domestic casualty, a man whose murderous deeds are fully sanctioned by the outrageous behavior of his wives. Francis Egerton El-lesmere's two-act burlesque reveals that "womankind are all alike, rebel-lious and unruly, / And can't be trusted any more . . . / Than in a hen-roost can a fox, or a cat in a china closet."[5]

When Ludwig Tieck, the German playwright and novelist who was also a contemporary of the Brothers Grimm, dramatized Bluebeard, he also framed one of the most severe indictments of the heroine's character. In his rendition, even Bluebeard's wife is appalled by her inability to resist temptation: "O curiosity," she declaims, "damned, scandalous curiosity! There's no greater sin than curiosity!" Her self-accusations are uttered in full view of a scene of carnage for which her brutish husband bears responsibility. Bluebeard confirms his wife's appraisal of her criminal be-havior and links her transgressions not only with sexual betrayal but more deeply with original sin: " 'Cursed curiosity! Because of it sin entered the innocent world, and even now it leads to crime. Ever since Eve was curious, every single one of her worthless daughters has been curious. . . . The woman who is curious cannot be faithful to her husband. The husband who has a curious wife is never for one moment of his life secure. . . . Curiosity has provoked the most horrifying murderous deeds.' "[6]

Anatole France, as noted earlier, thought along similar lines when he presented the "cold, naked Truth" about Bluebeard to the public. His "Seven Wives of Bluebeard" (1909) was to be a "true history," a corrective to the "glittering enchantments of Falsehood" produced in an earlier age by Charles Perrault. Bluebeard, France maintains, was not at all the "perfect model of cruelty" that Perrault made him out to be, but "generous and magnificent," the "victim" of a venal, corrupt, and ruthless family of conspirators. France's counternarrative, like today's upside-down stories which retell a traditional tale from the villain's point of view, systematically contests every point made in Perrault's "Bluebeard."

Although France's historical truths are told tongue in cheek, they are also consonant with the interpretive history of the Bluebeard story, which positions Bluebeard as victim of his wives' infidelities. Corrupt, licentious, and avaricious, the wives in France's story are guilty of more than intellectual curiosity. One betrays him "with every man of quality in the neighborhood"; another arranges for a tryst with her lover in the forbidden chamber. It is the seventh wife who concocts what the narrator perceives to be a moronic story about mutilated corpses, when in reality the so-called Cabinet of the Unfortunate Princesses contains nothing but wall paintings depicting scenes from tragic mythological stories. Those paintings show Dirce bound to the horns of a bull, Niobe pierced by arrows, and Procris inviting to her breast the javelin of Cephalus: "These figures had a look of life about them, and the porphyry tiles with which the floor was covered seemed dyed in the blood of these unhappy women."[7]

The story of Bluebeard as told by Perrault fits squarely into this sequence of tales about women threatened by some form of bodily mutilation, yet France insists that the artworks on display in the cabinet (along with the stories underlying the paintings) gave rise to myths that have distorted the historical truth. In other words, if the history of art—visual and verbal—tells one story about women imperiled by male assailants, history itself (in the form of "authentic documents" and "reliable evidence") tells quite another story. That the so-called evidence on which "The Seven Wives of Bluebeard" is based consists of Bluebeard's own version of the events, along with an anonymous complaint against his murderers, does not seem to unsettle the narrator's conviction that his character is the victim of malicious scandalmongers.

Bluebeard's murder is described by France as the "most atrocious, treacherous, and cowardly domestic crime of which the record has come down to us."[8] Despite the narrator's assurances that he will record the facts "with all possible restraint," "The Seven Wives of Bluebeard" is more emphatically an exercise in excess than virtually any other retelling of Perrault's tale. Its aggregation of superlative forms alone—"most atrocious, treacherous, and cowardly"—is telling. With a hero who is as shy, gentle, and benevolent as his wives are unscrupulous, deceptive, and malicious, France's Bluebeard story reveals just how powerfully a rewriting of the tale can reconfigure its sexual politics.

Donald Barthelme's "Bluebeard" (1987) intensifies the message of France's account by giving us a wife who, in the course of giving her side of the story, reveals the full extent of her deceitful behavior. In an almost offhand manner, Bluebeard's wife refers to the nun's habit that she wears during the midnight masses at which she meets her lover. Claiming to be "not at all curious by nature" and "obedient to the valid proscriptions my husband might choose to impose," this is a woman who is goaded into opening her husband's forbidden chamber once she realizes that there might be something there besides the corpses of her predecessors. Yielding to her "intense curiosity," she rushes to the prohibited chamber, turns the key, and finds "on hooks, gleaming in decay and wearing Coco Chanel gowns, seven zebras."[9] Monstrous hybrid figures, the zebras combine repulsive putrefaction with designer glamour to produce a surreal effect. "Jolly, don't you think?" is the lapidary comment of this Bluebeard who has finally succeeded in duping a conniving wife.[10]

France's "Seven Wives of Bluebeard" and Barthelme's "Bluebeard" may both be cast in the satirical mode, but the "truth" they reveal about the protagonists and their wives only reinforces myths about female duplicity that are embedded even in the stories that present Bluebeard's wives as victims. Though France's narrator claims to write against the grain of Perrault's story and Barthelme's wife of Bluebeard claims to know the story and hence is able to subvert its terms, both narrators deliver tales that are consonant with the ideological position articulated in the story found between the covers of *Tales of Mother Goose*. An appetite for knowledge rhymes with the desire for sexual adventures.

Given the wobbly ethics and loose morals of Bluebeard's wife, is it any wonder that Bluebeard himself begins to look like a cultural hero, a man who, even when he murders, has a mission to rid the world of women characterized by duplicitous behavior and predatory sexuality? As Aline Kilmer puts it, in her essay "The Case of Bluebeard" (1923), Bluebeard's wife is a "monster of ingratitude" who plays the "miserable, low, contemptible trick" of going through the pockets of a man who, at the least, deserves our "sympathy."[11] In both Chaplin's *Monsieur Verdoux* and Hitchcock's *Shadow of a Doubt*, women are the real monsters and both Monsieur Verdoux and Uncle Charlie are driven to a life of crime by their hatred of feminine excesses.

In a film subtitled "A Comedy of Murders," Charlie Chaplin gives us a Bluebeard who, though guilty of murder as well as of the infidelities with which Bluebeard's wives are usually charged, remains a victim. The long-suffering Monsieur Verdoux must not only subject himself to women with disagreeable dispositions, but also falls prey to an unstable economy, losing first his job, then his small fortune. *Monsieur Verdoux* begins with the voice-over confession of its title character, who explicitly identifies himself with Bluebeard: "For thirty years I was an honest bank clerk until the Depression of 1930, in which year I found myself unemployed. It was then I became occupied in liquidating members of the opposite sex. This I did as a strictly business enterprise to support a home and family. But let me assure you that the career of a Bluebeard is by no means profitable. Only a person with undaunted optimism could embark on such a venture. Unfortunately, I did. What follows is history."

Verdoux is not the only one to refer to himself as Bluebeard. A police detective also uses the term to describe the man whom he is pursuing: "He's a Bluebeard. A mass killer working in cities all over the country." And Chaplin himself used "Bluebeard" as the working title for the script, which was inspired by Orson Welles's idea of writing a screenplay about the crimes of Henri Landru.[12]

But Monsieur Verdoux does not at all look or sound the part of a Bluebeard. Our first glimpse of him is in a garden, cutting roses in a manner that is both effete and effeminate. This is a man who, like Max Frisch's Bluebeard (in the novel of that name), would not hurt a fly, and indeed he stoops to the ground to rescue a wayward caterpillar from the walkway. Cutting the figure of a narcissist rather than of a murderer, he stops to admire himself in the mirror and is endlessly sniffing the roses. But this is a man with a secret, and we get a hint of it from the puffs of smoke in the rear of the garden (Verdoux has disposed of his latest wife in his backyard incinerator). When the doorbell rings, Verdoux is cautious, putting his eye to the keyhole to ensure that no one is planning to violate the privacy of his domestic space.

Verdoux leads a double life: he is both cold-blooded serial murderer and tender-hearted husband, a man who thinks nothing of slipping poison into a woman's drink, then catching a train in time for drinks and dinner with his disabled wife. But the film makes it clear that Verdoux's split personality has a certain logic, for it is symptomatic of what it takes to survive in a capitalist economy. As important, Verdoux's crimes are given a certain justification in that they target only the "grossly materialistic" half of the population. When Verdoux is told that he appears to dislike women, he protests: "On the contrary, I love women, but I don't admire them." The source of Verdoux's contempt has something to do with women's lack of spirituality, their innate incapacity to transcend material things. "Women are of the earth, realistic, dominated by physical facts," he declares, and, from its opening scene in a dining room, the film repeatedly shows us women engaged in practical chores: raking, clearing dishes, dusting, and doing laundry.

Mona, Verdoux's wife, is another matter: we see her for the first time in an ethereal setting—a domestic angel seated in a wheelchair, reading a book. And indeed, when she senses that her husband's health is suffering, Mona appeals to him to trade their newly won prosperity for poverty. "If it means losing your health, I'd sooner go back to living in one room again," she pleads with him. Mona seems not of this world, and before the film ends, she has been translated into a higher sphere. In a sense, *Monsieur Verdoux* suggests that there are two regimes of women: one frail, self-sacrificing, and doomed to die young, the other robust, insatiable, and deserving to die, if not young, then at least middle-aged.

No one could form a more perfect contrast to Verdoux's wife than one of his intended victims, played by Martha Raye, a comedian whom the French film critic André Bazin aptly described as "Hollywood's number one pain in the neck."[13] Vulgar and shrewish, with an abrasive voice and abusive manner, her character Annabella recoils in fright from what she sees in the waters of a lake—"It's a monster," she shrieks, only to realize that it is her own reflection that has frightened her. In a grotesque reprise of the lake scene in Dreiser's *An American Tragedy* (doubled also in Humbert Humbert's failed murder attempt in Nabokov's *Lolita*), Verdoux unsuccessfully seeks to rid himself of this harridan.

It is Annabella, rather than the ethereal Mona, who in the end redeems Verdoux. She vindicates Verdoux's murderous career, turning him into an object of our compassion rather than our antipathy. Verdoux, as Bazin points out, manages to have his revenge on women without having to sacrifice his splendid role as victim. This is a Bluebeard who mobilizes our sympathy, not simply because he has lost his job as bank teller but because he is the little man perpetually tyrannized by the big woman.

A failure at the box office, *Monsieur Verdoux* has come under fire for sending mixed messages. One critic suggests that the film makes the fatal mistake of breaking the implied aesthetic contract between Chaplin and his audiences, offering social criticism rather than the pleasures of slap-stick.[14] The film's critique of capitalism did not sit particularly well with United States citizens, who had little patience for what they saw as a leftist denunciation of capitalism from a guest in their country. Verdoux's exoneration of himself as nothing more than a petty businessman whose crimes pale by comparison with state-sanctioned murders stretched the limits of their tolerance. "As for being a mass killer," Verdoux proclaims, "doesn't the world encourage it? Is it not building weapons of destruction for the sole purpose of mass killing? Has it not blown unsuspecting women and little children to pieces and done it very scientifically? As a mass killer, I am an amateur by comparison." And in a final declaration citing the Reverend Beilby Porteus's famous aphorism about state-sanctioned crime, Verdoux grandstands for himself by proclaiming: "One murder makes a villain, millions a hero. Numbers sanctify."

But what must have been more troubling—and what remains disturbing to audiences today—is the paradox of Verdoux's character. He is a devoted father and husband, an underdog who deserves our sympathy, the victim of a cold capitalist machine, yet he is also a hardened criminal. Chaplin referred to Verdoux as a "paradox of virtue and vice," and it is disconcerting to most audiences to find themselves rooting for a character who is so ruthlessly calculating (it is no coincidence that Verdoux starts out as a bank teller) as to try out a new poison on a bedraggled young woman who has lost her home.[15] Verdoux's vices—his pitiless attitude toward female victims, young and old—make it something of a challenge to embrace fully his virtues as a representative of the little man.

Yet in the end Verdoux, whose voice speaks to us from beyond the grave at the beginning of the film, triumphs, for his victims prove relentlessly unsympathetic, while the beneficiaries of his murders, his wife, Mona, and his son, Peter, are emphatically idealized. In pathologizing the victims of Verdoux's crimes, Chaplin's film sanctifies the homicidal impulses of its protagonist, turning him into a cultural hero who rids society of those guilty of enjoying in excess the things to which we ourselves feel entitled.

Dean MacCannell has precisely identified the flaws in the moral logic of Chaplin's character. Verdoux, MacCannell argues, is throughout "the perfect model of the modern man in general," a man who believes that he is at liberty to do whatever he wants so long as it is for the family. "Perfectly correct in every way," he is also "absolutely pitiless toward his victims" and "as a kind of by-product of the sense of propriety that causes him to kill—he enjoys wealth, freedom, exotic entertainments, and limitless sexual conquests, all of these being necessary to the performance of his duty toward his wife and child."[16] Verdoux's parting shot, "I will see you all very soon," implies that he is no guiltier than the rest of us, that we all participate in the perversions of a capitalist economy that dictates a ruthless appropriation of surplus value.

If the death of Perrault's Bluebeard brought a sigh of relief from readers, the execution of Monsieur Verdoux produces tragic effects from a man who was the master of comedy. Verdoux's crimes, committed in the name of financial survival, turn him into a saintly figure who claims to sacrifice himself, not his victims, on the altar of the family.

Uncle Charlie, the villain of Hitchcock's *Shadow of a Doubt*, is as shrewd and cynical as Monsieur Verdoux, but with the idealistic veneer removed. His pathology runs deeper than that of Verdoux and has the virtue of revealing more clearly what is at stake for this Bluebeard figure, who also murders for cash. In a speech delivered at the dinner table of his sister's family, the "Merry Widow murderer" reveals his powerful contempt for women. For Uncle Charlie, murder is not just a business, it is a passion:

> Women keep busy in towns like this. In the cities, it's different. The cities are full of women. Middle-aged widows, husbands dead, husbands who've spent their lives making fortunes, working and working. Then they die and leave their money to their wives. Their silly wives. And what do the wives do? These useless women. You see them in the hotels, the best hotels, every day by the thousands, drinking their money, eating their money, losing their money at bridge. Playing all day and all night, smelling of money. Proud of their jewelry, but nothing else. Horrible. Faded, fat, greedy women.

Charlie Newton, Uncle Charlie's niece and namesake, is an odd candidate for Bluebeard's wife. For starters, she is, of course, a blood relation rather than a spouse. But the relationship between Uncle Charlie and Charlie is a complicated one. "We're not just uncle and niece," Charlie asserts. "It's something else. I know you." Charlie and her uncle are the first characters we meet in the film, both introduced through Peeping Tom shots in which the camera tracks from shots of their respective towns into their bedrooms to observe both, recumbent on their beds, meditating on the dead ends in which they find themselves. "This coupling of the two characters lying in beds separated by a continent is the most striking indication of the relationship that exists between them," one critic writes. "There is a sly hint that what Charlie and her uncle are thinking about while lying in bed is of the other in bed."[17] In these paired scenes, there seems to be as much a touch of the morbid as of the erotic, for both characters are posed in such a way as to suggest a deathbed scene. With what appears to be telepathic precision, Charlie and her uncle simultaneously frame plans to telegraph the other with proposals for a family reunion.

If there is any doubt that the kinship between the two Charlies transcends blood ties, it is eliminated when the uncle takes his niece's hand and slips a ring on it. "Give me your hand, Charlie," he asks, and the profile of the two suggests a romantic engagement scene more than anything else. This symbolic marriage caps a scene that decisively takes us into the territory of the Bluebeard story. Charlie confides a powerful sense of kinship to her uncle at the same time that she asserts her knowledge of a secret in his past, an enigma that endows him with an aura of mystery. As her uncle's double, she not only feels confident that she can identify it, but also feels entitled to know it:

> CHARLIE: I know you. I know that you don't tell people a lot of things. I don't either. I have a feeling that inside you somewhere there's something nobody knows about.
>
> UNCLE CHARLIE: Something nobody knows . . .
>
> CHARLIE: Something secret and wonderful, and I'll find it out.
>
> UNCLE CHARLIE: Not good to find out too much.
>
> CHARLIE: But we're sort of like twins, don't you see. We have to know.

Charlie, like a true wife of Bluebeard or daughter of Eve, feels compelled to penetrate the mystery of her uncle's past. Slipping into the role of detective, she embarks on an investigation that transforms her from dutiful daughter in a family repeatedly described, albeit it tongue in cheek, as "average" to transgressive agent who becomes a disruptive presence both in her uncle's plans and in her "ordinary little town."

Determined to know her uncle (and here Charlie walks a treacherous tightrope between intellectual knowledge and carnal knowledge), she enters the forbidden space of the room in which he sleeps. That room, in a wonderful Hitchcockian twist, is her own bedroom converted into a guestroom for the visiting uncle. From it, she retrieves a clue that leads her to continue her investigation at the public library. On her way to the library, Charlie has two significant brushes with law and order. First she is halted by a policeman who takes her to task for jaywalking; then she is reprimanded by the librarian ("I'm surprised at you, Charlie!") for demanding entrance after the closing hour has struck. On the trail of her uncle's secret, she becomes contaminated by his criminal past, turning into something of a renegade herself who is perpetually disturbing the peace and enacting in unexpected new ways the powerful bond that links niece to uncle.

If Charlie becomes a true wife of Bluebeard, Joseph Cotten as Uncle Charlie slips right into the role of enraged husband, who feels compelled to murder the "clever" young woman who has gotten to the bottom of his past. His three foiled attempts to murder Charlie follow hard on his discovery of her detective work:

> "You think you know something, don't you? You think you're the clever little girl who knows something. There's so much you don't know. So much. What do you know really? You're just an ordinary little girl living in an ordinary little town. You wake up every morning of your life and you know perfectly well there's nothing in the world to trouble your life. You go through your ordinary little day, and at night you sleep your untroubled ordinary sleep, filled with peaceful, stupid dreams. And I brought you nightmares. Or did I? Or was it a silly, inexpert lie? You live in a dream. You're a sleepwalker, blind."

Uncle Charlie, for all his craft and shrewdness, has grossly miscalculated his niece. Charlie's life is troubled, but only because it feels so ordinary and average. What agitates her is the fact that she seems destined for a life of bovine stupidity: "You sort of go along and nothing happens. We're in a terrible rut. . . . Eat and sleep, and that's about all," Charlie complains to her father from her bed. "A family should be the most wonderful thing, and this family has just gone to pieces." Uncle Charlie brings melodrama and passion into the household, creating romance, mysteries, enigmas, and terrors that break the tedium of life in the average family. The excitement may turn out to be the excitement of a nightmare, but Charlie still manages to get out of the rut, to awaken from the stupor in which she finds herself, to witness the rejuvenation of her mother, and to experience real disturbances in what, until Uncle Charlie's arrival, has been an untroubled existence. In an ironic twist, it is precisely the brush with death that saves Charlie from the morbid boredom of small-town life, from the simulacrum of death that she stages for the viewer as she lies stretched out on her bed at the beginning of the film. And it is Uncle Charlie's undoing that his niece is unwilling to lie down and die in order to let him lie low and survive in the average little town of Santa Rosa.

Both Verdoux and Uncle Charlie are "ideal" men, "handsome, well-dressed, well-built, intelligent, entertaining, middle-class, and democratic." Functioning as what one critic calls "capitalist 'angels of death,'" they execute "fat cows feeding off of excess," those who have more than their fair share of material pleasures, but they also bring dash, charisma, and drama into the world.[18] Verdoux becomes a kind of tragic hero whose murders seem justified by the vulgarity of his victims and by the evils of capitalism; Uncle Charlie becomes a dark rescuer, a man who, though a scoundrel, saves Charlie from the humdrum routines of small-town life and also enables her to embrace the family life for which she once felt such deep scorn.

Charlie is one of the boldest of Hitchcock's many female investigators, yet for all her investigative savvy and her near clairvoyance when it comes to her uncle's secrets, she returns, after the excitement has died down, to a blissfully benighted state. The last scene, described by one critic as "maliciously ambiguous," shows Charlie and her new boyfriend, a detective named Graham, outside the church at which Uncle Charlie's funeral is taking place.[19] The conversation between Charlie and Graham forms an ironic counterpoint to the words spoken by the priest:

> PRIEST: Santa Rosa has gained and lost a son. A generous, kind . . . .
> CHARLIE: He hated the whole world. He said people like us had no idea of what the world is like.
> GRAHAM: It's not as bad as all that.
> PRIEST: . . . their sterling characters. . . .
> GRAHAM: Sometimes, the world needs a lot of watching. It goes a bit crazy now and then, like your Uncle Charlie.
> PRIEST: . . . the beauty of their souls, the sweetness of their characters live on with us forever.

Charlie has rid herself of her uncle and of his contaminating influence over her, but she has done so at the price of acquiescing to the lethal boredom of family life. "Those desires of independence and freedom almost do kill her," James McLaughlin points out, "yet she rids herself of them only to land in the tomb of marriage and family life."[20] Charlie's career as investigator and outlaw comes to an end after a brutal murder (she manages to push her uncle into the path of an oncoming train when he tries to kill her), and she reclaims her innocence by taking refuge in the family, declaring her allegiance to the hypocrisies of bourgeois family life uttered by the priest. In a flagrant betrayal of the heroic spirit that guided her to uncover her uncle's past, Charlie closes the door to self-knowledge and integrity, disavowing the quest on which she had embarked. Once a daughter of Eve, she willingly adapts to cultural expectations, bonding with a man of the law as the voice of a priest intones sacred lies in the background.

Marriage to Graham, as William Rothman observes, is not Charlie's "dream come true."[21] In the end, we are not even absolutely certain that Charlie will marry Graham. What we do know, however, is that Charlie's body language in the presence of Graham does not reveal anything of the passion, agitation, and excitement that appeared on screen when Uncle Charlie entered Santa Rosa. Can Charlie, her uncle's double and twin, ever settle for a life that lacks the romantic chemistry, the profound mysteries, and the investigative excitement that marked her affair with Uncle Charlie? Will she, like her father and his quirky friend Herb, resign herself to reading and analyzing detective stories? Beyond a shadow of a doubt, Charlie will have trouble finding a match to the charismatic criminality of her Uncle Charlie.

The cultural critic George Steiner has read one of the many cultural variants of "Bluebeard" as a map for understanding the human quest for knowledge. For Steiner, we are all—men and women alike—wives of Bluebeard, unable to reverse the move from innocence and ignorance to knowledge. Like Judith, in Béla Bartók's opera *Bluebeard's Castle*, "we cannot turn back." "We cannot choose," Steiner adds, "the dreams of unknowing. We shall, I expect, open the last door in the castle even if it leads, perhaps *because* it leads, onto realities which are beyond the reach of human comprehension and control. We shall do so with that desolate clairvoyance, so marvelously rendered in Bartók's music, because opening doors is the tragic merit of our identity." Steiner further celebrates the irresistible appetite for knowledge that is symbolized by the curiosity of Bluebeard's wife: "We open the successive doors in Bluebeard's castle because 'they are there,' because each leads to the next by a logic of intensification which is that of the mind's own awareness of being. To leave one door closed would be not only cowardice but a betrayal—radical, self-mutilating—of the inquisitive, probing, forward-tensed stance of our species. We are hunters after reality, wherever it may lead. The risk, the disasters incurred are flagrant. But so is, or has been until very recently, the axiomatic assumption and a priori of our civilization, which holds that man and the truth are companions, that their roads lie forward and are dialectically cognate."[22]

Charlie's likely decision to choose the "tomb of marriage and family" over intellectual excitement and melodramatic peril can be read as an abdication of the quest for self-knowledge, but on a deeper level it signifies a wholesale betrayal of Western cultural values that endorse the search for wisdom, truth, and personal integrity. In marrying Graham, Charlie would be tacitly accepting the false pieties of the priest ("the beauty of their souls, the sweetness of their characters live on with us forever") and acquiescing to the patriarchal values embodied in Graham's words about the need for supervision ("Sometimes, the world needs a lot of watching"). Turning back and choosing the "dreams of unknowing," Charlie would be losing Bluebeard and the intellectual energy he released, and, along the way, losing what is in some ways her better self.

If Steiner, in a curious twist to the customary affiliation of knowledge with patriarchy, identifies Enlightenment ideals with Bluebeard's wife, it is because his familiarity with the tale seems limited to the operatic tradition, in which the husband is associated with violence, darkness, and pessimism while the wife carries the banner for warmth, illumination, and knowledge. In Bartók's *Bluebeard's Castle*, Bluebeard remains a figure tragic in his existential isolation, while his wife, unable to turn back as Steiner observes, presses on with her quest for knowledge, even when it means facing self-defeating realities. Yet Bartók's Bluebeard, like the Bluebeards of the nineteenth-century operatic tradition who rarely murder any wives at all, is less ladykiller than a figure heroic in his tragic isolation.[23]

Paris and Budapest: in these two capitals, Bluebeard made, if not his operatic debut, his most celebrated operatic appearances.[24] In Paul Dukas's *Ariane and Blue Beard* (*Ariane et Barbe-bleue*, 1907), as in Bartók's opera, Bluebeard becomes a figure trapped in permanent existential loneliness. For the Belgian symbolist poet Maurice Maeterlinck, who wrote the libretto for *Ariane and Blue Beard*, the wealthy nobleman plays a subordinate role to the spirited Ariane. In Dukas's opera, as in Bartók's Hungarian work, Bluebeard's wife is given a name, in this case a name that aligns her with the heroic Greek woman who enabled Theseus to escape from the labyrinth and who was subsequently abandoned by him. Courageous and resourceful, the Greek Ariadne nevertheless fell victim to a treacherous spouse.

Maeterlinck's Ariane resists the role of tragic martyr. Recognizing the absurdity of dogged loyalty to an untrustworthy husband, she sets out to resurrect Bluebeard's previous wives. The subtitle to the libretto, "The Useless Rescue," is telling in its anticipation of Ariane's failed mission to liberate the wives, who seem to find perverse enjoyment in languishing in the cellar of Bluebeard's estate. Ariane herself triumphs in the end, refusing to relinquish hope despite the defeatist attitudes of the previous wives.

Maeterlinck's Ariane represents a radical break with the folkloric tradition, for this wife of Bluebeard is fearless in her resolve to undo the evils of a despot. The work in which she appears has been described as "a feminist answer to the male tyranny which has dominated . . . the Bluebeard tradition," and she herself has been heralded as "the prototype of the liberated woman."[25] Ariane is the first wife of Bluebeard to exult in defiance and to proclaim that she has an obligation to disobey orders that seem questionable. "He loves me," she declares, "I am pretty, and I'll know his secret. I must disobey him, that's the first duty when an order is threatening or incomprehensible." Dissatisfied with the treasures she finds behind the six doors to which she has been allowed access, Ariane presses on, despite the warnings from her nurse to avoid the seventh door, with its golden lock. "What we are allowed to see won't teach us anything," Ariane asserts in words that resonate with Steiner's views on forbidden doors as gateways to knowledge.[26]

Carrying a lamp to illuminate the dungeon in which Bluebeard's wives are imprisoned, Ariane brings light and life to the five women. Yet in the end these wives choose to stay with the wounded Bluebeard, and Ariane alone departs as the dawn is breaking to reveal a "world of hope" that stands in sharp contrast to the doom and gloom of Bluebeard's castle.[27] Ariane, alone of all her sex, becomes the champion of truth, the probing, inquisitive spirit who offers redemption even when it is spurned. Associated with "light and nature" and "opposed to the unnatural literal and metaphorical darkness of Bluebeard, his home and his past," Maeterlinck's heroine is positioned as a seeker of truths, who reverses an operatic tradition that—since Mozart's *Magic Flute*—associates bass and tenor voices with Enlightenment ideals.[28] And yet because her rescue is "useless" and she ends by saving no one but herself (and perhaps Bluebeard), her story can also be read as an antifeminist parody of woman's missionary zeal. Indeed, the biographical facts of Maeterlinck's life suggest that he may have been lampooning the passionate efforts of Georgette Leblanc, the actress and singer who was his companion for twenty years, to liberate beauty from oppression. "Will you help me," she wrote in *The Choice of Life* published in 1904, ". . . deliver beauty which doesn't know how to show itself and conviction which doesn't dare to act." "To deliver," she added with dazzling artlessness, "what a magical word!"[29]

Béla Balázs, an ardent admirer of Maeterlinck, wrote an essay on the author of *Pélleas et Mélisande* for a Hungarian journal. There he expressed his profound respect for the murky mysteries of Maeterlinck's dramas:

> That silence, that motionlessness locked up in those sullen castles, does it not undulate around me here as well? That invisible, all-ruling great mystery. For *that* is the hero of Maeterlinck's plays. . . . And as for the vast Unknowable, within whose breast we live as if in a dark forest: its most visible, most dramatic manifestation is death. Death is the hero of these dramas. But death here is not the terrible sad end, not burial pit and skeleton, but the dark secret, the lurker. *It is only a symbol of the great mystery.*[30]

The obsession with the unknown became evident in Balázs's publication of a collection of plays with the title *Mysteries: Three One-Acters*, a volume that appeared in 1912. Among the three plays, whose composition dates back to 1908, was *Bluebeard's Castle*, which was to serve as the libretto for Béla Bartók.[31] Although the opera was finished in 1911 in time for a competition organized in Budapest, the work was rejected as "unperformable," and its premiere did not take place until 1918.[32]

What is clear from reading Balázs's remarks on Maeterlinck's *Ariane and Blue Beard* is the librettist's lack of passion for the figure of Ariane. Balázs is less impressed with Ariane's heroic move to rescue Bluebeard's victims than with the bleak loneliness of the site at which Bluebeard has stored his victims. The librettist seems indifferent to what is usually the motor of the plot for Bluebeard tales—the secret that drives a wedge between husband and wife—and instead remains fixated on the mystery of life and how death is one manifestation of that impenetrable mystery.

Bartók's opera has only two voices, but there is a third presence that manifests itself in the form of the castle, a forbidding structure that asserts its dominance already in the work's title. Bluebeard's domicile, as many critics hasten to point out, stands for the soul of its inhabitant and becomes the stage on which the conflict between husband and wife is played out. In a gesture emphasizing the centrality of the structure and its symbolic significance, Balázs had included the castle in the list of dramatis personae in the first published version of the play (Bartók later removed the castle from the list). Some years after he had written the libretto, Balázs emphasized the identity between Bluebeard and his spectral habitation: "The castle is his soul. It is lonely, dark, and secretive: the castle of locked doors. . . . Into this castle, into his own soul, Bluebeard admits his beloved. And the castle (the stage) shudders, sighs, and bleeds. When the woman walks in it, she walks in a living being."[33]

The prologue to the opera situates Balázs's libretto squarely in a folkloric tradition by enunciating the traditional opening for Hungarian folktales: "Where did it happen? Where did it not happen?" That question is answered with another question—"Where is the stage: outside or inside?"—which in turn places the play within the tradition of symbolist literature (where appearances mirror essences) and also challenges members of the audience to ponder the relevance of the script to their own lives. This may be a familiar story, but it will take new twists and turns to create a more robust message with a new meaning for contemporary audiences.

The curtain to *Bluebeard's Castle* rises on an "empty, dark, cold cave of stone," with a staircase to one side, seven large doors to the other.

Bluebeard returns home, accompanied by his wife, Judith, who opens each of these doors as she makes her way into Bluebeard's soul. "I will open up the darkness. / Light will shine here, breezes blow here, love will live here, / In this house as light unending," she confidently declares.[34] Each of the doors opened by Judith emits a specific color of light, the first producing a blood-red glow to symbolize what Bluebeard describes as his "torture chamber." The second door is awash in yellow-red light and contains "instruments of terrible war." A golden beam of light emanates from the third door, behind which is Bluebeard's treasure chamber, filled with golden coins, diamonds, emeralds, and rubies. Behind a fourth door is the secret garden of Bluebeard's castle, lit up by blue-green hues. The fifth door is the gateway to Bluebeard's kingdom, and it is the last of the doors to produce light. The two remaining doors, once opened, bring darkness back onto the stage. The sixth door, with its "motionless mysterious waters," represents "weeping," though whether the tears are Bluebeard's or those of his former wives is not clear. The final door, which Judith insists on opening in order to discover the "terrible truth" about Bluebeard's past, reveals Bluebeard's three previous brides, bedecked with jewels and representing dawn, noon, and eventide. For her transgression, Bluebeard's wife will incarnate night and bring darkness back to the castle as she joins the three other living brides entombed behind the seventh door, while Bluebeard remains alone.

In the folkloric tradition, Bluebeard's wife usually remains unnamed. When she is given a name, it is, as noted earlier, usually the generic Fatima, an orientalizing nod in the direction of the *Arabian Nights*. Judith is a name so powerfully allusive and yet also so remote from the world of Bluebeard that it cries out for an explanation. Why would Balázs name Bluebeard's wife after a biblical heroine who saves the Israelite town of Bethulia by taking up the scimitar and beheading the Assyrian general Holofernes? The apocryphal story of Judith, after all, reverses the positions found in the Bluebeard tale, with the woman wielding a sword in the just defense of her people and the man falling victim to her blade.

The Judith of *Bluebeard's Castle* seems to have many kindred spirits, both literary and operatic. Like Ariane in Dukas's opera, Judith brings light, illuminating the castle through her vigorous curiosity. But Judith's project backfires. The tenacity of her desire to explore the darkest recesses of every chamber in the castle leads to separation and loss. In this sense, Judith's operatic trajectory closely resembles that of Elsa in Richard Wagner's *Lohengrin*. Both Lohengrin and Bluebeard plead with their wives to curb their curiosity, and both wives are unable to resist the desire to know what lies in the past of their husbands. Judith has also been linked to Wagner's *Flying Dutchman*, for she can be seen as a latter-day Senta, whose faith and grace hold the promise of redeeming a dark, brooding man in a state of spiritual crisis.

With the name Judith, however, Balázs firmly affiliated the heroine of his libretto with the long and venerable line of Judiths in the visual and literary arts. From Caravaggio and Artemisia Gentileschi to Friedrich Hebbel and Jean Giraudoux, Judith has figured prominently in the imagination of European artists. While the biblical account of Judith celebrates the courage of a woman who dares to challenge the power of an evil Oriental tyrant, the modern period transformed Judith from a heroic protector of her people to a woman who seduces through her beauty and deceives with her words. The story of her triumph was transformed into a cautionary tale warning men of the hazards of lust, or *luxuria*. In these rescriptings of the biblical narrative, Holofernes became the tragic protagonist whose hubris brought about his downfall. Symptomatic of the way he came to take center stage are the titles given to sixteenth- and seventeenth-century dramas based on the Book of Judith.[35] Just as Bluebeard's wife is effaced from the title of her story, Judith also yields the limelight to her antagonist in titles like *Holofernes* and *The Tragedy of Holofernes*.[36] And like Bluebeard, Holofernes becomes tragic victim rather than menacing threat.

Militant, seductive, and deceitful, the nineteenth-century Judith became, like Salomé, with whom she was often confused, a kind of femme fatale.[37] Friedrich Hebbel's 1840 play *Judith*, which Balázs knew well from his dissertation on Hebbel's dramatic theories, so powerfully sexualized its title figure that a biblical icon of feminine courage was suddenly transformed into an idol of perversity.[38] Balázs was surely aware of Judith's checkered past when he chose her name to attach to his construction of Bluebeard's wife. The curiosity of his Judith may have some positive overtones, but it also poses a threat so lethal to her husband that she must be entombed before she does any further harm.

The Judith of *Bluebeard's Castle* leaves her sword behind when she enters her husband's abode, just as Bluebeard wields no scimitar and proves to be more tenderhearted than tyrannical. If the biblical Judith is renowned as a manslayer and the folkloric Bluebeard builds his reputation on murdering wives, the Judith and Bluebeard of Bartók's opera are devoid of homicidal impulses and seem bent on establishing marital intimacy and accord. To Bluebeard, Judith reveals her deep love: "I came here because I love you: / Let each door be open for me."[39] Judith may be unable to resist the temptation to open those last two doors, but she seems to be a model of domestic devotion, resolved to ignore the rumors circulating about her husband, willing to part ways with her family, and determined to bring heat and light to a castle that resembles a dungeon. And Bluebeard seems genuinely grateful for the warmth that Judith's "fair hand" has brought to the castle.

Although folkloric versions of "Bluebeard" veered away from exploring the psychological complexities of the relationship between husband and wife, *Bluebeard's Castle* seems to focus almost single-mindedly on the mysteries of intimacy and love. As one commentator on the opera observes, "The story of Bluebeard and his wives came to be seen as one of mutual unhappiness between the lonely man who yearned for the enriching presence of a woman in his life but could not tolerate the spiritual closeness love demands, and the woman, or newest wife, who felt a mysterious attraction to this darkly violent man but could not—or would not—break down the emotional walls he had erected around his soul."[40] Bluebeard was no longer connected with murder and mayhem and instead became a target of compassion.

Despite the allegorical turn taken when Bluebeard anoints his fourth wife as night, *Bluebeard's Castle* resembles nothing so much as a story of domestic friction. Judith's undoing comes when she insists on learning about her husband's sexual history: "Tell me truly beloved, / Who possessed your love before me?" She wants full disclosure and demands details: "Tell me of the way you loved them, / Fairer than me? Dearer than me? / More than you love me, beloved?"[41] That she loses much of her sympathy through her insistence becomes evident when one critic refers to her "badgering," which becomes progressively more aggressive.[42] Another critic roundly condemns Judith for her lack of discretion and emphasizes the emotional "truth" of Bluebeard's need to protect his secrets: "In man's interior world, perhaps, there are secrets locked away; each one of us contains the best and the worst, by our material condition. . . . Only the shining intoxication of fresh love can sometimes dissipate this dark threat: but let the new woman in a man's life be discreet; the hidden places of the masculine self are forbidden to her and, above all, those where . . . past love lives."[43]

Bluebeard's warnings, for all their obvious gravity, fall on deaf ears, and Judith opens the final door to face the "terrible truth" of her husband's past. The previous wives, Bluebeard reveals, are part of his past and present: "They will always live beside me."[44] *Bluebeard's Castle* displays the perils of wanting to know too much, of pushing so hard for the truth about a husband's past that that past comes to life to destroy a marriage. Caught in the paradox of opening the door that is intended for her even as she loses her husband, Judith falls victim to her insistent curiosity and to her failure to take things on trust. Bluebeard, as tragic protagonist, is left alone on stage, engulfed by the darkness that symbolizes his lot when he puts an end to the quest for knowledge.

Recent commentators on the Bluebeard operatic tradition, most notably Stephen Benson, have contested readings that position Bluebeard as tragic victim of existential loneliness. Seeking to understand the significance of the darkness that engulfs Bluebeard, these observers have reflected on why the operatic tradition gives us "narratives of failure." The dystopian endings leave one heroine "defiant and vulnerable," the other incorporated into the very series of repetitions that she attempted to escape. For Benson, Bluebeard represents a "masculine darkness" that is symptomatic of "historically obsessed decline, a state of being borne down by the past." Ariane and Judith incarnate a "questing and questioning femininity" that avoids being "seduced into submission by the commodities Bluebeard has shored against his ruin," commodities that represent a retreat into preserving and sanctifying a questionable past, one that has been memorialized as torture chambers, tools of warfare, treasure chambers smeared with blood, secret gardens with blood seeping through them, endless domains beneath clouds of red, and mournful waters created from tears. These wives of Bluebeard are on a mission that transcends personal happiness and engages them with the troubled political as well as personal histories of their husbands.[45] They tell us that the tale of Bluebeard's domestic life has a larger significance and that the castle that is his home represents more than a marital space.

More recently, Claude Chabrol's *Landru* reminds us, once again, of the powerful link between private vices and public virtues and of how the carnage in the Bluebeard story is repeatedly implicated in military violence. Landru, for whom women are "monsters" with "cruel hearts," commits his crimes in secret on the home front, while his fellow countrymen enter war zones to murder other men. The Frenchman's crimes, enacted on screen in Technicolor, are cross-cut with historical footage from black-and-white newsreels documenting what goes on in combat. Whether Landru's crimes are a cynical comment on military violence or whether the military violence ennobles Landru's crimes and turns him into a heroic figure, it becomes clear that the battle of the sexes cannot be divorced from the broader social violence practiced on a grand scale by nations at war. The story of Bluebeard, for all its intense focus on the home front, mirrors problems writ large in the public sphere.

6

CHAPTER

The Art of Murder:
Bluebeard as Artist and Aesthete

I asked Celeste and her friends in and around that public
teenage athletic facility, if they knew who Bluebeard was. I
meant to mention Bluebeard in this book. I wanted to know
if I had to explain, for the sake of young readers, who
Bluebeard was.

Nobody knew. While I was at it, I asked them if they
recognized the names of Jackson Pollock, Mark Rothko, or
Terry Kitchen, or Truman Capote, or Nelson Algren, or Irwin
Shaw, or James Jones, all of whom had figured not only in
the history of arts and letters but in the history of the
Hamptons. They did not. So much for achieving immortality
via the arts and letters.

—Kurt Vonnegut, *Bluebeard*

As a double of Eve and Pandora, Bluebeard's wife is implicated in
issues of trust and betrayal, but she is also constructed in modern
times as a resourceful detective, even if her investigative projects
remain largely confined to the domestic sphere. As we have seen, Bluebeard, in his more recent incarnations, has come to be celebrated as a
cultural hero, a master criminal who kills in order to create a higher ethical order. But Bluebeard's work can also take an aesthetic turn, and fin-
de-siècle writers found in the folkloric villain a powerful model for the
artist who must preserve and nourish his creative energies by killing the
beloved and thereby shielding himself against the depleting effects of intimacy. While Bluebeard's wife continues to direct her erotic and intellectual energy toward the marriage project, Bluebeard himself has become a

152

figure with a certain ethical power and aesthetic vigor, a man who may not always murder, but who at least perseveres in the belief that murder is not always, in life as in art, a bad thing.

Henri de Régnier's short story "Bluebeard's Sixth Marriage" (1892) harks back to the Romantic cult of morbid beauty in its presentation of Bluebeard as an evil genius who creates art with his murders. Régnier's Bluebeard preserves the essences of his dead wives through their dresses, which become phantom works of art, each with its own perfumed chamber and haunting musical accompaniment. Like Grenouille, the olfactory genius in Patrick Süskind's best-selling German novel *Perfume* (1985), this Bluebeard kills in order to distill essences and create beauty. Savoring scents, sounds, and sights, Bluebeard makes the rounds of the chambers between marriages.[1] When wife number six has the wisdom to leave her wedding dress at home and enter the church without clothes, he finally settles down to live happily ever after.

Régnier's novella, which claims—like so many of its literary antecedents—to offer the historical truth about Perrault's Bluebeard, perpetuates the violence of stories that were part of an oral storytelling tradition, but many twentieth-century artistically inclined Bluebeards disavow the violence of their folkloric ancestors, creating art in ways that appear to do violence but in fact often do not. Like Barthelme's Bluebeard, who displays seven zebras wearing Coco Chanel gowns in his forbidden chamber, these Bluebeards traffic in art that does not require homicide. And yet there are still many Bluebeards who, like Edward Dmytryk's Bluebeard in the film of that title, shoot to kill and then display the corpses as objects of aesthetic contemplation.

What happens when Bluebeard declares that he has "only words to play with" and that he is in many ways powerless to translate homicidal desire into reality? Or when he keeps nothing but paintings locked in his forbidden chamber? Or when he has nothing at all that is worth reading or looking at? In short, what happens when Bluebeard sublimates his desire for violence and channels it into art rather than projecting it into life? Or, to move to the other extreme, what happens if Bluebeard needs to mediate his art through violence, to commit murder and create mayhem in order to transcend them through art? Twentieth-century literature and film offer up a variety of Bluebeards who write, paint, or photograph their way to immortality and notoriety in the arts.

Let us begin with the new breed of nonviolent Bluebeards, with characters who take control of the Bluebeard story and repudiate the notion that there is any violent edge at all to it. Vladimir Nabokov's *Lolita*, the story of Humbert Humbert and his eloquent passion for a twelve-year-old girl, seems at first blush not even distantly related to the Bluebeard story. And yet critics have been able to document the extent to which *Lolita* is replete with intertextual references to fairy tales, most notably *Bluebeard* and *Beauty and the Beast*. Although Nabokov's artful narrative may seem light years away from the roughhewn plots of fairy tales, the Russian émigré firmly believed in a powerful kinship between novels and folklore. In his *Lectures on Literature*, he pointed out that "great novels are above all great fairy tales," and he traced the origins of narrative to the moment when a boy first came running home crying "Wolf!" For Nabokov, fairy tales and novels are linked by the power of imagination, which invades everyday life to claim our attention with "news."[2]

Lolita is littered with references to fairy tales, most not obvious to the casual reader. There is Lolita's "crystal sleep," which is much like Snow White's; Ted Hunter, Cane, N.H. (a pseudonym for Humbert's rival Quilty and an anagram for "enchanted hunter"), seeks to rescue this nymphet, who wears a red cap at one point, from the predatory Humbert Humbert; like Charles Perrault's Donkeyskin, Lolita is threatened by a lecherous (step)father; Charlotte is a kind of wicked queen so beside herself with sexual envy that she sends her daughter out to languish, if not perish, in the wilderness of Camp Q. Humbert Humbert is a figure who represents a hybrid of Beast and Bluebeard, an abject yet also calculating figure who struggles against his own wretched state and also revels in it, hoping to undergo a transformation that will elevate him to the status of Prince Charming. Unable to liberate himself from the beastliness of pedophilia, he appears as a "comic, clumsy, wavering Prince Charming," a suitor who cannot win the hand of his beloved and live happily ever after with her. A European bon vivant whose "wives" are all dead by the time he suffers a coronary thrombosis in prison, Humbert Humbert arrives in the town of Ramsdale as a kind of Bluebeard figure who proves fatally seductive to both women residing in the house he enters.

Although Humbert Humbert is a man with a past, his real secret has to do with desires he feels in the present. When Charlotte becomes Mrs. Humbert, her husband is surprised to discover that his wife has a "possessive streak." Like Bluebeard's wife, Charlotte, the Haze woman, shows a "fierce insatiable curiosity," though in her case that curiosity is directed at her husband's erotic exploits: "She desired me to resuscitate all my loves so that she might make me insult them, and trample upon them, and revoke them apostately and totally, thus destroying my past" (75). To please Charlotte, Humbert embellishes his history and parades a series of invented mistresses before her imagination: "I presented my women, and had them smile and sway—the languorous blond, the fiery brunette,

154

the sensual copperhead" (75). For this Bluebeard, the key to success lies in excess. Taking pains to pad the account of his conquests, he makes himself even more attractive to his wife by killing off his mistresses, "destroying" his past.

Yet Humbert Humbert does not tell all, and he emphatically has something to hide. The words he has to play with are recorded in what he terms "exhibit number two" (39), a pocket diary in which he records the "hideous hieroglyphics" of his "fatal lust," his deviant passion for Lolita. In it, he spells out his revulsion for Charlotte and makes it clear that his marriage to the mother is nothing but a cover for gaining access to the daughter. Although Humbert Humbert believes that he has found the perfect hiding place for the key to that intimate diary in the groove of a velvet-lined case for his razor, he underestimates Charlotte's curiosity about the locked drawer of the imitation mahogany table (she suspects the existence of "love letters"). Returning from a medical appointment, Humbert Humbert discovers "the raped little table with its open drawer, a key hanging from the lock"—note that Charlotte becomes the agent of violence in the "rape" of her husband's private space.[3] In an interesting twist, this Bluebeard never has to lift a finger against his disobedient wife whose curiosity has gotten the better of her, for Charlotte is killed by a passing motorist. By keeping his journal, preserving in writing a record of his ardor for Lolita, Humbert Humbert has conspired with fate, "that synchronizing phantom," to produce the automobile accident that kills Charlotte: "Had I not been such a fool—or such an intuitive genius—to preserve that journal, fluids produced by vindictive anger and hot shame would not have blinded Charlotte in her dash to the mailbox" (96).

Humbert Humbert's writings, drafted in his "smallest, most satanic, hand" (40), figure as the weapon that does in Charlotte Haze. The words in the pocket diary may not murder directly, but in revealing the secret lust harbored by Humbert Humbert, they hit their mark and prove more effective than the scimitar wielded by the Bluebeards of fairy tales. *Lolita*, even more forcefully than the folklore of earlier ages, shows us the fatal effects of curiosity. In constructing a Bluebeard who is above all a writer and who has "only words" to play with, Nabokov suggests that the story of Bluebeard is as much about the terrible beauty and power of language as about sexual passion and murderous lust. *Lolita* tells us how words construct stories containing monstrous secrets that radiate a fierce brilliance, producing effects in the world outside it.

Lolita is, then, about both the beauty of words and the joy of their sounds as well as about the force of desire. Its opening sentence declares an investment in alliteration, assonance, literary allusiveness, and sculpted prose: "Lolita, light of my life, fire of my loins. My sin, my soul. Lo-lee-ta: the tip of the tongue taking a trip of three steps down the palate to tap, at three, on the teeth. Lo. Lee. Ta." A "pure and austere work," in the words of its author, *Lolita* can be read on one level as a novel of transcendent beauty that exempts itself from moral criticism. And yet as John Ray, Jr., fictional author of the preface to *Lolita* ("Confessions of a White Widowed Male"), insists, Humbert Humbert is a "shining example of moral leprosy" and his story is a "tragic tale tending unswervingly to nothing less than a moral apotheosis."

In *Lolita*, the aesthetic and the ethical are not two competing regimes. Rather, they exist side by side, in constant friction with each other. Like fairy tales, which pit beauty and goodness against monstrosity and evil, Nabokov's novel thrives on an engagement with both aesthetic and ethical issues, with the fair and the brutish in all the complex twists and turns of their manifestations. After his first night with Lolita, Humbert Humbert notes that "the beastly and beautiful merged at one point," and it is this point of convergence, which signals both the depths of depravity and the heights of sublime passion, that becomes the novel's center of narrative gravity.

Humbert Humbert is a Bluebeard whose reputation is established through writing rather than through murder or sexual conquests. The book *Lolita* gives us his bid for immortality. If he is deprived of the flesh and blood Lolita, he succeeds in re-creating her and endowing her with eternal life in the form of a book with the title *Lolita*. He exhorts the Lolita living in Alaska to feel no pity for Quilty: "One had to choose between him and H.H., and one wanted H.H. to exist at least a couple of months longer, so as to have him make you live in the minds of later generations." Through his writing, Humbert Humbert has endowed his own life and Lolita's with a kind of transcendent power: "I am thinking of aurochs and angels, the secret of durable pigments, prophetic sonnets, the refuge of art. And this is the only immortality you and I may share, my Lolita" (281).

If Humbert ultimately finds refuge in art and places his faith in the transcendent beauty of language, the hero of Kurt Vonnegut's 1987 novel *Bluebeard* has retreated from art, in part because the pigments he used to build his reputation were less than durable. Sateen Dura-Luxe, the paint that promised permanence but delivered unforeseen chemical reactions, ended by ruining Rabo Karabekian's artistic career. Karabekian's self-consuming artifacts are symbolic of the destructive side of abstract art, the way in which nonreferential painting liquidates itself in its determined refusal to engage with reality. What Karabekian is after, as he writes the story of his life and the diary of a summer, is a painting that will represent the violence and suffering of life yet will also disdain sacrifice and loss as the condition for artistic production.

Rabo Karabekian may have been married twice, but he seems to bear only the faintest resemblance to the legendary Bluebeard. Yet this artist, whose main identifying feature is a missing eye rather than a blue beard, embraces the role of Bluebeard, declaring to his confidante Circe Berman: "I am Bluebeard." Karabekian sees in that figure a kindred spirit in large part because he too possesses a secret in the form of a forbidden chamber. Locked in a potato barn on his estate on East Hampton, Long Island, is the "secret of a silly old man," a mystery to which the reader is not made privy until the final pages of the book.[4]

Circe Berman, the woman who moves into Karabekian's house, may have a platonic relationship with the Armenian painter, but she slips quickly into the role of Bluebeard's wife. "When I listen to her moving about this house," the diarist tells us, "I not only hear her footsteps: I hear the opening and closing of drawers and cupboards, too. She has investigated every nook and cranny, including the basement" (38). Predictably, what torments the "nosy widow Berman" is the potato barn, with its "six big padlocks and massive hasps" (39). Of all those familiar with the secret, Circe Berman is the one who finds the secret "most intolerable" (46). Karabekian's delight in withholding information from his energetic, candid, pragmatic houseguest is evident. He is fully aware of the way in which Bluebeard is "either a poor psychologist or a great one, since all his new wife can think about is what might be behind the door" (46). In a sense, he has produced a lure that tantalizes both Circe (whose name evokes the seductive siren who transforms men into swine) and, as important, the reader of his memoir, who keeps turning pages with the hope of discovering what is hidden in the potato barn.

Hidden in the potato barn is a painting, executed by Rabo Karabekian at age sixty-eight. Bearing the title *Now It's the Women's Turn*, its expansive 64′ × 8′ canvas is described by the painter as he and Circe contemplate it:

We were standing on the rim of a beautiful green valley in the springtime. By actual count, there were five thousand, two hundred and nineteen people on the rim with us or down below. The largest person was the size of a cigarette, and the smallest a flyspeck. There were farmhouses here and there, and the ruins of a medieval watchtower on the rim where we stood. The picture was so realistic that it might have been a photograph.

"Where are we?" said Circe Berman.

"Where I was," I said, "when the sun came up the day the Second World War ended in Europe." (281)

What Karabekian has produced is a canvas of epic proportions, one that depicts birth and death, suffering and liberation, a "gruesome Disneyland" that relies on photographic realism for its effect.

Vonnegut's *Bluebeard* gives us the history of Rabo Karabekian and allows us to enter the potato barn that houses his most intimate secret. That secret, like Humbert Humbert's, has more to do with aesthetics and ethics than with the past sexual or marital history of Karabekian. Vonnegut once noted that he made a point of avoiding depicting "adult sexual love" in his novels: "The minute you introduce that element the reader's not going to want to hear anything more about the factory system or about what it's like to be a parachutist. He's going to want to hear about the guy getting the girl and this is a terrible distraction unless you're really going to deal flat out with the sexual theme."[5] There may be an erotic edge to Karabekian's relationship with Circe Berman and there may be a marital history, but the real center of narrative energy lies in the debate staged in the novel about the merits of abstract art and representational art, and that debate is key to understanding the secret locked behind the door to the potato barn.

As a member of the American artistic movement known as Abstract Expressionism, Karabekian is committed to producing canvases that are "about absolutely nothing but themselves." This kind of art, while it can become wildly successful in commercial and professional terms, has a spiritual emptiness whose objective correlative appears in the self-destructing paintings done by Karabekian in Sateen Dura-Luxe. The eight panels of "Windsor Blue Number Seventeen," for example, end "in a locked chamber in the bottommost of the three basement floors under the Matsumoto Building" (272). Like the artist who painted them, the panels are "entombed," as good as dead to the world around them. Lacking soul and passion, they fail to express any kind of ethical or personal engagement. The secret to the past of this Bluebeard lies in that underground vault, a barren space that houses his art and is never sought out by the world.

What Circe Berman proposes to Rabo is a new kind of art, a representational mode that relies on the real and is charged with the task of preserving cultural memory. Dismissing the work of Jackson Pollock as unworthy of "houseroom," she suggests a portrait of Rabo's mother, a survivor of the Armenian massacre, feigning death under the corpse of an old woman killed by the Turks. "You could build a whole new religion, and a much needed one, too, on a picture like that" (24), she points out. The masterpiece in the potato barn shows us a transformed version of the mother's trauma: from the mouth of a dead gypsy queen come rubies and diamonds, like the jewels found in a dead woman's mouth by Karabeki-an's mother after the Armenian massacre. Instead of focusing on a "beau-tiful girl" who sees the diamonds and emeralds, we have a scene that resolutely shows us the horrors of war, refusing to camouflage or aesthet-icize the effects of its violence.

What Karabekian puts on display is a canvas, colossal in its propor-tions, epic in its scope (representing survivors ranging from concentration camp inmates through a Japanese army major to a Maori from the New Zealand Field Artillery), and monstrous in its depiction of human suffer-ing (men, women, and children are wounded, diseased, and dying). Yet he also shows a moment of triumph, the day "the sun came up" after World War II, the day that marks the triumph of the survivors. Small wonder that the one word he says to the shopkeeper from whom he buys the materials for the painting is "Renaissance."

Now It's the Women's Turn: this is the title that Karabekian bestows on the painting. What Karabekian recognizes is that he is prepared to abdicate a creative identity that is predicated on violence, on the depiction of mutilated, diseased, and dead bodies. Behind each of the figures on his canvas lies a story, and each of those stories is heartbreaking. As one critic puts it, what Karabekian's autobiography gives us is "a study of men at war—in and with themselves, with the women who serve and are abused by them, with other times and cultures they seek to dominate, with the ways they've learned to recreate and relish their world in art."[6]

In the potato barn, Rabo Karabekian has housed a new identity, one that declares itself prepared for a different representational regime. Blue-beard's secret turns out to hinge on a decision to abandon violence and to embrace a true renaissance, a rebirth that will avoid the sterile solipsism of Abstract Expressionism and the banal pathos of mimetic art. In the end, this artistic Bluebeard has found his soul, and with a "happy heart," he has decided that the time has come for women to generate new paint-ings that tell new stories about the figures of lived experience and about the wonders of an imagined world.

Both Nabokov and Vonnegut use forbidden spaces to house words and images that constitute the true identities of their protagonists. Humbert Humbert's diary exposes the secret life of the writer who produces the novel *Lolita*; Rabo Karabekian's painting reveals that the inner life of its creator is more than a monolithic canvas with no signs of life outside itself. What drives the plots of both these novels has much to do with the need of each protagonist to protect his identity, to establish a preserve in which the private self can express its authentic feelings. But the real narrative tension in both works is produced by the friction between efforts to guard that secret and attempts to identify it. Humbert and Rabo are perpetually hounded by meddlers, snoops, and busybodies determined to disclose their clandestine operations. Charlotte and Quilty dog Humbert; Circe Berman is determined to enter Rabo's potato barn.

Humbert Humbert may disavow the violence of his folkloric antecedents by using "only words," and Rabo Karabekian may refuse to live up to his reputation for violence by renouncing it, but popular cinema has kept alive Bluebeard's savage side. In a remarkable series of horror films dating back to the 1940s, a number of artists and aesthetes—in the tradition of Dracula, Frankenstein's monster, and Jack the Ripper—revive Bluebeard's notoriety as a lady-killer.

Edgar G. Ulmer's *Bluebeard* (1944) is the first in a trio of films that reveal a reciprocal relationship between artistic creativity and sexual performance. Whether these Bluebeards paint and photograph in order to erase sexual trauma or evoke sexual trauma in order to produce art is not always clear. But for all of them, art is always in some way implicated in murder. Ulmer's Bluebeard, a painter and puppeteer named Gaston Morrell, once aspired to be a great artist, to paint "something really worthwhile, something fine." While nursing back to health a young woman who collapsed in the streets of Paris, he paints her on her sickbed and finds that he has created a masterpiece. Jeanette recovers, but Gaston discovers to his disgust that she has become "a low, coarse, loathsome creature," a woman of the night who is "defiling the image that I had created of her, degrading my work." And so he finds himself engaged in serial painting and serial murder, always killing at the moment he finishes a portrait, compensating for the libidinal loss of the woman with the aesthetic reward of the painting. For the Parisian art dealer who is his partner in crime (and who plays Mephisto to Gaston's Faust as the puppet play of Goethe's *Faust* staged in the film suggests), the artistic capital generated by Morrell's paintings is quickly translated into financial gain.

Gaston's art reveals the dark secret that, according to Klaus Theweleit and other critics, has haunted artistic production ever since Orpheus turned around to look at Eurydice and gained artistic immortality through his song even as he lost his beloved: transcendental artistry is predicated on the sacrifice of beautiful women.[7] Much as Gaston tries to channel his aggression into other outlets—he becomes a puppeteer in order to produce works of art that allow him to destroy a counterfeit version of the woman he loves—he is unable to stop himself, killing as soon as he realizes that his ideal image of a woman has been tainted by reality.

An advertising poster for the film hints that sexual crisis may be responsible for Gaston's murderous rampages: "I search for beauty hidden in a woman's soul. . . . In my arms many were beautiful. . . . But the flame of passion exposed their soul's ugliness . . . ugliness I destroy." As soon as Jeanette recovers from the illness that disables her to become a woman of flesh and blood who may feel passion, Gaston murders her. Suffering from performance anxiety as much as from aggrieved aesthetic sensibilities, Gaston is a Bluebeard who murders in part because he is unable to live up to his reputation as a figurative lady-killer.

In *The Two Mrs. Carrolls* (1947), the artist Geoffrey Carroll (improbably played by Humphrey Bogart) worries more about his art than about anything else. For him, the completion of a painting marks a point of depletion, the exhaustion of inspiration and artistic energy. In order to renew himself, to reinvigorate his artistic power, he must find a new muse, a wife willing to sit for a portrait. Carroll's art feeds on fresh blood, and it is no coincidence that he enters his second wife's room during the night through an upper-story window. Poised over her like a vampire, he is prepared to put an end to her life so that he can reanimate himself over her dead body. Just as Uncle Charlie in Hitchcock's *Shadow of a Doubt* is represented as a vampiristic figure (he hovers over the city streets from a rooftop perch), Geoffrey Carroll is presented as a creature who feeds on his victims in order to renew his art.[8]

When Geoffrey remarks that "Beauty is worth any sacrifice," he reveals a kinship with Gaston Morrell, for he aspires to sacrifice women both to renew his art and to find ever more attractive muses to inspire him. Yet if Geoffrey is linked with Dracula in the art of his murders, Gaston is connected with a very different model of murder, for this Bluebeard suffocates his victims. Gaston, operating in Paris, seems more like a debonair French version of Jack the Ripper, painting, puppeteering, and murdering his victims with elegant silk ties. Though called Bluebeard, his story bears a closer resemblance to historical serial killers like Jack the Ripper than to the Bluebeard of folklore. Geoffrey, by contrast, though never linked explicitly with Bluebeard, marries his victims, has a forbidden chamber (the studio in which he completes the bloodcurdling portrait of his wife), is paired with a curious wife, and undertakes the obligatory business trip that conveniently takes him out of town.

As the Bluebeard story is recycled, it also comes to be contaminated with other cultural stories of multiple murders, marriages to strangers, transgression, and betrayal. Dracula and Jack the Ripper figure most prominently in the pantheon of cinematic cousins to Bluebeard. A newspaper contest proposed by publicity agents for Ulmer's *Bluebeard* reveals that product differentiation may have motivated the decision to use the name Bluebeard. Four photographs, each displaying a set of menacing eyes gazing out at the viewer, must be recognized to qualify for first prize. The first gives a shot of the actor John Carradine as Bluebeard, the second Bela Lugosi as Dracula, the third Boris Karloff as Frankenstein's monster, and the last Laird Cregar as Jack the Ripper in Hitchcock's *The Lodger*.

Publicity agents for *Bluebeard* proposed that theater owners could "make a killing" with Bluebeard. Under the banner of the term "Exploitation" (refreshing in its candor), they urged a campaign that emphasized drawing attention to the film's title, its cast, its setting, and its aura of mystery. Bluebeard, they claimed, is "the most terrifying character in all fiction, yet one which has taken on color with the years." Beyond that, Bluebeard has become "a symbol of man's mad lust for woman." The story figures as "a legend which has persisted through the years and one which is based on fact. . . . the theme holds fascination for all ages. . . . It is the spirit of evil incarnate." That Ulmer's Bluebeard, who is as much aesthete as artist, is also intended as a kind of criminal cultural hero, a lady's man whose dangerous sexuality will draw crowds, becomes evident from a proposal to have female viewers write letters to their local newspapers on the topic: "Why do dangerous men fascinate most women?"[9]

The effete artist, scarred by trauma but with powerful sexual charisma, was reprised by Edward Dmytryk in his *Bluebeard* (1972), a film featuring Richard Burton in the lead role. Dmytryk gives us Bluebeard as a man for all seasons. Richard Burton plays Baron Kurt von Sepper, a photographer who shoots his dead wives both figuratively and literally, then puts them on aesthetic display in cold storage. A veteran and war hero who, according to his physician, is unable to consummate his marriages because of trauma suffered in combat, he is also still "in love with his mother." Murder, as his last wife declares, is "the only thing you know how to do in war and peace."

Anne, a carefree American singer who manages to escape from Bluebeard's freezer, functions as both detective and analyst. She may appear to practice a shallow form of Freudianism, but she has the courage and wits to explore the baron's villa, discover his previous wives, and delay her own execution by suggesting a talking-cure to Bluebeard: "It might give you a better understanding of why you did it." While the Baron insists that his wives were "monsters," "depraved" women, and "liars," his wife is able to figure out the exact score. "They were just women. Their only fault was that they wanted a little love, and you weren't able to give it to them, were you?"

What makes Dmytryk's *Bluebeard* especially compelling is the way in which it enters into dialogue with so many previous versions of the story while at the same time parodying the notion of Bluebeard as homicidal artist with its visual excesses. The film builds on the tradition of Bluebeard as voyeur, as a man who derives visual pleasure rather than sexual satisfaction from the women he marries. Like Angela Carter's Marquis, Dmytryk's aristocrat suffers from a form of ennui that can be relieved only by visual stimulation, but he is never able to consummate his marriages. He follows in the footsteps of Humbert Humbert and Rabo Karabekian in building his reputation through art, in this case the mysterious images he produces when each wife expires, but he needs violence in order to sustain his art. In the tradition of excess associated with horror, this Bluebeard poses the corpses themselves in his freezer to produce what resembles a wax museum of beautiful murder victims, while the director, in a gesture of grim appreciation, provides a coda in which each murdered women is put on display, with a voice-over proclaiming how each was killed. It seems somehow fitting that the final scene of the film displays the dead body of Bluebeard, laid out to rest, while Anne (with a nod in the direction of Perrault's Sister Anne) and her youthful fiancé cheerfully take leave of the old villain.

Dmytryk's *Bluebeard* indulges in the art of excess in its presentation of Bluebeard as a depraved aristocrat and of his wives as grotesquely monstrous creatures. The camp portrayals of Baron von Sepper and his wives stretch the plot to the point of parody, reminding us that the story was never intended to be taken literally. The grotesque turns taken by Dmytryk's film point up, more than anything else, the flaws in Bluebeard's interpretive history, showing, for example, the absurdity of using a vulgarized form of psychoanalysis to cure a man who poses his dead wives as works of art in his castle's room-size freezer.

At the other end of the stylistic spectrum, we have Bluebeard stories that diminish the power of the plot by attenuating the strength of the tale's two most vital ingredients: the curiosity of a woman and the secrets of a man. It comes as no surprise that efforts to rewrite the story can founder when the hermeneutic crisis fails to materialize, reducing the man's secret to something that no one wants to know or so limiting the woman's curiosity that the mysteries of the man's psyche have no appeal to her whatsoever. When secrets no longer stimulate desire for knowledge, when women curb their investigative energy, and when transgressive drives are converted into compliance, there is no longer much of a story to tell.

In two very different cultural climates, one Canadian, the other Swiss, the Bluebeard story, for two very different reasons, loses much of its narrative power. In L. M. Montgomery's *Blue Castle*, the heroine may rebel against her family and marry an eccentric stranger with a secret writing habit, but she willingly accepts the role of compliant domestic angel who finds contentment and magic at the hearth. Never once moved to pry, she is perfectly happy to accommodate her husband's desire to keep a secret chamber. Max Frisch, by contrast, gives us a Bluebeard whose diary reveals that he has not only no closeted desires, but no desires whatsoever. These Bluebeards may still construct their identities through writing, but it is an art that lacks a transgressive edge, creating one Bluebeard who is far too tame to support the premises of the folkloric plot and another Bluebeard who seems invested in entirely subverting its terms.

L. M. Montgomery's novel *Blue Castle* (1926) is perhaps the first work to present Bluebeard as a writer. Its heroine, Valancy Stirling, falls in love with a colorful local figure named Barney Snaith, elopes, and retires with him to the "Blue Castle," an island retreat that allows them to leave behind the "realm of everyday and things known" to enter a "realm of mystery and enchantment where anything might happen."[10]

At the blue castle, Valancy is given free rein over every space, save a "lean-to" that is Barney's preserve. " 'You can't tidy the lean-to,' Barney declares. 'You can't even enter it. The door will be locked and I shall keep the key.' " Valancy, who seems fearless about taking almost any other risk, proclaims her willingness to acquiesce in Barney's wishes. Dwelling in what appears to be an enchanted domain, she immediately makes an association to the story of Bluebeard, but disavows the role of the curious wife: " 'Bluebeard's chamber,' said Valancy. 'I shan't even think of it. So long as they're really dead. I don't care how many wives you've got hanging up in it. So long as they're really dead' " (133).

Barney is an enigma. He is described by his own father as a "secretive young devil" (190); he smiles an "enigmatical smile" (150); he is said to be "notorious" (28); and he is a man about whom people tell "terrible tales" (202). Add to that the scandalous fact that he often does not shave for days on end—a clear nod in the direction of Bluebeard for this man whose real name is "Redfern," and it becomes obvious why he is seen as an "outlaw" (29). But the stories put into circulation about Barney are a product of gossip and invention, tales told to add spice to the dull lives of the local folk. The dozen wives rumored to be a part of Barney's past and the various crimes of which he is accused are nothing more than wishful thinking.

Valancy has no evident interest in penetrating the secrets of Barney's past. Although her husband shuts himself up in what comes to be known as "Bluebeard's Chamber," she has "no desire to peer into the locked chambers of Barney's house of life. His past and his future concerned her not. Only this rapturous present" (153). When she finally makes the decision to cross the threshold and enter Bluebeard's Chamber, she does so "absently," expecting to find it locked. In search of a pencil, Valancy is, tellingly, "only looking for something to write with" when she enters Barney's room: "There was not the slightest curiosity in her as she went into the lean-to" (195).

When Barney confronts her with the fact of her intrusion into his private sphere, Valancy emphatically declares that curiosity did not lead her to the forbidden door: "I forgot you had told me, not to go in—I forgot—" (209). No Bluebeard, but well tutored in the fine points of his story, Barney tells Valancy that there is no need to call Sister Anne, for he is not planning to kill his wife and hang her up on the wall. Without a moment's hesitation, he provides his wife with all the details of his life history.

Valancy, unlike most of Bluebeard's other wives, is a woman with an untroubled marriage. She is "happy—gloriously and entirely so." What makes life especially agreeable has something to do with its beauty, unpredictability, and mystery: "She seemed to be living in a wonderful house of life and every day opened a new, mysterious room" (147). While her husband's cryptic past and his secret chamber exercise little fascination over Valancy, the daily routines of life are charged with magic, charm, and enchantment. Valancy has entered a world utterly different from home, a space that drove her to distraction with its empty rituals and predictable routines. "Every door has always been shut to me," she declared in her family home. There everything seems scripted, with no deviations from the norm. A typical evening dinner drags "its slow length" along, true to family form: one uncle makes his "perennial joke"; an aunt tells "the same old story"; another uncle tells his "favorite prosy tale"; and the cousins discourse on about grievances and funerals, "as usual" (57). Valancy feels "bound" and "enmeshed" in that world, as if she were caught in a "spider's web of steel" (13).

Valancy managed to escape the drab routines at home by building a powerful fantasy about a second home, or "Blue Castle," in the clouds. In this abode, she has "quite a few lovers," though never more than one at a time. Rather than "murdering" these lovers as she outgrows them, she simply lets them "fade away" (5). This daydream, in which Valancy plays the role of a Lady Bluebeard, is supplanted by a second secret, one that allows Valancy to translate the fantasy about the Blue Castle into the reality of life with Barney Snaith on their island utopia. In a move that shocks her family, Valancy proposes to Barney Snaith, discloses her medical secret to him, and retires with him to his island retreat.

Barney's forbidden chamber conceals the secret of his second identity as John Foster, a successful author of meditations on nature. Valancy's few moments of joy derive from reading his books, which "yield glimpses of a world into which she might once have entered" and offer the "tantalizing lure of a mystery never revealed—some hint of a great secret just a little further on—some faint, elusive echo of lovely, forgotten things—John Foster's magic was indefinable" (9). Drawn to the books as much as to their author, Valancy is more intensely trained on acquiring knowledge about the expanses of nature than about probing the scope of human nature.

What enables Valancy to move from a dreary existence in which she is condemned to play the role of "old maid" to a life that holds forth the promise of perpetual fascination, thrills, and excitement is the lure of the forbidden. "Have you ever thought, Uncle James," she reflects, "how dull life would be without the Ten Commandments? It is only when things are forbidden that they become fascinating" (66). John Foster's books have taught her that "fear is the original sin" and that "all the evil in the world has its origin in the fact that someone is afraid of something" (25–26). Through his writings, Valancy acquires the courage to defy convention and to open the doors that have been shut to her. Barney Snaith becomes her perfect companion, for, though his past may have become an open book, he declares himself to be a perpetual mystery: "I never satisfy curiosity" (115). As author, he will presumably continue to supply Valancy with the mysteries of nature, to avert boredom and repetition by endlessly feeding her imagination.

Barney Snaith's books, the writing that he produces in Bluebeard's Chamber, become a source of liberation, freeing him from the hated role of a millionaire's entitled child and opening doors for his wife Valancy. Bluebeard's wife, for once, has nothing to fear from entering the chamber that has been forbidden to her. Montgomery may have disavowed the transgressive curiosity that gives the Bluebeard story its narrative energy, but she has reinvested some of that energy in the books produced by John Foster and read surreptitiously by Valancy at her home. Those books become a source of knowledge that transcends personal relationships and that transforms Valancy from a dutiful daughter to a rebel who may find her salvation in nature, books, and marriage, but who also ranks among the least curious and the tamest of Bluebeard's many brides.

Montgomery's novel, unlike Nabokov's *Lolita* and Vonnegut's *Bluebeard*, gives us the perspective of Bluebeard's wife. It relies on Valancy's felt experience to communicate life with a man whose secret identity is constituted through writing rather than through murder. Moving in the mode of the romance novel, it is marked by a kind of overstatement and excess that culminates in the plenitude of a fairy-tale ending. Barney Snaith will continue writing his magical books; Valancy will continue to be fascinated and fascinating; and the marriage will remain untroubled.[11]

There are a number of disturbing elements in this formulaic plot, not the least of which is the investment of the domestic arena with a charm and mystery that it often lacks in real life. Valancy's accidental search for a writing instrument also hints that Barney can count on some possible competition from a wife who seems blissfully unaware of her real ambitions and desires. Even as Montgomery endorses Valancy's rebellious break with her family and suggests her potential for something greater than keeping house for Barney, she also produces a well-lacquered version of domestic life, endowing it with mystery and magic despite its drab realities.

If any narrative deflates the notion that modern Bluebeards can live happily ever after, it is the dreary *Bluebeard* (1982), by the Swiss writer Max Frisch. Some latter-day Bluebeards are able to reconstitute their identities through their art, but Frisch's protagonist attains little more than psychic disintegration and self-eradication. This is a work that gives us ground zero of the Bluebeard story, an effort to create an endgame for a fairy tale that has led a robust afterlife in the artistic production of countless cultures. Frisch's Bluebeard story may still retain a violent edge, but his protagonist has no edge whatsoever.

Felix Schaad, a physician on trial for the murder of his seventh wife, suffers from what is repeatedly described as a form of "pathological jealousy."[12] Although his six previous wives are all alive, well, and willing to testify, Schaad (whose surname resembles the German "Schade," meaning harm or injury, even as his first name suggests happiness and good fortune) has committed something resembling soul murder. Possessive to an extreme yet at the same time indifferent to his wives (Schaad spends most of the trial meditating on how to line up good billiard shots), Schaad seems to have lost touch with any real affect. Described as a "person who would not hurt a fly," he has descended into a state of utter isolation, unable to make any kind of contact whatsoever. Schaad's wives are the victims of murderous indifference rather than of murderous jealousy.[13]

Schaad, like his literary cousins, keeps a diary in which he expresses his secret thoughts—feelings that he is unable to communicate with his wives.

But this "secret diary" (86) turns out to be of no interest whatsoever to his wife. "So did you snoop?" the prosecutor asks, only to learn that the woman on the witness stand had no desire to read her husband's diary. That lack of interest is, of course, symptomatic of a marriage gone awry, of a woman who is utterly indifferent to her husband's inner life. The "dozens" of notebooks in which Schaad scribbles down his thoughts "instead of saying what he thought in open argument" (86) testify to the physician's discontent and to his refusal to engage in a discussion of that discontent. Locked in a partnership with his diary, he is unable to form bonds with the wives that pass through his life. That the diaries fail to spark any curiosity reveals that Frisch's Bluebeard has been defeated in his quest to forge an alternate identity as writer. This Bluebeard, rather than building his reputation by confiding in a diary, gradually liquidates his identity, as husband, as physician, as writer, and finally as the Bluebeard of his story's title.[14]

Despite his confession, Schaad cannot even claim the role of the fairy-tale criminal, for a "Greek student with a black beard" admits to murdering his wife. His initial guilt, based on the intertextual reference in his story's title, proves illusory.[15] One critic sees Frisch's work as moving in the direction of eradicating not only his protagonist but the story to which he is affiliated as well: "It is as if Frisch, standing within a Western patriarchal tradition that he knows is moribund, feels an ethical obligation to help destroy the tradition that fathered it."[16] Another finds that the Swiss author reveals, through *Bluebeard*, that he can create "nothing original or new, but only endless versions of the same 'story' of his own life."[17] The story of Bluebeard, in its serial repetition of the same plot, mimes Frisch's own inability to construct a fresh, new fiction. And yet despite the Swiss writer's efforts to eradicate Bluebeard by eviscerating him, the villain lives on as powerfully as ever, preserved by cultural memory in the form of folktales and forever haunting cultural production with new words and images.

EPILOGUE

Perhaps, in the beginning, there was a curious room, a room
like this one, crammed with wonders; and now the room and
all it contains are forbidden you, although it was made just
for you, had been prepared for you since time began, and you
will spend all your life trying to remember it.
—Angela Carter, "Alice in Prague or The Curious Room"

Angela Carter's observation about a room that is both "curious" and
"forbidden" captures the powerful mix of aesthetics and ethics
that inspires our fascination with the story of Bluebeard. Her
Kafkaesque curious room, which arouses desire because it is "crammed
with wonders," is also the site of a moral paradox, for that very room is
also the chamber destined for the person who trespasses in crossing its
threshold. For Bluebeard's wife, it is both fated and (nearly) fatal, yet, as
we have seen, it also contains vibrant, if morbid, attractions beyond the
moral dilemmas at its entryway.

Eudora Welty once observed that "there is absolutely everything in
great fiction but a clear answer." And yet a clear answer is what many
readers demand. Well before Charles Perrault added his two morals to
the story of Bluebeard, the tellers of tales embedded explicit advice and
wisdom about life in their narratives. The fate of "Bluebeard"—its transformation through adaptation, appropriation, and revision—reveals the
degree to which writers, artists, and thinkers have been drawn to the folktale and engaged with its terms, at least in part because they wished to
revise its message, to enter into dialogue with what it broadcast to the

culture in which it was told. Part of the pleasure of every story derives from its engagement with social mores, cultural values, and ethical principles. Fairy tales, in the words of G. K. Chesterton, can be enjoyed "because they are moral." At the same time, he added, "morality can be enjoyed because it puts us in fairyland, in a world at once of wonder and of war."

"Bluebeard" considers the complexities of intimacy and marriage, of a relationship that is driven by considerations both physical and spiritual, aesthetic and ethical. What becomes evident, in the face of the cumulative weight of variations on a theme, is that Bluebeard and his wife form a powerful generative couple, ceaselessly engendering permutations of themselves that work through their relationship in new ways. Like King Schahriyar and Scheherazade, that other narrative couple of folklore, they reproduce themselves in stories, creating not just a thousand and one nights, but what Jorge Luis Borges has called "infinite, countless nights, endless nights."

Italo Calvino has told us that the moral dimension to a tale can be found "not in the subject matter but in the very nature of the folktale, in the mere fact of listening and telling." And it is that listening and telling—that dialogical discourse—that produces a proliferation of stories, each responding in different ways to the story as it was told once upon a time. In these unending efforts to "get the story right," we articulate what is at stake for us at the deepest level of human relationships.

It is for precisely this reason that efforts to reduce the lessons of this and other fairy tales to one-liners inevitably misfire. In *The Book of Virtues*, William J. Bennett tells us, for example, that "Beauty and the Beast" offers an "unforgettable lesson in how appearances can be deceiving, and how character lies beneath the skin."[1] In his failure to look beyond Madame de Beaumont's moral (to ask, for example, about Beauty and whether her appearances deceive) and his universalizing tendency (suggesting that every version of "Beauty and the Beast" broadcasts the same message), Bennett ignores the fact that new messages, values, and morals emerge in the dialogue about the story rather than through what is articulated in an eighteenth-century French version of a fairy tale.

The absurdity of trying to read a lesson into "Bluebeard" becomes evident from Winfried Menninghaus's survey of the interpretive activity surrounding Bluebeard, of efforts to create "sense" from the story. "Is Bluebeard perhaps impotent, and does he kill his wives because they make him aware of his incapacity and are witness to it? . . . Or does the fairy tale issue a warning to young girls not to consent to marry a (repugnant) man in anticipation of great wealth? . . . Or does the story of the forbidden chamber evocatively support the prudent psychological maxim that each person should be allowed his secrets—even in marriage—and that it is wrong and dangerous to intrude into a person's privacy against his will? Or do the corpses in the cellar represent Bluebeard's own repressed femininity, which perhaps he unconsciously even hopes to recover through his wives?" These interpretive gambits, I would argue, are less "fragments of meaning" than efforts, in particular times and at particular places, to extract sense from a story that resists any kind of totalizing interpretation.[2]

The moral wars that Chesterton finds in fairy tales are resolved through dialogue, but the wonder, to which he also alludes, emerges from the tale itself. Storytelling traffics in secrets and mysteries, stimulating our powers of imagination, investigation, and analysis. Reading books or watching films, we stand on the threshold of new worlds, opening doors that take us into the hidden chambers of unfamiliar mansions and into the secret spaces of other minds. Magic, as I noted at the beginning of this volume, often happens on that threshold, and if, as in the Bluebeard story, that magic has more to do with the great existential mysteries than with wondrous delights, then fairy tales clearly traffic in the art of excitement and revelation rather than in the pleasures of enchantments. Many of our most compelling cultural stories rely on the "lure of the forbidden," what adults talk about in hushed tones, to engage the curiosity of both character and reader.[3]

It is a rare novel or play that is able to hold our attention without constructing some kind of enigma, without challenging us to scrutinize, explore, and finally solve a mystery. Even the dullest narrative will have what Roland Barthes has identified as a hermeneutic code, the formal terms by which "an enigma can be distinguished, suggested, formulated, held in suspense, and finally disclosed."[4] Fairy tales, the most plot-driven of all narratives, tend to present their mysteries in visible form and to conduct their investigations in physical domains. Rooms harbor the unknown; doors open to reveal secrets; and protagonists are perpetually driven by curiosity to enter forbidden arenas. "Every door is an object of some vague symbolism," Barthes reminds us, and each is bound up with "a whole complex of death, pleasure, limit, secret."[5] Barthes's words remind us of how the doors to the forbidden chamber in Bluebeard narratives become charged with symbolic power, holding out the promise of both horror and pleasure in return for the rewards of transgressive curiosity.

The Bluebeard story enlists our desire for knowledge in order to keep us reading and to keep us alive through a sense of curiosity, wonder, and awe. And as important, rather than extinguishing that desire once the last page is turned, the story reignites it as we turn from the pages of the book to the realities of our lives.

In 1861 the New England writer Rose Terry Cooke penned a poem entitled "Blue-Beard's Closet," ending each of the seven strophes with the words "*The chamber is there!*" That phrase, in its repetition, is a dark reminder that violence, despite our efforts to liberate ourselves from it, remains ever present and even inviting: "Quicken, mad footsteps, / On pavement and stair; / Look not behind thee, / *The chamber is there!*" Forbidden and forbidding, Bluebeard's chamber still beckons us to enter, explore, and begin to understand its mysteries.

The war and wonder in "Bluebeard," as I have tried to show, cannot be fully understood without considering the gender trouble in the story. If the story has been continually recycled to draw attention to women's curiosity and its effects, tales about curious men have undergone a process of cultural repression. Fairy tales with animal brides—seal maidens, swan maidens, or peacock brides—occasionally comment on the consequences of male curiosity and how a man who wants to know too much can destroy his marriage. Consider "The Crane's Gift," a Japanese tale that tells of a young man and his marriage to a woman who magically appears at his doorstep after he pulls an arrow from a wounded crane and heals the bird. But one day, "filled with curiosity, the husband peeks through a crack in the door to the wife's weaving shed and discovers that the woman to whom he is married can transform herself into a crane. 'Now that you've broken your promise and have seen me,' she tells him, 'I can no longer stay here with you.' "[6] This story, even in its European cognate forms, has receded from cultural memory even as "Bluebeard" grows more prominent.

Bluebeard's wife is constructed as both agent of sexual betrayal and resourceful investigator, but in projects that often remain confined to the domestic sphere. The first part of this volume addressed the origins of "Bluebeard," showing how it emerged in literary works as a blueprint for mapping the risks of marriage, tracing its powerful but unconscious reemergence in cinematic culture of the 1940s when men were at war, and documenting its reappropriation by feminist writers, who revised the story to reflect anxieties about the marriage trap in the 1970s and 1980s. The final chapters of this volume gave us the husband's side of the story, showing how Bluebeard has come to be celebrated as a cultural hero, either as the master criminal who kills in order to create a higher moral order or as the artist who must shield himself against intimacy in order to foster his creative energies. Bluebeard has thus become a figure with a certain ethical power and aesthetic vigor, while Bluebeard's wife continues to direct her intellectual and erotic energy largely to the marriage project. "Bluebeard" has left its fingerprints in many obvious and not so obvious places, and we obsessively return to it to try to understand marital discord, unaware that the story itself has dictated certain cultural terms, in much the way that the biblical account of Eve and the mythical story of Pandora have shaped our thinking. Hence the importance of investigating the story, looking at how it reflects our anxieties as cultural symptom, yet also probing the reach of its cultural effects as it continues to shape our fantasies and desires.

Cultural Variants of "Bluebeard"

BLUEBEARD
From Charles Perrault, Contes, *1697.*

There was once a man who owned grand estates, in both the country and the city. He had dinner services of gold and silver, beautifully upholstered furniture, and carriages covered in gold leaf. But this man also had the misfortune of having a blue beard, which made him look so hideously ugly that women and girls alike fled at the sight of him.

One of his neighbors, a highly regarded lady, had two daughters, both of whom were perfect beauties. He asked for the hand of one of the two in marriage, leaving the choice up to the mother. Neither of the two girls wanted to marry him, and the offer went back and forth between them, since both were reluctant to marry a man with a blue beard. Their feelings of revulsion intensified when they learned that the man had been married several times before and that no one knew what had become of his wives.

To get to know the family better, Bluebeard invited the girls and their mother, three or four of their closest friends, and a few young people from the neighborhood to one of his country houses, where they stayed for a whole week. Every day there were festive activities: picnics, hunting, fishing, dancing, and dining. They caroused all night long and no one slept a wink. Everything went so well that the younger sister started imagining that the lord of the manor had a beard that was not really so blue after all and that he was in fact a fine man. As soon as they got back to town, the marriage took place.

After a month had gone by, Bluebeard told his wife that he had to take care of some urgent business in the provinces and that he would be away for at least six weeks. He wanted her to enjoy herself while he was away and encouraged her to invite all her friends and think about going out to the country, anything that would make her happy.

He handed her a bunch of keys, saying: "These open my two large store rooms. These are for the gold and silver china that is too good for every-day use. Here are the keys for my strongboxes, where I keep my gold and silver. Here are the ones for the caskets in which I store my jewels. And finally, here is the master key that opens every room in the house. This last key here is the key that opens the small room at the end of the long passage on the lower floor. Open anything you want. Go anywhere you want. But I absolutely forbid you to go into that one room, and if you open it so much as a crack, my anger will know no limits."

The wife promised to do exactly as he had told her. Bluebeard kissed her, got into the carriage, and set out on his journey.

Friends and neighbors did not wait for invitations. They were so impatient to see the splendors of the house that they came to call on the young bride right away. While the husband was at home, they had not dared to call, for the blue beard had frightened them off. In no time at all, they were darting around in the rooms, opening the closets and the wardrobes, each of which was more magnificent and sumptuous than the next. They went up the stairs to the storerooms, and there they could not find words to describe the great numbers of beautiful tapestries, beds, sofas, cabinets, nightstands, and tables. There were looking glasses in which you could see yourself from head to toe. Some of them had frames of glass, others of silver or gilded lacquer, but all of them were more grand and splendid than anyone could have imagined.

The visitors lavished praise on the young woman even as they could not help but feel some envy at her good fortune. Unable to get any pleasure at all from these riches, the bride could not wait to get into the room on the lower floor. She was so tormented by her curiosity that she did not stop to think how rude it was to desert her guests, and she raced down the back stairs so fast that two or three times she thought she was going to break her neck. When she reached the door to the room, she stopped for a moment to recall how her husband had forbidden her to open it, and she reflected on the punishment she might incur for being disobedient. But the temptation was too strong for her to resist. She took the little key and, trembling, she opened the door.

At first she could see nothing at all, for the windows were shuttered. After a few moments, it dawned on her that the floor was covered with clotted blood and that in those pools of blood were reflected the corpses of several women, hung up on the walls (these were all the women Bluebeard had married and whose throats he had cut one after another).

She was sure that she would die of fright, and the key to the room, which she was about to pull out of the lock, dropped from her hand. She pulled herself together, picked up the key, locked the door, and went back up to her bedroom to compose herself. But her nerves were too frayed to allow her to recover completely. After noticing that the key to the room was stained with blood, she wiped it two or three times, but the blood would not go away. She tried to rinse it off and scrubbed it with sand and grit as well. But the bloodstain remained because the key was enchanted, and there was no way to remove the blood from it. When you got the stain off one side of the key, it came back on the other side.

Bluebeard unexpectedly returned from his journey that very evening and reported that, on the way, he had received letters informing him that the business which had called him away had been settled to his satisfaction. His wife did everything she could to make it appear that she was delighted with his early return. The following day, he asked for his keys, and she returned them, but with a hand shaking so badly that he knew right away what had happened.

"Why isn't the key to the little room here with the others?" he asked.

"I must have left it upstairs on my dressing table," she replied.

"Don't forget to bring it right back to me," Bluebeard told her.

She made one excuse after another, but finally she had to bring him the key. Bluebeard inspected it, then said to his wife: "How did you get blood on this key?'

"I have no idea," the poor woman answered, and she turned pale as death.

"You have no idea," Bluebeard replied. "But I have an idea how. You tried to get into that little room. Well, madam, now that you have opened it, you can walk right in and take your place beside the ladies whom you saw there."

She threw herself at her husband's feet, weeping and begging forgiveness, with every sign that she felt genuine regret for disobeying him. This beauty in distress would have melted a heart of stone, but Bluebeard's heart was harder than stone.

"Madam, you must die," he declared. "Your time has come."

"Since I must die," she replied, gazing at him, her eyes filled with tears, "give me just a moment to say my prayers."

"I will give you a quarter of an hour," Bluebeard replied, "but not a second longer."

When she was alone, she called for her sister and said to her: "Sister Anne"—for that was her name—"I beg you, go to the top of the tower to see if our brothers are on the way here. They promised that they were coming to visit today. If you catch sight of them, send them a signal to hurry."

Sister Anne climbed to the top of the tower, and, from time to time, the poor woman cried out to her: "Anne, Sister Anne, can you see anyone coming?"

Sister Anne replied: "I see nothing but the sun shining and the green grass growing."

In the meantime, Bluebeard raised his enormous scimitar and shouted as loud as he could up to his wife: "Come down here at once, or I'll go up there to get you!"

"Just give me one more second, I'm begging you," his wife replied and then she whispered loudly: "Anne, Sister Anne, do you see anyone heading this way?"

"I see a great big cloud of dust heading in this direction," replied Sister Anne.

"Is it our brothers?"

"No, oh no, sister dear, it's just a flock of sheep."

"Are you coming down here or not?" Bluebeard roared.

"Just one more second," his wife replied, and then she called out: "Anne, Sister Anne, do you see anyone heading this way?"

"I see two horsemen heading this way, but they're still far away," she replied. A moment later she called out: "Thank God, it must be our brothers. I'll send them a signal to hurry up."

Bluebeard roared so loudly that the entire house shook. His poor wife came downstairs in tears, her hair disheveled. She threw herself at her husband's feet.

"That won't do you any good," said Bluebeard. "Prepare to die." Taking her by the hair with one hand and raising his scimitar with the other, he was getting ready to chop off her head. The poor woman turned to him and, with dimmed eyes, begged him to stop and give her a moment to prepare for her death.

"No, no," Bluebeard said. "Prepare to meet your maker." And lifting his arm . . .

Just then there was a pounding at the gate so loud that Bluebeard stopped in his tracks. The gate was opened. Two men on horseback—swords in hand—galloped in, heading straight for Bluebeard, who realized that the men—one a dragoon, the other a musketeer—must be his wife's brothers. He fled at once, hoping to escape, but the two pitiless

178

brothers closed in on him before he could get to the stairs. They ran their swords through him and left him for dead. Bluebeard's wife was almost as lifeless as her husband. She barely had the strength to rise and embrace her brothers.

It turned out that Bluebeard had left no heirs, and so his wife was able to take possession of the entire fortune. She used some of it to marry her sister Anne to a young gentleman who loved her dearly. And some of it went to buying commissions for her two brothers. The rest she used to marry herself to a very worthy man, who helped her banish the memory of the terrible days she had spent with Bluebeard.

Moral

Curiosity, with its many charms,
Can stir up serious regrets;
Thousand of examples turn up every day.
Women give in, but it's a fleeting pleasure;
Once satisfied, it ceases to be.
And always it proves very costly.

Another Moral

Take the time to stop and think,
And to ponder this grim little story.
You surely know that this tale
Took place many years ago.
No longer are husbands so terrible,
Demanding the impossible,
Acting unhappy and jealous.
They toe the line with their wives.
And no matter what color their beards,
It's not hard to tell who is in charge.

THE ROBBER BRIDEGROOM
From Jacob and Wilhelm Grimm, Kinder- und Hausmärchen, *1857.*

There once lived a miller who had a beautiful daughter. He wanted to be sure that she was provided for and that she married well once she was grown up. He thought: "If the right kind of suitor comes along and asks for her hand, I shall give her to him."

Before long a suitor turned up who seemed to be rich, and since the miller could find nothing wrong with him, he promised him his daughter. But the girl didn't care for him in the way that a girl should care for her betrothed, and she did not trust him at all. Whenever she looked at him or when her thoughts turned to him, she was filled with dread.

One day he said to her: "You're engaged to me, and yet you've never once visited me."

The girl replied: "I don't know where you live."

The bridegroom told her: "My house is out in the dark forest."

The girl made all kinds of excuses and claimed that she would not be able to find the way there. But the bridegroom said: "Next Sunday you have to come to my place. I've already invited the guests, and I'll strew ashes on the path so that you can find your way through the woods."

When Sunday arrived and the girl was supposed to leave, she became dreadfully frightened without knowing exactly why, and she filled both her pockets with peas and lentils to mark the way. When she entered the woods, she found the trail of ashes and followed it, but at every step she threw some peas on the ground, first to the right, then to left. She walked almost all day long until she got to the middle of the forest, where it was the gloomiest. There she saw a house standing all alone, but she didn't like the look of it because it seemed dark and spooky. She walked in. It was deadly silent, and there was no one around. Suddenly, a voice cried out:

> "Turn back, turn back, my pretty young bride,
> In a house of murderers you've arrived."

The girl looked up and realized that the voice was coming from a bird in a cage hanging on the wall. Once again it cried out:

> "Turn back, turn back, my pretty young bride,
> In a house of murderers you've arrived."

The beautiful bride walked all around the house, going from one room to the next, but it was completely empty and there was not a soul in it. Finally, she went down to the cellar, where she found a woman, as old as the hills, her head bobbing up and down.

"Can you tell me if my betrothed lives here?" the girl asked.

"Oh, you poor child!" said the old woman. "How did you get here? This is a den of murderers. You think you're a bride about to be married, but the only wedding you'll celebrate is one with death. Look over here! I had to heat up this big pot of water for them. When you get into their hands, they'll show no mercy and will chop you into pieces, cook you, and eat you, for they are cannibals. You're lost unless I take pity on you and try to save you."

The old woman hid her behind a big barrel, where no one could see her. "Be still as a mouse," she said. "Don't stir and don't move or that'll be the end of you. At night, when the robbers are asleep, we'll escape. I've been waiting a long time for this moment."

No sooner had she spoken those words when the wicked crew returned home, dragging another maiden behind them. They were drunk and paid no attention to her screams and sobs. They gave her wine to drink, three glasses full, one white, one red, one yellow, and before long her heart burst in two. They tore off her fine clothes, put her on the table, chopped her beautiful body into pieces, and sprinkled them with salt.

The poor girl was trembling and shaking from her hiding place behind the barrel, for she now understood what the robbers had in store for her. One of them caught sight of a golden ring on the little finger of the murdered girl, and when he couldn't pull it off right away, he took an ax and chopped the finger off. The finger went flying through the air up over the barrel and landed right in the girl's lap. The robber took a candle and wanted to go looking for it but couldn't find it. One of the other robbers asked: "Have you looked over there behind that big barrel?" Just then the old woman called out: "Come and eat! You can look again tomorrow. The finger isn't going to go running off."

"The old woman's right," the robbers said, and they put an end to their search and sat down to eat. The old woman put a few drops of a sleeping potion in their wine, and soon they retired to the cellar where they were snoring away in their sleep.

When the bride heard them snoring, she came out from behind the barrel and made her way over the sleeping bodies arranged on the ground in rows. She was terrified that she might wake one of them up, but God guided her footsteps. The old woman went up the stairs with her, opened the door, and they ran as fast as they could from the den of murderers. The wind had scattered the ashes, but the peas and lentils had sprouted and showed the way in the moonlight. The two walked all night long. In the morning they reached the mill, and the girl told her father about everything that had happened.

When the day of the wedding celebration arrived, the groom appeared, as did all the friends and relatives invited by the miller. When they sat down for dinner, each person was asked to tell a story. The bride sat quietly and didn't utter a word. Finally the bridegroom said to his bride: "Don't you have anything to say, my love? You have to tell us something."

"Very well," she replied, "I will tell you about a dream I had. I was walking alone through the woods and came across a house. Not a soul was living in it, but on the wall there was a cage, and in it was a bird that cried out:

'Turn back, turn back, my pretty young bride,
In a house of murderers you've arrived.'

"Then it repeated those words. My dear, I must have been dreaming all this. Then I walked from room to room, and each one was completely empty. Everything was so spooky. Finally I went down to the cellar, and there I saw a woman as old as the hills, her head bobbing up and down. I asked her: 'Does my betrothed live here?' She replied: 'Oh, you poor child, you have stumbled into a den of murderers. Your betrothed lives here, but he is planning to chop you up and kill you, and then he'll cook you and eat you up.' My dear, I must have been dreaming all this. The old woman hid me behind a big barrel, and no sooner was I hidden when the robbers returned home, dragging a maiden with them. They gave her three kinds of wine to drink, white, red, and yellow, and her heart burst in two. My dear, I must have been dreaming all this. Then they tore off her fine clothes, chopped her beautiful body into pieces, and sprinkled it with salt. My dear, I must have been dreaming all this. One of the robbers caught sight of a gold ring on her finger and since it was hard to pull off, he took an ax and chopped it off. The finger flew through the air up behind the big barrel and landed in my lap. And here is the finger with the ring."

With these words, she pulled it out and showed it to everyone there.

The robber, who had turned white as a ghost while she was telling the story, jumped up and tried to escape, but the guests seized him and turned him over to the authorities. He and his band were executed for their dreadful deeds.

FITCHER'S BIRD
From Jacob and Wilhelm Grimm, Kinder- und Hausmärchen, *1857.*

There was once a wizard who used to disguise himself as a poor man and go begging from door to door in order to capture pretty girls. No one knew what he did with them, for they disappeared without a trace.

One day he appeared at the door of a man with three beautiful daughters. He looked like a poor, weak beggar and had a basket strapped on his back, as if he were collecting hand-outs. He asked for something to eat, and when the eldest girl came to the door to give him a crust of bread, all he had to do was touch her, and she jumped right into the basket. Then he made long legs and hurried away to bring her back to his house, which was in the middle of a dark forest.

Everything in the house was splendid. He gave the girl everything she wanted and told her: "Dearest, I'm sure you'll be happy here with me, for you'll have whatever your heart desires." After a few days had gone by, he said: "I have to go on a trip and will leave you alone for a short while. Here are the keys for the house. You can go anywhere you want and look around at anything you want, but don't go into the room that this little key opens. I forbid it under the punishment of death."

He also gave her an egg and said: "Carry it with you wherever you go, because if it gets lost, something terrible will happen." She took the keys and the egg and promised to do exactly as he had told her. After he left, she went over the house from top to bottom, taking a good look at everything in it. The rooms were filled with glittering silver and gold, and she thought that she had never seen anything so magnificent. When she finally got to the forbidden door, she was about to walk right past it when curiosity got the better of her. She inspected the key and found that it looked just like the others. Putting it into the lock, she turned it just a little bit and the door shot open.

Imagine what she saw when she entered! In the middle of the room there was a big basin full of blood, and in it were the chopped-up pieces of dead bodies. Next to the basin was a block of wood with a gleaming ax on it. She was so horrified that she dropped the egg she was holding into the basin. Even though she took it right out and wiped off the blood, it didn't help. The stain came right back. She wiped and scraped, but it just wouldn't come off.

It wasn't long before the man returned from his journey, and he asked for the key and the egg right away. She gave them to him, but she was trembling, and when he saw the red stain, he knew that she had been in the bloody chamber. "You went into the chamber against my wishes," he said. "Now you will go back in against yours. Your life has reached its end."

He threw her down, dragged her into the chamber by her hair, chopped her head off on the block, and hacked her into pieces so that her blood ran down all over the floor. Then he tossed her into the basin with the others.

"Now I'll go and get the second one," said the wizard, and he went back to the house dressed as a poor man begging for charity. When the second daughter brought him a crust of bread, he caught her as he had the first just by touching her. He carried her off, and she fared no better than her sister. Her curiosity got the better of her: she opened the door to the bloody chamber, looked inside, and when the wizard came back she had to pay with her life.

The man went to go get the third daughter, but she was clever and sly. After handing over the keys and the egg, he left, but she put the egg in a safe place. She explored the house and entered the forbidden chamber. And what did she see! There in the basin were both her sisters, foully murdered and chopped into pieces. But she set to work gathering all the body parts and put them back where they belonged: heads, torsos, arms, and legs. When everything was in place, the pieces began to move and to knit back together. Both girls opened their eyes and came back to life. Overjoyed, they kissed and hugged.

On his return home, the man asked right away about the keys and egg. When he was unable to find a trace of blood on the egg, he declared: "You have passed the test, and you shall be my bride." He no longer had any power over her and had to do her bidding. "Very well," she replied. "But first you must take a basketful of gold to my father and mother, and you must carry it on your back. In the meantime, I'll make the plans for the wedding."

She ran to her sisters, whom she had hidden in a little room and said: "Now is the time when I can save you. That brute will be the one who carries you home. But as soon as you get back there, send help for me."

She put both girls into a basket and covered them with gold until they could not be seen. Then she summoned the wizard and said: "Pick up the basket and start walking, but don't you dare stop to rest along the way. I'll be looking out my little window, keeping an eye on you."

The wizard put the basket up on his shoulders and started walking with it. But it was so heavy that sweat began to pour down his forehead. He sat down to rest for a while, but within moments one of the girls cried out from the basket: "I'm looking out my little window, and I see that you're resting. Get a move on." Whenever he stopped, the voice called out, and he had to keep going until finally, gasping for breath and groaning, he carried the basket with the gold and with the two girls in it back to their parents' house.

Meanwhile the bride was preparing the wedding celebration, to which she had invited all the wizard's friends. She took a skull with grinning teeth, crowned it with jewels and a garland of flowers, carried it upstairs, and set it down at an attic window, facing to the outside. When everything was ready, she crawled into a barrel of honey, cut open a featherbed and rolled around in the feathers until she looked like a strange bird that no one could have recognized. She left the house and, on her way, she met some wedding guests, who asked:

"Oh, Fitcher's feathered bird, where from, where from?"
"From feathered Fitze Fitcher's house I've come."
"And the young bride there, how does she fare?"
"She's swept the house all the way through,
And from the attic window, she's staring down at you."

She then met the bridegroom, who was walking back home very slowly. He too asked:

"Oh, Fitcher's feathered bird, where from, where from?"
"From feathered Fitze Fitcher's house I'm come."
"And the young bride there, how does she fare?"
"She's swept the house all the way through,
And from the attic window, she's staring down at you."

The bridegroom looked up and saw the decorated skull. He thought it was his bride, nodded, and waved to her. But when he got to the house with his guests, the brothers and relatives who had been sent to rescue the bride were already there. They locked the doors to the house so that no one could get out. Then they set fire to it, and the wizard and his crew were burned alive.

MR. FOX

From Joseph Jacobs, English Fairy Tales, *1890.*

Lady Mary was young, and Lady Mary was fair. She had two brothers and more lovers than she could count. But of them all, the bravest and most gallant was a Mr. Fox, whom she met when she was down at her father's country house. No one knew who Mr. Fox was; but he was certainly brave, and surely rich, and of all her lovers Lady Mary cared for him alone. At last it was agreed upon between them that they should be married. Lady Mary asked Mr. Fox where they should live, and he described to her his castle, and where it was; but, strange to say, did not ask her or her brothers to come and see it.

So one day, near the wedding day, when her brothers were out, and Mr. Fox was away for a day or two on business, as he said, Lady Mary set out for Mr. Fox's castle. And after many searchings, she came at last to it, and a fine strong house it was, with high walls and a deep moat. And when she came up to the gateway she saw written on it:

Be bold, be bold.

But as the gate was open, she went through it, and found no one there. So she went up to the doorway, and over it she found written:

> Be bold, be bold, but not too bold.

Still she went on, till she came into the hall, and went up the broad stairs till she came to a door in the gallery, over which was written:

> Be bold, be bold, but not too bold.
> Lest that your heart's blood should run cold.

But Lady Mary was a brave one, she was, and she opened the door, and what do you think she saw? Why, bodies and skeletons of beautiful young ladies all stained with blood. So Lady Mary thought it was high time to get out of that horrid place, and she closed the door, went through the gallery, and was just going down the stairs, and out of the hall, when who should she see through the window but Mr. Fox, dragging a beautiful young lady along from the gateway to the door. Lady Mary rushed downstairs, and hid herself behind a cask, just in time, as Mr. Fox came in with the poor young lady, who seemed to have fainted. Just as he got near Lady Mary, Mr. Fox saw a diamond ring glittering on the finger of the young lady he was dragging, and he tried to pull it off. But it was tightly fixed, and would not come off, so Mr. Fox cursed and swore, and drew his sword, raised it, and brought it down upon the hand of the poor lady. The sword cut off the hand, which jumped up into the air, and fell of all places in the world into Lady Mary's lap. Mr. Fox looked about a bit, but did not think of looking behind the cask, so at last he went on dragging the young lady up the stairs into the Bloody Chamber.

As soon as she heard him pass through the gallery, Lady Mary crept out of the door, down through the gateway, and ran home as fast as she could.

Now it happened that the very next day the marriage contract of Lady Mary and Mr. Fox was to be signed, and there was a splendid breakfast before that. And when Mr. Fox was seated at table opposite Lady Mary, he looked at her. "How pale you are this morning, my dear." "Yes," she said, "I had a bad night's rest last night. I had horrible dreams." "Dreams go by contraries," said Mr. Fox; "but tell us your dream, and your sweet voice will make the time pass till the happy hour comes."

"I dreamed," said Lady Mary, "that I went yestermorn to your castle, and I found it in the woods, with high walls, and a deep moat, and over the gateway was written:

> Be bold, be bold."

"But it is not so, nor it was not so," said Mr. Fox.

"And when I came to the doorway, over it was written:

Be bold, be bold, but not too bold."

"It is not so, nor it was not so," said Mr. Fox.

"And then I went upstairs, and came to a gallery, at the end of which was a door, on which was written:

Be bold, be bold, but not too bold.
Lest that your heart's blood should run cold."

"It is not so, nor it was not so," said Mr. Fox.

"And then—and then I opened the door, and the room was filled with bodies and skeletons of poor dead women, all stained with their blood."

"It is not so, nor it was not so. And God forbid it should be so," said Mr. Fox.

"I then dreamed that I rushed down the gallery, and just as I was going down the stairs I saw you, Mr. Fox, coming up to the hall door, dragging after you a poor young lady, rich and beautiful."

"It is not so, nor it was not so. And God forbid it should be so," said Mr. Fox.

"I rushed downstairs, just in time to hide myself behind a cask, when you, Mr. Fox, came in dragging the young lady by the arm. And, as you passed me, Mr. Fox, I thought I saw you try and get off her diamond ring, and when you could not, Mr. Fox, it seemed to me in my dream, that you out with your sword and hacked off the poor lady's hand to get the ring."

"It is not so, nor it was not so. And God forbid it should be so," said Mr. Fox, and was going to say something else as he rose from his seat, when Lady Mary cried out:

"But it is so, and it was so. Here's hand and ring I have to show," and pulled out the lady's hand from her dress, and pointed it straight at Mr. Fox.

At once her brothers and her friends drew their swords and cut Mr. Fox into a thousand pieces.

How the Devil Married Three Sisters
From Thomas Frederick Crane, Italian Popular Tales, *1885.*
Revised by Maria Tatar.

Once upon a time the Devil was seized with the desire to marry. He decided to leave Hell and took on the form of a handsome young man. After building a fine, large house, he furnished it in high style and introduced himself to a family with three pretty daughters. He began courting the eldest of the three girls. The handsome man pleased the maiden, and her parents were glad to see that she wanted to marry a man who would provide for her. Not much later, the wedding was celebrated.

When the Devil took his bride home, he presented her with a very tastefully arranged bouquet. He took her into all the rooms of the house, and finally to a closed door. "The whole house is at your disposal," he said, "only I must ask one thing of you. You must not, on any account, open this door."

Of course the young wife promised faithfully. But she could really scarcely wait for the moment to come when she could break her promise. When the Devil left the house the very next morning, under the pretext of going hunting, she ran as fast as she could to the forbidden door, opened it, and saw a terrible abyss full of fire that shot up toward her and singed the flowers she was wearing. When her husband came home and asked whether she had kept her promise, she unhesitatingly said "Yes." But he could see from the flowers that she was telling a lie.

"I will not put your curiosity to the test any longer. Come with me. I myself will show you what is behind the door," he said. With that, he took her to the door, opened it, and gave her such a big push that she fell all the way down into Hell. And he shut the door again.

A few months later, he wooed the next sister, and won her hand. Everything that happened with the first wife was repeated exactly with the second. Finally he courted the third sister. She was a shrewd maiden, and she said to herself: "I'm sure that he has murdered my two sisters, but then again this is a splendid match. I will try to see whether I can have better luck than they did." And so she consented to the marriage. After the wedding, the bridegroom gave her a beautiful bouquet, and he also forbade her to open the door which he made a point of showing her.

Not a whit less curious than her sisters, the third sister also opened the forbidden door after the Devil had gone hunting. But she put the flowers in water before opening the door. Behind the door she saw the fatal abyss and her sisters who were in it. "Ah!" she exclaimed, "poor creature that I am. I thought that I had married an ordinary man, and instead he is the Devil! How will I ever get away from him?" She pulled her two sisters carefully out of Hell and hid them. When the Devil came home he looked at the bouquet right away, and his wife was still wearing it. He saw that the flowers were fresh, and he didn't ask any questions. Now he was certain that his secret could remain a secret, and, for the first time, he really loved his bride.

After a few days, the bride asked her husband if he would consent to take three chests to her parents' house, without putting them down or resting on the way. "And," she added, "you must keep your word, for I shall be watching you."

The Devil promised to doing exactly as she wished. The next morning, she put one of her sisters in a chest and positioned it on her husband's shoulders. The Devil, who is very strong but who is also very lazy and not accustomed to do any work at all, soon grew tired of carrying the heavy chest and was hoping to rest before he had left the street on which he lived. But his wife called out to him, "Don't put it down. I can see you!"

The Devil walked on reluctantly with the chest on his back until he turned the corner. Then he said to himself, "She can't see me here. I will rest for a little while."

But scarcely had he started to put the chest down when the sister inside cried out, "Don't put it down; I can still see you!" Cursing, he dragged the chest on into another street and was about to put it down on a doorstep, when he again heard the voice, "Don't put it down, you rascal. I can still see you!"

"What eyes my wife must have," he thought, "to be able to see around corners as well as straight ahead and through walls as if they were made of glass!" While he was thinking about her eyes, he arrived at last, perspiring and worn out, at the house of his mother-in-law, to whom he hastily delivered the chest. He then hurried home to strengthen himself with a good breakfast.

The same thing happened the next day with the second chest. On the third day the girl herself was to be taken home in the chest. And so she prepared a figure that she dressed in her own clothes and placed on the balcony, under the pretext of being able to watch her husband better. She slipped quickly into the chest and had the maid put it on the Devil's back. "The deuce with it!" he said, "this chest is even heavier than the others. And today, with her sitting on the balcony, I will have even less of a chance to rest." By dint of the greatest exertions, he managed to carry the chest to his mother-in law without stopping, and then he hurried back home, cursing under his breath, with his back almost broken.

Quite contrary to what usually happened, his wife did not come out to meet him, and there was no breakfast ready. "Margerita, where are you?" he called out, but there was no reply. As he was running through the corridors, he looked out the window and saw the figure on the balcony. "Margerita, have you fallen asleep? Come downstairs. I am dog tired, and as hungry as a wolf." But there was no answer. "If you don't come down this instant I will go up and get you," he cried angrily. But Margerita would not stir. Enraged, he rushed up to the balcony and gave her such a box on the ears that her head flew off. Then he realized that the head was nothing but a milliner's form, and the body just a bundle of rags. In a rage, he rushed down the stairs and searched the entire house, but in vain. He found nothing but his wife's empty jewelry box. "Ha!" he cried, "she has been stolen from me, along with her jewels!" And he ran off at once to tell her parents of the terrible misfortune. But when he got near the house, to his great surprise, he could see on the balcony above the door all three sisters, his wives, who were looking down on him and laughing scornfully at him.

The three wives scared the Devil so badly that he took off as fast as he could. Since then, he has lost his taste for marriage.

The Hen Is Tripping in the Mountain
From Peter Christen Asbjørnsen and Jørgen Moe,
Norske Folkeeventyr, *1852.*

O nce there was an old widow who lived with her three daughters in a corner of the parish, high up under a mountain ridge. She was so poor that she had nothing but a hen, which was the apple of her eye. She cackled to it and took care of it day and night.

One day, out of the blue, the hen disappeared. The old woman combed her cabin, searching and calling, but the hen was gone, and gone it stayed.

"You'll have to go out and look for the hen," the old woman said to her oldest daughter. "We have to get it back, even if we end up digging it out of the mountain."

The oldest daughter went out to look for the hen. She went back and forth, searching and calling, but she could not find the hen. Then, all at once, from the wall of the mountain, she heard a voice call out:

> "The hen is tripping in the mountain!
> The hen is tripping in the mountain!"

When she went over to find out what was going on, she fell right through a trap door in the mountain wall and landed way down below in an underground vault. She made her way through many different rooms, each one finer than the next, and in the innermost room a big, ugly mountain troll walked right up to her.

"Will you be my beloved?" he asked.

"No," she replied, "Never." She wanted to go back up and keep looking for the hen that had disappeared.

The mountain troll was so enraged that he grabbed her, twisted her head off, and flung her body and head down into the cellar.

The mother was sitting at home, waiting patiently, but her daughter did not return. She waited a good while longer, but when she had neither heard a word nor seen a thing of her, she told her second daughter that she would have to go out and look for her sister. "And you can call the hen at the same time," she said.

The second sister went out, and the same thing that happened to the first sister befell her. She was walking and searching and calling, when out of the blue she also heard a voice from a wall in the mountain saying:

"The hen is tripping in the mountain!
The hen is tripping in the mountain!"

She thought that strange and went over to see what was going on when she too fell through a trap door, landing way down low in the vault. She walked through all the rooms, and in the innermost room the mountain troll walked up to her and asked if she would be his beloved. No, she would not, never. She wanted to go back up at once and keep on looking for the hen that had disappeared. The mountain troll flew into a rage. He took her and twisted off her head and flung her head and body down into the cellar.

The old woman sat and waited a long, long time for the second daughter to return, but no daughter was to be seen or heard. And so she said to the youngest: "You'll have to go out and look for your sisters. It was bad enough that the hen disappeared, but it would be even worse if we never found your sisters again. You can always look for the hen at the same time!"

The youngest daughter left home. She went back and forth, searching and calling, but she could not find the hen, and her sisters were nowhere to be seen. At long last, she reached a wall in the mountain and heard a voice saying:

"The hen is tripping in the mountain!
The hen is tripping in the mountain!"

She found this strange and was about to go over and have a good look when she also fell through the trap door way down into the vault. She walked through one room after another down there, one room was finer than the next. But she was not frightened and took her time, looking at one thing and the other. Then she caught sight of the cellar door. She looked down in there, and at once she recognized her sisters, who were lying on the floor.

Just as she was closing the cellar door, the mountain troll walked over to her.

"Will you be my beloved?" he asked.

"With all my heart," the girl replied, for she had figured out what must have happened to her sisters.

When the troll heard these words, he was so happy to find someone who would be his beloved that the girl was given the finest clothing she could desire, along with everything else she wanted.

After the girl had been down there for a while, there came a day when she was very downhearted and quiet. The mountain troll asked why she was moping.

"Oh," the girl replied, "it's because I can't go visit my mother. She's probably hungry and thirsty, and she has no one to keep her company either."

"Well, you can't go visit her," the troll replied. "But if you put some food in a sack, I'll take it to her."

The girl thanked him for the offer, and she said that she would do as he said. At the bottom of the sack she put much gold and silver, then covered them with a layer of food. She told the troll that the sack was ready and that he must not look into it. He agreed to what she said.

After the mountain troll had departed, she looked out at him through a tiny hole in the trap door. When he had walked a part of the way, he said, "This sack is so heavy. I'm going to take a look and see what's in it." He was about to untie the string when the girl shouted: "I can see what you're doing! I can see what you're doing!"

"Those are mighty sharp eyes you've got in your head!" the troll said. After that, he didn't dare take a look.

When he arrived at the widow's house, he threw the sack in through the door. "Here's some food from your daughter! She has everything she could ever want!" he said.

One day, after the girl had been in the mountain for a while, a billy goat fell through the trap door. "Who sent for you, you shaggy beast?" the troll demanded. He was so wild with rage that he took the goat, twisted off its head, and threw it down into the cellar.

"Oh, no! Why did you do that?" asked the girl. "I could have used it to amuse me down here."

"Don't mope around about it," said the troll. "I can bring that goat back to life if I want." With that he took down a jar that was hanging on the wall, got the head of the goat, and rubbed some salve from the jar on the head and put it back on the body. The goat was restored to life.

"Aha," the girl thought, "that jar is certainly worth something." After staying with the troll a while longer, she waited for a day when the troll was away, then put the head back on the body of her older sister. She rubbed the salve from the jar around her neck, the way that the troll had done with the billy goat, and the sister sprang back to life. The girl put her sister in a sack and covered her up with food. When the troll came back home, she said to him, "My dear friend, now you will have to take some food to my mother again. She's probably thirsty and hungry, poor thing, and quite alone as well. But don't you dare look into the sack!"

He would take the sack all right, he promised, and he would also not look inside it. But when he had gone a part of the way, he found the sack heavy, and when he had gone a bit farther, he thought he would take a look in the sack. "No matter how sharp her eyes are, she can't see me now!" he thought to himself.

Just as he was about to open the sack, the girl who was inside it said: "I can see what you're doing! I can see what you're doing!"

"Those are mighty sharp eyes you've got in your head!" said the troll, for he thought that the girl back home was speaking. He didn't dare take another look, but carried the sack as fast as he could to the mother's house. When he got to the cabin, he threw the sack in through the door. "Here's some food from your daughter! She has everything she could ever want!" he said.

After the girl had been in the mountain for some time, she did to the second sister what she had done to the older sister. She put her head on her body, rubbed some salve from the crock around her neck, and put her in the sack. This time she filled the sack with as much silver and gold as possible, and on top she placed a layer of food.

"My dear friend," she said to the troll, "You must take some food to my mother again, but don't look inside the sack!" The troll was perfectly willing to let her have her way, and he promised that he would not look into the sack. But when he had gone a part of the way, he found that the sack had grown terribly heavy. He went a bit farther, and he was downright worn out. After he put the sack down to catch his breath, he thought he would untie its fastenings and look inside it.

The girl who was in the sack shouted: "I can see what you're doing! I can see what you're doing!"

"Those are mighty sharp eyes you've got in your head," said the troll, and he did not dare to look in the sack and went as fast as he could with the sack to the mother's house. When he got to the cabin, he threw the sack in through the door. "Here's some food from your daughter! She has everything she could ever want!" he said.

The girl had been there for a while, when the troll decided to go out. The girl pretended to be sick and ailing, and she moaned and carried on. "There's no use coming home before twelve o'clock," she said, "for I'm feeling so miserable and weak that I won't be able to get dinner ready before then," she said.

When the troll was out of sight, she stuffed her clothes with straw and placed the girl of straw over in a corner near the hearth with a stirrer in her hand. It looked just like her. Then she hurried home and asked a hunter to stay with her in her mother's cabin.

When it was twelve o'clock or a little later, the troll came home. "Bring in the food!" he said to the girl of straw. But there was no reply. "Bring the food I said!" the troll shouted. "I'm hungry!" But there was no answer.

"Bring the food!" the troll screeched a third time. "Listen to what I'm saying or else I'll make sure you wake up!" But the maiden didn't move.

The troll became enraged and gave her a kick that sent the straw flying about the walls and ceiling. When he saw what had happened, he suspected mischief and began searching high and low until he got down in the cellar. Both sisters were gone, and he now realized what had happened. Well, she would soon pay for that! he thought, and he set out for the mother's cabin. But when he got there, the hunter fired a shot. The troll did not dare enter, for he thought it was thunder. He wanted to go home as fast as he could, but just when he reached the trap door, the sun rose, and he burst into pieces. There is plenty of gold and silver still there, if you can just find someone who knows how to get to the trap door.

THE WHITE DOVE

Told by Mr. Puivert, Aude, in September 1950. Taken down by Gaston Maugard in Contes des Pyrénées, *1955.*

A prince and his wife lived in their palace with two children, a son and a daughter. When the young prince turned twenty, he got married and made his home in the family castle, as is the custom. The daughter, on the other hand, had strange ideas. She refused each and every marriage proposal and swore that she would marry only if she found a prince with a blue beard.

One day, the trumpet of the guard announced the arrival of a magnificent carriage. It was a giant who was said to be a great hunter, and this giant had a blue beard. He accepted the customary hospitality. The girl was presented to him, and he was pleasing to the headstrong child. The following day the marriage was celebrated, and the father gave a hunting party in which the son-in-law distinguished himself.

The day for departure arrived, and the giant was planning to take his wife away to his distant castle.

The mother, who loved her daughter dearly, asked her: "What dowry can I give you, my child? Gold? But where you're going, there will be a castle and treasures. Horses? The giant has fabulous horses. I think I'll give you these three birds, the pride of my aviary, a black dove, a white dove, and a red dove. That way we can get news from you, for you will be living far away. Listen carefully: if you're in good health and living in peace with your husband, send the red one. If you become ill, send the white one; but if there is discord or some kind of bad luck, send the black dove right away." The father and mother accompanied the young wife to her new home, but, as is customary, they returned after a few days.

Bluebeard had but one pastime and one passion, hunting, and he devoted himself to it all day long.

One day, taking leave of his wife, he gave her a bunch of keys. "My wife, here are nine keys. Each of them opens up a chamber in the castle. But I forbid you to go into the room at the end of the hall or to use the ninth key, which will open its door."

"Very well, my lord."

Bluebeard called his hounds and left on horseback. Meanwhile his wife took a tour of the castle. All women are curious; the lady of the manor went into eight of the chambers, but that was not enough for her. Her fingers wanted to turn the lock that fit the ninth key.

"I'm going to go into this last chamber after all."

The key turned; the door opened. The princess saw a great basin filled with blood. She raised her eyes. The key slipped from her fingers because above the basin she saw, swinging in the dim light, the corpses of eight women, all hanging from chains hooked into the ceiling. She had just enough strength to pick up the key and close the door. But rubbing the key was useless: the bloodstain would not come out. She awaited her husband's return with anxiety and grew increasingly terrified.

"Woman, hand over the key!"

"I'll give it to you in a minute, my lord."

"Give me my keys at once."

She had to bring the nine keys even though she didn't want to.

"Ha! I see that you counted the corpses. Now you too will die. Go upstairs and put on your loveliest dress, and in one hour—at most in an hour and a half—you will end up hanging on a hook with the others! Go and get dressed for the last time!"

The poor woman, her heart pounding, still found the strength to climb up to the tower. She sent the black dove to her father's house.

"Black dove, go quickly and tell them that I am going to die in an hour. And you, white dove, stay on the roof."

The unhappy woman returned to her chamber, where she was supposed to get dressed for the last time. From time to time the windows opened up, and she asked the bird: "My white dove, do you see anyone coming?"

Downstairs, her husband had lit a great fire and was boiling oil in an enormous cauldron. He stoked the fire, threw logs into the brazier, and then stirred the liquid with a big wooden stick. From time to time the house shook with his shouts. The strokes of the stick beat time like a clock:

> *"Down, down, come right down,*
> *No more stalling, come right down."*

And the lady replied from upstairs:

> "Let me just don
> The dress of a bride,
> The hour is up,
> White Dove, is there no hope?"

"I see nothing but sun and wind."
Downstairs the oil was boiling.

> *"Down, down, come right down,*
> *No more stalling, come right down."*
> "Let me just don
> The veils of a bride
> The hour is up,
> White Dove, is there no hope?"

"I see nothing but sun and wind."
"Down, down, come right down," the stick beat darkly, "No more stalling, come right down!"

> "Let me just don
> The skirts of a bride
> The hour is up,
> White Dove, is there no hope?"

"I see nothing but sun and wind."

> *"Down, down, come right down,*
> *No more stalling, come right down."*
> "Let me just don
> The train of a bride
> The hour is up,
> White Dove, is there no hope?"

"A cloud of dust on the horizon."

> *"Down, down, down,"*

The oil is boiling,

> *"Are you finally coming down?"*
> "Let me just don
> The shoes of a bride
> The hour is up,
> White Dove, is there no hope?"

"Through a cloud of dust I can see two knights in the distance."
Downstairs the oil was boiling in the cauldron.

> *"Down, down, down,*
> *I'll come up if you stay down!"*
> "Let me just don
> The cap of a bride
> The hour is up,
> White Dove, is there no hope?"

"Two knights are halfway down the road."

> *"Down, down, down,"*

And the oil was boiling,

> *"I order you to come down!"*
> "I'm coming, I'm coming,
> My bouquet in hand.
> The hour is up,
> White Dove, is there no hope?"

"The horses are here!"
Bang! Bang! Bluebeard was counting the steps in the staircase. Naturally he had put the great wooden bar across the portals. The knights were already battering against them, but the door was barricaded. What

could they do? When they pushed their horses up against the portals to break them down, the doors opened up. The two visitors entered on horseback, sabers in their fists.

"What's going on, my dear brother-in-law?" cried the prince.

"You arrived in the nick of time," the giant replied, without missing a beat. "It's just perfect. My wife got dressed for dinner. Let's have ourselves a feast."

They all enjoyed a hearty meal with plenty of meat and wine. Finally, Bluebeard fell into a deep sleep. Had he had too much to drink? Or had someone poured a sleeping potion into his wine? Whatever had happened, he was snoring with his mouth wide open. With the help of a funnel, the guests took a big dipper full of boiling oil and poured it down his throat. He choked to death on it. Then they washed the key with the oil, and the bloodstain disappeared.

Their work done, the princess left the castle with her father and brother. She inherited rightfully all of the land of her dead husband so that her family now had two castles. It's a very sad truth that in this world some have too much money, while others, like me, never have enough.

I've gone as far as my fields extend,
And so my tale has found its end.

Mr. Fox

Compiled from tellings by R. M. Ward of Beech Creek,
North Carolina, and by Polly Johnson of Norton, Virginia.
From Richard Chase, American Folk Tales and Songs, *1956.*

One time there was a young woman named Polly. They called her Pretty Polly. She wasn't married and she lived by herself. All her folks were dead. And one day a stranger came into that settlement. Said his name was Fox. Slick-lookin' feller, and he went to courtin' Pretty Polly right off. He'd come to see her of a Saturday night, and they'd talk. Then one day he asked her would she meet him the next Saturday night under a big pin out on a ridge there. So she told him she would. But when he left, she got to studyin' about him askin' her to meet him away off like that and she decided she didn't like it much.

Well that Saturday night came and she didn't feel like goin', but she fixed up and went on anyhow. Hit was cold and the wind was blowin' something awful when she got out on that ridge. She got to the pine tree but he wasn't there. She thought first she'd wait, then she thought she'd run back; and before she could make up her mind she heard him comin' up the holler. Then she thought she'd hide but there wasn't any place to hide. She happened to look up in that tree, and it had a few low branches to it, so she caught hold on them and cloomb right on up till she was in the thickest part of that big pine.

She could see down through the branches a little, see what was right under the tree. And directly here came Mr. Fox carryin' a lantern. She saw him put the lantern on a big rock and sit down to wait. He waited and waited. Then, after a right long time, he reached over beyond a rock and she saw him lift out a mattick and shovel. He started diggin'. She watched. He kept on diggin' and Polly saw the place he dug was about six-foot long and three-foot wide. She kept watchin', and then she knew it was a grave, and that he was diggin' it for her.

Mr. Fox got the grave started and then he sat down again. He 'uld look and listen, turn his head up this way and that. Then he'd act restless-like: jump in that grave and just dig and dig. He kept on diggin' and waitin' and diggin' till 'way up in the night.

Pretty Polly nearly froze up there. The wind kept blowin' the top of the tree over to one side, and the branches 'uld creak and rattle, but she kept holdin' on. And fin'lly she heard a rooster crow 'way off in the settlements somewhere, so she knew it must be close to midnight. Well, pretty soon after that she saw Mr. Fox pick up his tools and throw 'em across his shoulder, and he picked up his lantern and left. Polly she waited till he was good-and-gone, and then she got down from there in a hurry and struck out for home by all the near cuts she could figger.

Well, Mr. Fox he quit comin' to see her after that.

Then hit wasn't long till Pretty Polly heard folks talking about how three young women had disappeared from around the settle-ment. Some said Mr. Fox had been courtin' all three of 'em. He'd not come to any of their houses: met 'em out somewhere. But nobody had any evidence on him, so they couldn't do nothing about it. They'd tried to find out where he lived but nobody had any notion where his house was at.

Then one day he came to Pretty Polly's place again. She didn't let on like she knowed a thing, and they got to talkin' and directly he asked her would she come with him to his house. She told him, "Well I might, sometime."

"Come on and go with me now. Hit's not far."

"No," she says. "I can't go today."

"Can you come next Saturday?"

"I don't know where you live at."

"I'll come after you."

"No," she says to him. "If I come, I'll come by myself."

Mr. Fox he studied about that a minute, says, "If you'll give me a poke of flour I'll lay you a trail."

Polly went and got him a little sack of flour and he took it and went on off. He 'uld sift out a little of that flour every few steps.

Well—Polly she didn't go that next Saturday. It was the time after that she decided what she 'uld do. She was brave. It hadn't rained nor been very windy that two weeks, so she found the trail all right. She followed it on and on till fin'lly she came to an old rickety house awa-a-ay out in the woods. She hid and watched. Then she saw Mr. Fox come out of the house and go off. And when he was out of sight she went to the house and went on in.

Now there was a parrot in there and hit talked to her. Polly looked around, and when she went up the stairs and started to open a door, the parrot hollered at her, says,

> Don't go in, pretty lady!
> You'll lose your heart's blood.

But she opened the door anyhow, and looked in. It was like a slaughter room in there: women hung up all around the walls with their heads cut off. Polly shut the door right quick, and started runnin' down the stair-steps. Then she heard a racket sounded like a woman screamin'. Slipped to the window and peeked out, and there came Mr. Fox a-drag-in' a woman by the arm. "Law me! What'll I do now!"

> Hide! Pretty lady!
> Hide! Hide!

"Don't tell him I'm here!"

> No, pretty lady!
> No! No!

Polly ran and hid under the old rickety stair-steps.

Mr. Fox came on in the house jerkin' that girl along and dragged her on up the stairs. She reached out and caught the stair-rail a-tryin' to hold back. Mr. Fox took out his sword and hacked her hand off and it fell through the cracks of the stair-steps, landed right at Pretty Polly's feet.

Mr. Fox stopped, and asked that bird, "Has anybody been here?"

> No, sir!
> No! Oh no!

So he pushed the girl in his slaughter room and went on in after her and shut the door. Pretty Polly she reached and grabbed up that girl's hand, and slipped out the door and ran for life.

Well, in about a week or two after that there was a play-party in the settlement. Everybody went, and when Pretty Polly got there she saw Mr. Fox in the crowd. So all of 'em were having a good time dancin' and playin' kissin' games and first one thing and then another, and 'way up late in the night they all sat down close to the fireplace where the old folks were at, and they got to tellin' tales, and tellin' dreams and singin', and askin' riddles.

Pretty Polly slipped out and got that hand: brought it back wrapped up in a piece of cloth. She sat down again and unwrapped that hand under her apron where nobody could see. Sat right on listenin' to what somebody was tellin', didn't say a thing. Then directly she says: "I've got a riddle."

"What is it? Tell us!"

So she told 'em, says,

> Riddle to my riddle to my right!
> Where was I that Saturday night?
> All that time in a lonesome pine.
> I was high and he was low.
> The cock did crow, the wind did blow.
> The tree did shake and my heart did ache
> To see what a hole that fox did make.

They all tried to guess. Mr. Fox sat right still.

"What's the answer?" they all asked her. "Tell us the answer."

"Not now," she told 'em. "I'll tell you directly." Says, "I dreamt me a quare dream the other night. You might like to hear that."

"Ain't nothin' in dreams," says Mr. Fox.

They all begged her to tell her dream. Polly folded her hands under her apron and she told 'em, says, "I dreamed that I went to Mr. Fox's house. He wasn't at home, but I went on in to wait for him. There was a bird there and when I went to look in one of the rooms hit told me, says,

> Don't go in, pretty lady!
> You'll lose your heart's blood.

But I cracked the door just a little anyhow, and I saw a lot of dead women in there—hangin' on the walls."

"Not so! Not so!" says Mr. Fox. And the young men there all looked at him. Pretty Polly kept right on. "Then I dreamed I heard a woman screamin' and cryin', and I looked out and there came Mr. Fox a-draggin' a woman after him."

"Not so! Not so!" says Mr. Fox. "It couldn't 'a been me!"
And a couple of the men there moved back against the wall.
"That bird told me to hide and I ran and hid under the stair-steps. Then
I dreamed that girl grabbed hold on the rail and Mr. Fox took out his
sword and hacked her hand off, and it fell through the stairs and landed
right where I was at."

Old Mr. Fox jumped up, says,

> But it was not so,
> and it is not so,
> and God forbid it ever should be so!

And several young men moved over between Mr. Fox and the door.
Polly paid Mr. Fox no mind.

"Then I dreamed he shoved the girl in his slaughter room and went on
in and shut the door. And I grabbed up that hand and ran away from
there fast."

Old Mr. Fox hollered out again,

> But it was not so!
> And it is not so!
> And God forbid it ever should be so!

Then Pretty Polly answered him back, says,

> But it was so!
> And it is so!
> For here's the very hand to show!

And she took that hand out from under her apron and held it up right
in Mr. Fox's face. Then all the men there, they took hold on Mr. Fox and
they sure did handle him.

And after they took Mr. Fox out, everybody recollected Pretty Polly's
riddle and asked her about it, and she told 'em about that grave and all.

They took Mr. Fox on to town, and they tried him on Pretty Polly's
evidence and he was hung.

How the Helpmate of
Blue-beard Made Free with a Door
From Guy Wetmore Carryl, Grimm Tales Made Gay, 1902.

A maiden from the Bosphorus,
With eyes as bright as phosphorus,

Once wed the wealthy bailiff
Of the caliph
Of Kelat.
Though diligent and zealous, he
Became a slave to jealousy.

(Considering her beauty,
'Twas his duty
To be that!)

When business would necessitate
A journey, he would hesitate,
But, fearing to disgust her,
He would trust her
With his keys,
Remarking to her prayerfully:
"I beg you'll use them carefully.
Don't look what I deposit
In that closet,
If you please."

It may be mentioned, casually,
That blue as lapis lazuli
He dyed his hair, his lashes,
His mustaches,
And his beard.
And, just because he did it, he
Aroused his wife's timidity:
Her terror she dissembled,
But she trembled
When he neared.

This feeling insalubrious
Soon made her most lugubrious,
And bitterly she missed her
Elder sister
Marie Anne:
She asked if she might write her to
Come down and spend a night or two,
Her husband answered rightly
And politely:
"Yes, you can!"

Blue-Beard, the Monday following,
His jealous feeling swallowing,
Packed all his clothes together
In a leather-
Bound valise,
And, feigning reprehensibly,
He started out, ostensibly
By traveling to learn a
Bit of Smyrna
And of Greece.

His wife made but a cursory
Inspection of the nursery;
The kitchen and the airy
Little dairy
Were a bore,
As well as big or scanty rooms,
And billiard, bath, and ante-rooms,
But not that interdicted
And restricted
Little door!

For, all her curiosity
Awakened by the closet he
So carefully had hidden,
And forbidden
Her to see,
This damsel disobedient
Did something inexpedient,
And in the keyhole tiny
Turned the shiny
Little key:

Then started back impulsively,
And shrieked aloud convulsively—
Three heads of girls he'd wedded
And beheaded
Met her eye!
And turning round, much terrified,
Her darkest fears were verified,
For Blue stood behind her,
Come to find her
On the sly!

Perceiving she was fated to
Be soon decapitated, too,
She telegraphed her brothers
And some others
What she feared.
And Sister Anne looked out for them,
In readiness to shout for them
Whenever in the distance
With assistance
They appeared.

But only from her battlement
She saw some dust that cattle meant.
The ordinary story
Isn't gory,
But a jest.
But here's the truth unqualified.
The husband wasn't mollified
Her head is in his bloody
Little study
With the rest!

The Moral: Wives, we must allow,
Who to their husbands will not bow,
A stern and dreadful lesson learn
When, as you've read, they're cut in turn.

BLUE-BEARD'S CLOSET
Rose Terry Cooke, Poems, 1861

Fasten the chamber!
Hide the red key;
Cover the portal,
That eyes may not see.
Get thee to market,
To wedding and prayer;
Labor or revel,
The chamber is there!

In comes a stranger—
"Thy pictures how fine,
Titian or Guido,
Whose is the sign?"

Looks he behind them?
Ah! have a care!
"Here is a finer."
The chamber is there!

Fair spreads the banquet,
Rich the array;
See the bright torches
Mimicking day;
When harp and viol
Thrill the soft air,
Comes a light whisper:
The chamber is there!

Marble and painting,
Jasper and gold,
Purple from Tyrus,
Fold upon fold,
Blossoms and jewels,
Thy palace prepare:
Pale grows the monarch;
The chamber is there!

Once it was open
As shore to the sea;
White were the turrets,
Goodly to see;
All through the casements
Flowed the sweet air;
Now it is darkness;
The chamber is there!

Silence and horror
Brood on the walls;
Through every crevice
A little voice calls:
"Quicken, mad footsteps,
On pavement and stair;
Look not behind thee,
The chamber is there!"

Out of the gateway,
Through the wide world,

Into the tempest
Beaten and hurled,
Vain is thy wandering,
Sure thy despair,
Flying or staying,
The chamber is there!

UNTITLED BLUEBEARD SONNET
From Edna St. Vincent Millay, Renascence and Other Poems, *1917.*

This door you might not open, and you did;
So enter now, and see for what slight thing
You are betrayed. . . . Here is no treasure hid,
No cauldron, no clear crystal mirroring
The sought-for truth, no heads of women slain
For greed like yours, no writhings of distress,
But only what you see. . . . Look yet again—
An empty room, cobwebbed and comfortless.
Yet this alone out of my life I kept
Unto myself, lest any know me quite;
And you did so profane me when you crept
Unto the threshold of this room to-night
That I must never more behold your face.
This now is yours. I seek another place.

NOTES

Introduction

1. Frances Hodgson Burnett, *The Secret Garden* (New York: Signet, 1986), p. 74.

2. Herman Melville, *Moby-Dick*, ed. Harrison Hayford and Hershel Parker (New York: W. W. Norton, 1967), p. 16.

3. J.R.R. Tolkien, "On Fairy-Stories," in *The Tolkien Reader* (New York: Ballantine, 1966), p. 32.

4. Mark S. Madoff elaborates on the nature of transgression and locked rooms. See his "Inside, Outside, and the Gothic Locked-Room Mystery," in *Gothic Fictions: Prohibition/Transgression*, ed. Kenneth W. Graham (New York: AMS Press, 1989), pp. 49–62.

5. E. Sidney Hartland, "The Forbidden Chamber," *Folk-Lore Journal* 3 (1885): 193.

6. Theodore Ziolkowski, *The Sin of Knowledge: Ancient Themes and Modern Variations* (Princeton: Princeton University Press, 2000), pp. 3, 70; Roger Shattuck, *Forbidden Knowledge: A Landmark Exploration of the Dark Side of Human Ingenuity and Imagination* (San Diego: Harcourt Brace & Co., 1996), p. 50. See also Bonnie St. Andrews's critique of the gender asymmetries in cultural stories about the acquisition of knowledge: *Forbidden Fruit: On the Relationship between Women and Knowledge in Doris Lessing, Selma Lagerlöf, Kate Chopin, and Margaret Atwood* (Troy, N.Y.: Whitson, 1986).

7. Millay, Edna St. Vincent, [Untitled Bluebeard sonnet], in *Collected Poems*, ed. Norma Millay (New York: Harper, 1956).

8. Stephen King, *The Shining* (New York: Signet, 1978), pp. 182–83. Subsequent page references in the text are to this edition. On intertextual references to "Bluebeard" and "Hansel and Gretel" in *The Shining*, see Ronald T. Curran, "Complex, Archetype, and Primal Fear: King's Use of Fairy Tales in *The Shining*," in *The Dark Descent: Essays Defining Stephen King's Horrorscope*, ed. Tony Magistrale (Westport, Conn.: Greenwood, 1992), pp. 33–46.

9. Isaac Disraeli, *Vaurien: or, Sketches of the Times: Exhibiting Views of the Philosophies, Religions, Politics, Literature, and Manners of the Age* (London: T. Cadell, Junior, and W. Davies, 1797), pp. 192–93. As D. A. Miller points out, "sensation is felt to occupy a natural site entirely outside meaning, as though in the breathless body signification expired." See his *The Novel and the Police* (Berkeley: University of California Press, 1988), p. 147.

10. Walter Benjamin, "The Storyteller: Reflections on the Works of Nikolai Leskov," in Benjamin, *Illuminations*, ed. Hannah Arendt, trans. Harry Zohn (New York: Schocken, 1968), p. 86.

11. Ibid., p. 102.

12. As Mark Edmundson points out, "The best terror Gothic woke its eighteenth-century readers up. It roused them from the smug self-assurance often induced by enlightenment rationalism. Gothic was a blow against the sanitized, empirical philosophies of the age. In Gothic novels readers discovered, or were reacquainted with, the night side of life." See *Nightmare on Main Street: Angels, Sadomasochism, and the Culture of Gothic* (Cambridge, Mass.: Harvard University Press, 1997), p. 8.

13. Salman Rushdie, *Haroun and the Sea of Stories* (London: Penguin, 1990), pp. 71–72.

14. Margaret Atwood, "Grimms' Remembered," in *The Reception of Grimms' Fairy Tales: Responses, Reactions, Revisions*, ed. Donald Haase (Detroit: Wayne State University Press, 1993), p. 292.

Chapter One: The Attractions of "Bluebeard"

1. Willa Cather, *O Pioneers!* (New York: Penguin, 1994), p. 80.

2. Cited by Anthony Minghella, *The Talented Mr. Ripley: A Screenplay* (New York: Hyperion, 1999), p. xi.

3. J.R.R. Tolkien, "On Fairy-Stories," in *The Tolkien Reader* (New York: Ballantine, 1966), p. 26.

4. Charles Dickens, "Nurse's Stories," in *The Commercial Traveller*, in *The Oxford Illustrated Dickens* (Oxford: Oxford University Press, 1989), p. 153.

5. Aline Kilmer, "The Case of Bluebeard," in Kilmer, *Hunting a Hair Shirt and Other Spiritual Adventures* (New York: George H. Doran, 1923), p. 95.

6. Richard Wright, *Black Boy* (New York: Harper & Row, 1966), p. 48.

7. Emil Heckmann, *Blaubart: Ein Beitrag zur vergleichenden Märchenforschung* (Schwetzingen: A. Moch, 1932), p. 11.

8. Paul Delarue, *Le conte populaire français* (Paris: Editions Erasme, 1957), pp. 182–99.

9. Margaret Atwood, *True Stories* (Toronto: Oxford University Press, 1981).

10. Marc Beckwith, "Italo Calvino and the Nature of Italian Folktales," *Italica* 64 (1987): 261.

11. Charles Perrault, "La Barbe Bleue," in Perrault, *Contes*, ed. Marc Soriano (Paris: Flammarion, 1989), pp. 257–62.

12. Anatole France, "The Seven Wives of Bluebeard," *Spells of Enchantment: The Wondrous Fairy Tales of Western Culture*, ed. Jack Zipes (New York: Viking, 1991), p. 567.

13. The literature on Bluebeard and Gilles de Rais is extensive, despite the tenuous connection between the two figures. From the end of the nineteenth century through the twentieth century, Gilles de Rais became a kind of Bluebeard figure, even if he was not the model for the Bluebeard of folklore. See especially Thomas Wilson, *Bluebeard: A Contribution to History and Folk-lore, Being the History of Gilles de Retz of Brittany, France* (New York: Putnam's, 1897); Ernest Alfred Vizetelly, *Bluebeard: An Account of Comorre the Cursed and Gilles de Rais* (London: Chatto & Windus, 1902); Louis Vincent, *Gilles de Rais: The Original Bluebeard* (London: A. M. Philpot, 1926); Harriet Mowshowitz, "Gilles de Rais and the Bluebeard Legend in France," *Michigan Academician* 1 (1973): 83–92; Marina Warner, *From the Beast to the Blonde: On Fairy Tales and Their Tellers* (New York: Farrar, Straus and Giroux, 1994), pp. 260–65; and Carl S. Leafstedt, *Inside* Bluebeard's Castle: *Music and Drama in Béla Bartók's Opera* (New York: Oxford University Press, 1999), pp. 168–73. J. K. Huysmans's *Là-bas* offers a fascinating account of a figure who establishes a cult of Gilles de Rais. See *Là-bas*, trans. Keene Wallace (New York: Dover, 1972).

14. Michel Pastoureau, *Blue: The History of a Color* (Princeton: Princeton University Press, 2001), pp. 49, 63.

15. Hartwig Suhrbier, *Blaubarts Geheimnis* (Cologne: Eugen Diederich, 1984), pp. 27–34. On the color of the beard, see also Fabienne Raphoz, *Les femmes de Barbe-Bleue: Une histoire de curieuses* (Geneva: Metropolis, 1995), pp. 9–12.

16. Warner, *From the Beast to the Blonde*, pp. 241–242.

17. The critical voices are cited and documented in Maria Tatar, *The Hard Facts of the Grimms' Fairy Tales* (Princeton: Princeton University Press, 1987), p. 161.

18. Lydia Millet, "The Wife Killer," in *Mirror, Mirror on the Wall: Women Writers Explore Their Favorite Fairy Tales*, ed. Kate Bernheimer (New York: Doubleday, Anchor Books, 1998), p. 230.

19. Francis Egerton Ellesmere, *Bluebeard; or, Dangerous curiosity & justifiable homicide* (London: T. Brettell, 1841), p. 27.

20. Luisa Valenzuela, *Symmetries*, trans. Margaret Jull Costa (London: Serpent's Tail, 1998), pp. 148–49.

21. Barbara M. Benedict points out that curious spectators came to be seen as monsters who cross borders and slip out of conventional categories. See her *Curiosity: A Cultural History of Early Modern Inquiry* (Chicago: University of Chicago Press, 2001).

22. For the statement on Eve's sin, see J. C. Cooper, *Fairy Tales: Allegories of the Inner Life* (Wellingborough, Northamptonshire: Aquarian Press, 1983), pp. 72–73. The Scottish version of "Bluebeard" is cited by Humphrey Carpenter and Mari Prichard, *The Oxford Companion to Children's Literature* (London: Oxford University Press, 1984), p. 67.

23. On Bluebeard as tyrannical aristocrat in an operatic tradition that begins with Grétry's *Raoul Barbe-Bleue*, first performed in France in 1789, see Pierre Cadars, "Sept compositeurs pour une Barbe-Bleu," *L'avant-scène opéra* 149–50 (November/December 1992): 82–85.

24. Andrew Lang, *The Blue Fairy Book*, ed. Brian Alderson (New York: Penguin, 1987), p. 358.

25. Hartwig Suhrbier points out that George Colman's "grand dramatic romance" of 1798 with the title "Bluebeard; or Female Curiosity" first used the name Fatima for Bluebeard's wife (*Blaubarts Geheimnis*, p. 37).

26. Lauritis Bødker, Christina Hole, and G. D'Aronco, eds., *European Folk Tales* (Copenhagen: Rosenkilde and Bagger, 1963), pp. 158–60.

27. Stephen King, *The Shining* (New York: Doubleday, 1977), p. 169.

28. Cristina Bacchilega, *Postmodern Fairy Tales: Gender and Narrative Strategies* (Philadelphia: University of Pennsylvania Press, 1997), p. 111.

29. Millet, "Wife Killer," p. 243.

30. Minghella, *The Talented Mr. Ripley*, p. 106. I refer to the screenplay because Patricia Highsmith's novel of the same title does not contain the allusions to the Bluebeard story.

31. Mark Edmundson, *Nightmare on Main Street: Angels, Sadomasochism, and the Culture of Gothic* (Cambridge, Mass.: Harvard University Press, 1997), p. 115.

32. The phrase is Christina Bacchilega's. See *Postmodern Fairy Tales*, p. 111.

33. Juliet McMaster describes the tale in starker terms as one about "feminine curiosity and masculine brutality." See "Bluebeard: A Tale of Matrimony," *Room of One's Own* 11 (1976): 10.

34. Bruno Bettelheim, *The Uses of Enchantment: The Meaning and Importance of Fairy Tales* (New York: Knopf, 1976), p. 306.

35. Gaston Leroux, *The Phantom of the Opera* (New York: Harper, 1987), pp. 286–87.

36. Lawrence Stone, *The Family, Sex, and Marriage in England, 1500–1800*, abr. ed. (New York: Harper & Row, 1977), pp. 208–9.

37. Michelle Perrot, ed., *From the Fires of Revolution to the Great War*, vol. 4 of *A History of Private Life* (Cambridge, Mass.: Harvard University Press, 1990), p. 154.

38. Jurij M. Lotman, "The Origin of Plot in the Light of Typology," *Poetics Today* 1 (1979): 167.

39. Carol J. Clover, *Men, Women, and Chainsaws: Gender in the Modern Horror Film* (Princeton: Princeton University Press, 1992), p. 17.

40. Catherine Clément, *Opera, or the Undoing of Women*, trans. Betsy Wing (Minneapolis: University of Minnesota Press, 1999), p. 31.

41. Paul Delarue, *Le conte populaire français* (Paris: Erasme, 1957), 1: 182–99.

42. Bødker, Hole, and D'Aronco, *European Folk Tales*, pp. 158–59.

43. Reider Thorwald Christiansen, ed., *Folktales of Norway*, trans. Pat Shaw Iverson (Chicago: University of Chicago Press, 1964), pp. 228–33.

44. Sharon Rose Wilson, *Margaret Atwood's Fairy-Tale Sexual Politics* (Jackson: University of Mississippi Press, 1993), p. 34. On the crone-helper in "The Robber Bridegroom," see Daniela Hempen, "Bluebeard's Female Helper: The Ambiguous Role of the Strange Old Woman in the Grimms' 'Castle of Murder' and 'The Robber Bridegroom,' " *Folklore* 108 (1997): 45–48.

45. Italo Calvino, ed., *Italian Folktales*, trans. George Martin (New York: Harcourt Brace Jovanovich, 1980), pp. 26–30.

46. Stephen Benson's essay on the Bluebeard tale highlights the craftiness of certain heroines. See his *Cycles of Influence: Fiction, Folktale, Theory* (Detroit: Wayne State University Press, 2003), pp. 167–246.

47. Stephen Benson points out that tales like "Silvernose" hint at a connection between female curiosity and female craftiness (*Cycles of Influence*, p. 188).

48. Clarissa Pinkola Estés, *Women Who Run with the Wolves: Myths and Stories of the Wild Woman Archetype* (New York: Ballantine Books, 1992), pp. 71–72.

49. Katharine M. Briggs, *A Dictionary of British Folk-tales in the English Language* (London: Routledge & Kegan Paul, 1970), 1: 446–47.

50. Laura Mulvey, *Fetishism and Curiosity* (Bloomington: Indiana University Press, 1996), p. 59.

51. Romer Wilson, ed., *Red Magic: A Collection of the World's Best Fairy Tales from All Countries* (London: Jonathan Cape, 1930), p. 45.

52. Mulvey, *Fetishism and Curiosity*, p. 55.

53. Froma I. Zeitlin, "Travesties of Gender and Genre in Aristophanes' *Thesmophoriazousae*," in *Reflections of Women in Antiquity*, ed. Helene B. Foley (New York: Gordon and Breach, 1981), p. 207.

54. Mulvey, *Fetishism and Curiosity*, p. 59.

55. Sarah B. Pomeroy, *Goddesses, Whores, Wives, and Slaves* (New York: Schocken, 1975), p. 4.

56. On the connections between Eve and Pandora, see Marina Warner, *Monuments and Maidens: The Allegory of the Female Form* (New York: Atheneum, 1985), pp. 213–22. Philip Lewis points out that the relationship between Bluebeard and his wife is "essentially identical, in its structure, to the one that Yahweh established with Adam (before the creation of Eve) in order to refrain from eating the fruit produced by the tree of knowledge of good and evil in the Garden of Eden" (*Seeing Through the Mother Goose Tales: Visual Turns in the Writings of Charles Perrault* [Stanford: Stanford University Press, 1996], p. 221).

57. R. M. Dawkins, ed., *Modern Greek Folktales* (Oxford: Clarendon Press, 1953), pp. 89–95. Graham Anderson points out the similarities between the story of Persephone and Bluebeard in his *Fairytale in the Ancient World* (London: Routledge, 2000), p. 100.

58. *The Book of the Thousand Nights and One Night*, trans. Powys Mathers (London: Routledge, 1986), p. 5.

59. Warner, *From the Beast to the Blonde*, p. 263.

60. Alistair Boyle, *Bluebeard's Last Stand* (Santa Barbara: Allen A. Knoll, 1998), p. 153.

61. Françoise Gilot and Carlton Lake, *Life with Picasso* (New York: McGraw-Hill, 1964), p. 242. Subsequent page references in the text are to this volume.

Chapter Two: "Have you ever really been afraid? . . . of a man?
. . . of a house? . . . of yourself?"

1. Tania Modleski, *Loving with a Vengeance: Mass-Produced Fantasies for Women* (Hamden, Conn.: Archon Books, 1982), p. 20.

2. Joanna Russ, "Somebody's Trying to Kill Me and I Think It's My Husband: The Modern Gothic," *Journal of Popular Culture* 4 (1973): 667–68.

3. Cited by Fred Botting, *Gothic* (London: Routledge, 1996), p. 44.

4. Peter Messent discusses the "immortal outcast" and the "masterful, vaunting villain" of Gothic fiction in his "Introduction" to *Literature of the Occult: A Collection of Critical Essays*, ed. Peter B. Messent (Englewood Cliffs, N.J.: Prentice-Hall, 1981), p. 13.

5. Maggie Kilgour, *The Rise of the Gothic Novel* (London: Routledge, 1995), p. 9.

6. Mary Ann Doane, *The Desire to Desire: The Woman's Film of the 1940s* (Bloomington: Indiana University Press, 1987), p. 123.

7. Mary Shelley, *Frankenstein or The Modern Prometheus* (New York: Oxford University Press, 1980), p. 10. On the way in which the "compositional vocabulary" of the Gothic tradition continues to manifest itself, see *Modern Gothic: A Reader*, ed. Victor Sage and Allan Lloyd Smith (Manchester: Manchester University Press, 1996).

8. Charlotte Brontë, *Jane Eyre*, 2nd ed. (New York: W.W. Norton, 1987), p. 25. Subsequent page references in the text are to this edition.

9. Helene Moglen sees the childhood scenes in *Jane Eyre* as modeled on tales of the "dispossessed princess," in which "the princess must pass through a number of trials—choose among alternative possibilities—which test and prove her moral worth" (108). See *Charlotte Brontë: The Self Conceived* (New York: W.W. Norton, 1976). Sandra M. Gilbert and Susan Gubar describe Jane in the following manner: "the smallest, weakest, and plainest child in the house, she embarks on her pilgrim's progress as a sullen Cinderella, an angry Ugly Duckling, immorally rebellious against the hierarchy that oppresses her" (Sandra M. Gilbert and Susan Gubar, *The Madwoman in the Attic: The Woman Writer and the Nineteenth-Century Literary Imagination* [New Haven: Yale University Press, 1984], p. 342).

10. Karen E. Rowe, " 'Fairy-born and human-bred': Jane Eyre's Education in Romance," in *The Voyage In: Fictions of Female Development*, ed. Elizabeth Abel, Marianne Hirsch, and Elizabeth Langland (Hanover, N.H.: University Press of New England, 1983), p. 80. Abundant textual evidence for the way in which Jane's curiosity is "shunted aside" is provided by Michel Massé, *In the Name of Love: Women, Masochism, and the Gothic* (Ithaca, N.Y.: Cornell University Press, 1992), pp. 221–22.

11. Mei Huang, *Transforming the Cinderella Dream: From Frances Burney to Charlotte Brontë* (New Brunswick, N.J.: Rutgers University Press, 1990), p. 117.

12. On the problematics of Rochester's marriage to Bertha Mason, see Susan Zlotnick, "Jane Eyre, Anna Leonowens, and the White Woman's Burden: Governesses, Missionaries, and Maternal Imperialists Mid-Victorian Britain," in *Victorian Institute Journal* 24 (1996): 27–56, and Nancy Pell, "Resistance, Rebellion, and Marriage: The Economics of *Jane Eyre*," *Nineteenth-Century Fiction* 31 (1997): 397–420.

13. *Variety* 140:10 (13 November 1940): 5. Cited by Jeffrey Sconce, "Narrative Authority and Social Narrativity: The Cinematic Reconstitution of Brontë's *Jane Eyre*," in *The Studio System*, ed. Janet Staiger (New Brunswick, N.J.: Rutgers University Press, 1995), 140–61. Sconce also cites the statement about Selznick's desire to avoid any resemblance to *Rebecca* (145). On the cinematic transformation of Brontë's novel, see Patsy Stoneman, *Brontë Transformations* (London: Prentice Hall, 1996).

14. Daphne du Maurier, *Rebecca* (New York: Avon, 1971), p. 130.

15. Richard Michael Kelly, *Daphne du Maurier* (Boston: Twayne Publishers, 1987), p. 54. Robin Wood points out that Maxim's attachment to his second wife is "entirely dependent upon her willingness to remain a helpless child under his patriarchal protection and control." See "Rebecca Reclaimed," *Cineaction* 29 (1992): 100.

16. Margaret Forster, *Daphne du Maurier* (London: Chatto & Windus, 1993), p. 132.

17. "Like many another Gothic heroine," Michel Massé notes, "[the narrator] clandestinely uses the voyeur's role to seek knowledge forbidden by others and even by herself, but she quickly denies her own scopophilia and the knowledge she might have gained" (p. 155). See *In the Name of Love*.

18. Kelly, *Daphne du Maurier*, p. 65. Alison Light points out that *Rebecca* ends, not with "conjugal bliss" but with "middle-aged resignation and exile." See *Forever England: Femininity, Literature, and Conservatism between the Wars* (London: Routledge, 1991), p. 158. Daphne Watson similarly notes that there is "no transcendence and blissful union in the love and marriage of the de Winters." See *Their Own Worst Enemies: Women Writers of Women's Fiction* (London: Pluto Press, 1995), p. 21.

19. Nina Auerbach, *Daphne du Maurier: Haunted Heiress* (Philadelphia: University of Pennsylvania Press, 2000), p. 103. Sally Beauman, "Rereading *Rebecca*," *New Yorker* (8 November 1993): 130–31, 133–34.

20. Tania Modleski, *The Women Who Knew Too Much: Hitchcock and Feminist Theory* (New York: Routledge, 1988), p. 47.

21. François Truffaut, *Hitchcock*, rev. ed. (New York: Simon & Schuster, 1985), pp. 129–30.

22. Donald Spoto, *The Dark Side of Genius: The Life of Alfred Hitchcock* (New York: Ballantine Books, 1983), p. 483.

23. Truffaut, *Hitchcock*, p. 132.

24. Ibid., p. 131.

25. Ibid., p. 131.

26. Tania Modleski, *Loving with a Vengeance*, p. 31. I am indebted to Modleski's analysis of masculine brutality as a sign of sexual attractiveness.

27. Sarah Holland, *Bluebeard's Bride* (Toronto: Harlequin, 1985), p. 80.

28. Modleski, *Loving with a Vengeance*, p. 36.

Chapter Three: Investigative Pleasures

1. Francis Iles, *Before the Fact* (New York: Doubleday, 1932), p. 1.

2. Joseph C. Goulden comments on marriages as mistakes and on the high postwar divorce rates in *The Best Years: 1945–1950* (New York: Atheneum, 1976), p. 41. Coleman R. Griffiths writes on the problems of reentry into civilian life in "The Psychological Adjustments of Returned Servicemen and Their Families," *Marriage and Family Living* 4 (1944): 66.

3. Goulden, *The Best Years*, p. 38.

4. Andrea S. Walsh, *Women's Film and Female Experience: 1940–1950* (New York: Praeger, 1984), pp. 83–85.

5. Roland Barthes, *Image Music Text*, trans. Stephen Heath (London: Fontana, 1977), p. 160.

6. Joanna Russ, "Somebody's Trying to Kill Me and I Think It's My Husband: The Modern Gothic," *Journal of Popular Culture* 4 (1973): 666–91; Mary Ann Doane, "Paranoia and the Specular," in Doane, *The Desire to Desire: The Woman's Film of the 1940s* (Bloomington: Indiana University Press, 1987), p. 123; Walsh, *Women's Film and Female Experience*, p. 169; Thomas Elsaesser, "Tales of Sound and Fury: Observations on the Family Melodrama," in *Home Is Where the Heart Is: Studies in Melodrama and Woman's Film*, ed. Christine Gledhill (London: British Film Institute, 1987), p. 59; Kahane focuses on the locked "forbidden center of the Gothic," which she reads as the "spectral presence of a dead-undead mother, archaic and all-encompassing" (Claire Kahane, "Gothic Mirrors and Feminine Identity," *Centennial Review* 24 (1980): 47–48; Marjorie Rosen, *Popcorn Venus* (New York: Avon, 1974), p. 237; Michael Walker, "Secret beyond the Door," *Movie* 34/35 (1990): 17; and Diane Waldman writes about the move from a denial to a validation of the woman's point of view in the "gothic romance film" (Diane Waldman, " 'At last I can tell it to someone!': Feminine Point of View and Subjectivity in the Gothic Romance Film of the 1940s," *Cinema Journal* 23 [1983]: 29).

7. Walker, "Secret beyond the Door," p. 29.

8. Richard Maltby, "Film Noir: The Politics of the Maladjusted Text," *Journal of American Studies* 18 (1984): 53.

9. Stanley Cavell, *Pursuits of Happiness: The Hollywood Comedy of Remarriage* (Cambridge, Mass.: Harvard University Press, 1981), p. 1.

10. Elizabeth Cowie, "*Film Noir* and Women," in *Shades of Noir: A Reader*, ed. Joan Copjec (London: Verso, 1993), p. 135.

11. Elsaesser, "Tales of Sound and Fury," p. 58. As Michael Walker has pointed out, what is fundamental to many of the films in this genre is "the heroine's failure

to understand what is going on: the paranoia is located not in the heroine's responses but in the film's structure" (Walker, "Secret beyond the Door," p. 17).

12. Carl Freedman, "Towards a Theory of Paranoia: The Science Fiction of Philip K. Dick," *Science-Fiction Studies* 11 (1984): 15.

13. See Patrick McGilligan, *George Cukor: A Double Life* (New York: St. Martin's, 1991), p. 176.

14. Patrick Hamilton, *Angel Street* (New York: Samuel French, 1939), p. 37.

15. William Rothman reads Alex's secret in psychoanalytic terms: "Bergman has betrayed him by giving another man the key to the room to which only he and his mother had access, the room that contains the secret which grounds his intimate relationship with his mother. The suggestion is that the key marked *Unica* (union, eunuch) which unlocks the Grant/Bergman relationship and ultimately unites them unlocks as well that secret that Rains is sexually not really a man." See "Alfred Hitchcock's *Notorious,*" *Georgia Review* 4 (1975): 908–9.

16. Michael Renov, "The Male System of Hitchcock's *Notorious,*" *Wide Angle* 4 (1980): 35.

17. Tania Modleski, *The Women Who Knew Too Much: Hitchcock and Feminist Theory* (New York: Routledge, 1988), p. 62.

18. Slavoj Žižek, *Looking Awry: An Introduction to Jacques Lacan through Popular Culture* (Cambridge: MIT Press, 1992), pp. 90–91. Stephen Jenkins discusses the "battle of voice(over)s" in *Secret beyond the Door* in "Lang: Fear and Desire," in his *Fritz Lang: The Image and the Look* (London: BFI Publishing, 1981), p. 109.

19. Slavoj Žižek, " 'The Thing That Thinks': The Kantian Background of the Noir Subject," in *Shades of Noir: A Reader,* ed. Joan Copjec (London: Verso, 1993), p. 223.

20. Doane, *The Desire to Desire,* p. 152.

21. Cowie, "*Film Noir* and Women," p. 158.

22. Ibid., p. 158.

23. Žižek, " 'The Thing That Thinks,' " p. 216.

24. Walter Benjamin, "The Flaneur," in Benjamin, *Charles Baudelaire: A Lyric Poet in the Era of High Capitalism,* trans. Harry Zohn (London: New Left Books, 1973), p. 41.

25. Doane, *The Desire to Desire,* p. 136; Linda Williams, "When the Woman Looks," in *Re-vision: Essays in Feminist Film Criticism,* ed. Mary Ann Doane, Patricia Mellencamp, and Linda Williams (Los Angeles: American Film Institute, 1984), pp. 83–99.

26. Iles, *Before the Fact,* p. 287.

Chapter Four: Rewriting "Bluebeard"

1. Margaret Atwood, "Significant Moments in the Life of My Mother," in Atwood, *Bluebeard's Egg and Other Stories* (New York: Ballantine, Fawcett Crest, 1983), pp. 14–15. Subsequent page references in the text are to this edition of the story.

2. As Robert Fulford points out, "narrative began its life on earth in the form of gossip, simple stories told by one individual to another. Gossip remains a folk-art version of literature, the back-fence way of compressing events and exploring their meaning." See his *Triumph of Narrative: Storytelling in the Age of Mass Culture* (Toronto: Anansi, 1999), p. 1.

3. Marina Warner, *From the Beast to the Blonde: On Fairy Tales and Their Tellers* (New York: Farrar, Straus and Giroux, 1994), p. 49.

4. Margaret Atwood, *The Robber Bride* (New York: Doubleday, 1993), p. 292. For an intriguing analysis of the novel and its relation to detective stories and reading, see Casie Hermansson, *Reading Feminist Intertextuality through Bluebeard Stories* (Lewiston, N.Y.: Edwin Mellin, 2001), pp. 229–37.

5. Margaret Atwood, "Bluebeard's Egg," p. 176.

6. Atwood, according to Sharon R. Wilson, has always preferred the Grimms' "Fitcher's Bird" to Perrault's "Barbe Bleue," because the heroine of the Grimms' tale relies on her own resources to escape the wizard. See "Bluebeard's Forbidden Room: Gender Images in Margaret Atwood's Visual and Literary Art," *American Review of Canadian Studies* 16 (1986): 385–97. On Atwood's use of the Bluebeard tale, see Sherrill E. Grace, "Courting Bluebeard with Bartók, Atwood, and Fowles: Modern Treatments of the Bluebeard Theme," *Journal of Modern Literature* 11 (1984): 245–62. For Gloria Onley, Atwood's narratives function as "iconoclastic keys to getting mentally outside of Bluebeard's Castle." See "Power Politics in Bluebeard's Castle," *Canadian Literature* 60 (1974): 41. Atwood's early exposure to Grimms' fairy tales is documented in Nathalie Cook, *Margaret Atwood: A Biography* (Toronto: ECW Press, 1998), p. 24, and by Frank Davey, *Margaret Atwood: A Feminist Poetics* (Vancouver: Talonbooks, 1984), pp. 9–10.

7. As Sharon R. Wilson points out, in the Grimms' "Crystal Ball," a "red hot egg" releases a king's daughter from the spell of an enchantress and restores her beauty. See "Bluebeard's Forbidden Room," p. 393. W. J. Keith discusses the ending in "Interpreting and Misinterpreting 'Bluebeard's Egg,' " in *Margaret Atwood: Writing and Subjectivity, New Critical Essays*, ed. Colin Nicholson (New York: St. Martin's Press, 1994), pp. 248–57.

8. Barbara Godard analyzes embedded narratives in "Bluebeard's Egg." See her "Tales within Tales: Margaret Atwood's Folk Narratives," *Canadian Literature* 109 (1986): 54–84.

9. Margaret Atwood, *Power Politics* (Toronto: Anansi, 1972), p. 50. On the rich ambiguities of these lines, see Barbara Hill Rigney, *Margaret Atwood* (London: Macmillan, 1987), pp. 62–63.

10. Joseph Jacobs, "Mr. Fox," in *Classic Fairy Tales*, ed. Maria Tatar (New York: Norton, 1999), pp. 154–56.

11. Angela Carter, "Notes from the Frontline," in Carter, *Shaking a Leg: Collected Writings*, ed. Jenny Uglow (New York: Penguin, 1997), p. 38.

12. Angela Carter, *The Sadeian Woman and the Ideology of Pornography* (New York: Pantheon, 1978), pp. 18–20.

13. Robin Ann Sheets explores Carter's demystification of "Bluebeard" in "Pornography, Fairy Tales, and Feminism: Angela Carter's 'The Bloody Chamber,' " *Journal of the History of Sexuality* 1 (1991): 633–57.

14. Anna Katsavos, "An Interview with Angela Carter," *Review of Contemporary Fiction* 14 (1994): 12.

15. Angela Carter, "The Bloody Chamber," in Carter, *The Bloody Chamber and Other Stories* (New York: Penguin, 1979), p. 38. Subsequent page references in the text are to this edition.

16. Sheets, "Pornography, Fairy Tales, and Feminism," p. 646.

17. Ibid.

18. As Elaine Jordan points out in an analysis of "The Bloody Chamber," women can be complicit "with what captivates and victimizes them, even or especially in their adventurousness." See her "The Dangers of Angela Carter," in *New Feminist Discourses: Critical Essays on Theories and Texts,* ed. Isobel Armstrong (London: Routledge, 1992), p. 130. Patricia Duncker objects to precisely this aspect of Carter's work. See "Re-imagining the Fairy Tales: Angela Carter's Bloody Chambers," *Literature and History* 10 (1984): 3–12. And Kari E. Lokke points out that Carter reveals the importance of a "feminist redefinition of sexual pleasure and desire" (*"Bluebeard* and *The Bloody Chamber:* The Grotesque of Self-Parody and Self-Assertion," *Frontiers* 10 [1988]: 12).

19. Angela Carter, "Notes from the Frontline," p. 37.

20. Ibid., p. 42.

21. George Steiner, "The Great Ennui," in Steiner, *In Bluebeard's Castle: Some Notes towards the Redefinition of Culture* (New Haven: Yale University Press, 1971), p. 3.

22. Laura Mulvey, "A Phantasmagoria of the Female Body: The Work of Cindy Sherman," *New Left Review* 188 (July/August 1995): 136–50.

23. Catherine Morris, *The Essential Cindy Sherman* (New York: Harry N. Abrams, 1999), p. 79.

24. Ibid., p. 82.

25. Glen Harper, "Interview with Cindy Sherman," *Art Papers* (July/August 1995): 7.

26. Walter Benjamin, "The Storyteller: Reflections on the Works of Nikolai Leskov," in Benjamin, *Illuminations,* ed. Hannah Arendt, trans. Harry Zohn (New York: Schocken, 1968), p. 102.

27. Cindy Sherman, *Fitcher's Bird,* photography by Cindy Sherman, based on a tale by the Brothers Grimm (New York: Rizzoli, 1992), n.p.

28. Jane Campion comments on the pantomime in an interview with Thomas Bourguignon and Michel Ciment, "Entretien avec Jane Campion," *Positif* (June 1993): 6. In an interview conducted by Vincent Ostria and Thierry Jousse, Campion observes that she read "Bluebeard" after finishing the screenplay and before filming *The Piano:* "Entretien avec Jane Campion," *Cahiers du cinéma,* 467/8 (1993): 20. Sara Halprin points out that the pantomime prefigures Stewart's attack on Ada: "The silhouetted figure of Bluebeard brandishing an axe at his wife

is echoed in the image of Stewart striding home with his axe; the script tells us that when Ada hands Flora the fateful piano key, 'her black shadow behind the sheet recalls the macabre play.' " See "A Key to *The Piano*," *Women's Review of Books* (July 1994): 35.

29. Barbara Johnson, "Muteness Envy," in *Human, All Too Human*, ed. Diana Fuss (New York: Routledge, 1996), p. 161.

30. Jane Campion and Kate Pullinger, *The Piano* (New York: Miramax, 1994), p. 35. Subsequent page references in the text are to this volume.

31. Sue Gillett comments on Stewart's acquisitive nature. See her "Lips and Fingers: Jane Campion's *The Piano*," *Screen* 36 (1995): 285.

32. Lynda Dyson, "The Return of the Repressed? Whiteness, Femininity and Colonialism in *The Piano*," *Screen* 36 (1995): 273.

33. Stella Bruzzi, "*The Piano* Debate: Tempestuous Petticoats: Costume and Desire in *The Piano*," *Screen* 36 (1995): 259.

34. Mererid Puw Davies makes this point in " 'Du bist in einem Mörderhaus': Representing German History through the *Märchen* of 'Blaubart' and 'Der Räuberbräutigam' in Works by Dieter Hildebrandt and Helma Sanders-Brahms," in *Representing the German Nation*, ed. Mary Fulbrook and Martin Swales (Manchester: Manchester University Press, 2000), pp. 118–35.

35. Karin Struck, *Blaubarts Schatten: Roman* (Munich: List, 1991), p. 261.

36. Ibid., p. 282.

37. Elisabeth Reichart, "Die Kammer," in Reichart, *La Valse: Erzählungen* (Salzburg: Otto Müller, 1992), pp. 103–16.

38. Mererid Puw Davies, " 'In Blaubarts Schatten': Murder, 'Märchen,' and Memory," *German Life and Letters* 50 (1997): 504. See also her *The Tale of Bluebeard in German Literature: From the Eighteenth Century to the Present* (Oxford: Clarendon Press, 2001).

39. Ingeborg Bachmann, *The Book of Franza and Requiem for Fanny Goldmann*, trans. Peter Filkins (Evanston, Ill.: Northwestern University Press, 1999). I use the term "Case" to translate *Der Fall Franza*, because it is important to capture the notion of a "case study" in the work's title.

Chapter Five: Monstrous Wives

1. Robin Walz, *Pulp Surrealism: Insolent Popular Culture in Early Twentieth-Century Paris* (Berkeley: University of California Press, 2000), pp. 76–77.

2. Michel Foucault, *Discipline and Punish: The Birth of the Prison*, trans. Alan Sheridan (New York: Random House, Vintage Books, 1979), pp. 68–69.

3. Diane Wolfe Levy, "History as Art: Ironic Parody in Anatole France's *Les Sept Femmes de la Barbe-Bleue*," *Nineteenth-Century French Studies* 4 (1976): 361.

4. Charles Dickens, *The Pickwick Papers* (Harmondsworth: Penguin, 1972), p. 355.

5. Francis Egerton Ellesmere, *Bluebeard; or, Dangerous curiosity & justifiable homicide* (London: T. Brettell, 1841), p. 27.

6. Ludwig Tieck, *Ritter Blaubart: Ein Ammenmärchen in vier Akten*, in Tieck, *Werke*, ed. Richard Plett (Hamburg: Hoffmann und Campe, 1967), pp. 226, 238.

7. Anatole France, "The Seven Wives of Bluebeard," in *Spells of Enchantment: The Wondrous Fairy Tales of Western Culture*, ed. Jack Zipes (New York: Viking, 1991), p. 568.

8. Ibid., p. 580.

9. Donald Barthelme, "Bluebeard," in Barthelme, *Forty Stories* (New York: Putnam, 1987), p. 97.

10. Casie Hermansson describes the zebras as "a bizarre simulacrum emptied of all possible pre-texts." See *Reading Feminist Intertextuality through Bluebeard Stories* (Lewiston, N.Y.: Edwin Mellen Press, 2001), p. 258.

11. Aline Kilmer, "The Case of Bluebeard," in Kilmer, *Hunting a Hair Shirt and Other Spiritual Adventures* (New York: George H. Doran, 1923), pp. 94, 97.

12. On "Bluebeard" as working title for *Monsieur Verdoux*, see David Robinson, *Chaplin: His Life and Art* (New York: Da Capo, 1985), p. 520.

13. André Bazin, "The Myth of Monsieur Verdoux," in Bazin, *What Is Cinema?* trans. Hugh Gray (Berkeley: University of California Press, 1967), p. 116.

14. Charles J. Maland, *Chaplin and American Culture: The Evolution of a Star Image* (Princeton: Princeton University Press, 1989), p. 233.

15. Charles Spencer Chaplin, *My Autobiography* (New York: Simon and Schuster, 1964), p. 435.

16. Dean MacCannell, "Democracy's Turn: On Homeless *Noir*," in *Shades of Noir: A Reader*, ed. Joan Copjec (London: Verso, 1993), pp. 292–93.

17. James McLaughlin, "All in the Family: Alfred Hitchcock's *Shadow of a Doubt*," in *A Hitchcock Reader*, ed. Marshall Deutelbaum and Leland Poague (Ames: Iowa State University Press, 1986), p. 142.

18. MacCannell, "Democracy's Turn," p. 293.

19. McLaughlin, "All in the Family," p. 148.

20. Ibid., p. 149.

21. William Rothman, *Hitchcock: The Murderous Gaze* (Cambridge, Mass.: Harvard University Press, 1982), p. 244. "Graham," he adds, "knows only that realm of the ordinary within which, but also apart from which, Charlie is fated to stand."

22. George Steiner, *In Bluebeard's Castle: Some Notes towards the Redefinition of Culture* (New Haven: Yale University Press, 1971), pp. 140, 136. Note Susan McClary's identification of Bluebeard's wife with Judith in her discussion of feminism and musicology in "Introduction: A Material Girl in Bluebeard's Castle," in McClary, *Feminine Endings: Music, Gender, and Sexuality* (Minnesota: University of Minnesota Press, 1991), pp. 3–5.

23. Pierre Cadars, "Sept compositeurs pour une Barbe-Bleu," *L'avant-scène opéra* 149–50 (November/December 1992): 82–85.

24. On other musical works, including ballets, that invoke the Bluebeard story, see Carl Leafstedt, *Inside* Bluebeard's Castle: *Music and Drama in Béla Bartók's Opera* (New York: Oxford University Press, 1999), p. 174.

25. Mike Ashman, "Around the Bluebeard Myth," in *The Stage Works of Béla Bartók* (London: John Calder, 1991), p. 38. Ivan Sanders describes Ariane as the "liberated" woman. See his "Symbolist and Decadent Elements in Early-Twentieth-Century Hungarian Drama," *Canadian-American Review of Hungarian Studies* 4 (1977): 30.

26. Maurice Maeterlinck, *Ariane and Blue Beard: A Lyric Story in Three Acts* (New York: Rullman, 1910), p. 6.

27. Ibid., p. 35.

28. Stephen Benson, "The Afterlife of 'Bluebeard,'" *Marvels and Tales* 14 (2000): 244–67.

29. Austin B. Caswell, "Maeterlinck's and Dukas' *Ariane et Barbe-Bleue*: A Feminist Opera?" *Studies in Romanticism* 27 (1988): 219.

30. Cited by Leafstedt, *Inside* Bluebeard's Castle, p. 39.

31. Emil Haraszti sees Balázs's play as an attempt "to compress Maeterlinck's three-act tragedy into a one-act drama." See his *Béla Bartók: His Life and Works* (Paris: Lyrebird Press, 1938), p. 72.

32. Paul Banks, "Images of the Self: 'Duke Bluebeard's Castle,'" in *The Stage Works of Béla Bartók* (London: John Calder, 1991), p. 12.

33. Quoted in Leafstedt, *Inside* Bluebeard's Castle, p. 126.

34. Béla Bartók, *Duke Bluebeard's Castle*, trans. John Lloyd Davies, in *The Stage Works of Béla Bartók* (London: John Calder, 1991), p. 49.

35. As Mary Garrard puts it, Judith's image changed "from that of a paragon of chastity, strength, and courage to a dangerous and deceitful *femme fatale*." See her *Judith: Sexual Warrior. Women and Power in Western Culture* (New Haven: Yale University Press, 1998), p. 301.

36. Garrard lists these titles in ibid., p. 291.

37. Nadine Sine, "Cases of Mistaken Identity: Salomé and Judith at the Turn of the Century," *German Studies Review* 11 (1988): 9–29.

38. The term is borrowed from Bram Djikstra, who points out how Judith was a "paragon of self-sacrificial martyrdom for a noble cause" in the Bible and was then unmasked by nineteenth-century painters as "a lustful predator, an anorexic tigress." See *Idols of Perversity: Fantasies of Feminine Evil in Fin-de-Siècle Culture* (New York: Oxford University Press, 1986), p. 377. Marina Warner points out that although Judith is "the foremost biblical exemplar of Fortitude and Justice, the pattern of heroic virtue," in visual depictions of her, we see "a killer all the same." See Warner's *Monuments and Maidens: The Allegory of the Female Form* (New York: Atheneum, 1985), p. 175.

39. Bartók, *Duke Bluebeard's Castle*, p. 52.

40. Leafstedt, *Inside* Bluebeard's Castle, p. 176.

41. Bartók, *Duke Bluebeard's Castle*, p. 57.

42. Julian Grant, "A Foot in Bluebeard's Door," in *The Stage Works of Béla Bartók* (London: John Calder, 1991), p. 30.

43. Serge Moreux, *Béla Bartók* (London: Harvill Press, 1953).

44. Bartók, *Duke Bluebeard's Castle*, p. 58.

45. Benson, "The Afterlife of 'Bluebeard,' " pp. 259–60. See also McClary, "Introduction: A Material Girl in Bluebeard's Castle," pp. 3–34, and Anja Suschitzky, "*Ariane et Barbe-Bleue*: Dukas, the Light, and the Well," *Cambridge Opera Journal* 9 (1997): 133–61.

Chapter Six: The Art of Murder

1. Henri de Régnier, "Le sixième mariage de Barbe-Bleue," *Entretiens politiques et littéraires* 32 (November 1892): 221–32; Patrick Süskind, *Das Parfum: Die Geschichte eines Mörders* (Zurich: Diogenes, 1985).

2. See especially Steven Swann Jones, "Folk Characterization in *Lolita*," *Western Folklore* 39 (1980): 269–83, and Vladimir Nabokov, *The Annotated Lolita*, ed. Alfred Appel, Jr., rev. ed. (New York: Random House, Vintage Books, 1970), pp. 345–47.

3. Vladimir Nabokov, *Lolita* (New York: Putnam's, 1955), p. 89.

4. Kurt Vonnegut, *Bluebeard* (New York: Delacorte, 1987), p. 40. Subsequent page references in the text are to this edition.

5. David Rampton, "Into the Secret Chamber: Art and the Artist in Kurt Vonnegut's *Bluebeard*," *Critique: Studies in Contemporary Fiction* 35 (1993): 26.

6. Paul Skenazy, "Poking Holes in the Social Fabric," in *Critical Essays on Kurt Vonnegut*, ed. Robert Merrill (Boston: G. K. Hall, 1990), p. 66. On Karabekian's art, see also Cliff McCarthy, "*Bluebeard* and the Abstract Expressionists," in *The Vonnegut Chronicles: Interviews and Essays*, ed. Peter J. Reed and Marc Leeds (Westport, Conn.: Greenwood Press, 1996), pp. 165–77; Lawrence R. Broer, "*Bluebeard*: Redemption and Unwavering Light," in *Sanity Plea: Schizophrenia in the Novels of Kurt Vonnegut* (Ann Arbor: UMI Research Press, 1989), pp. 161–75; and Donald E. Morse, "Thinking Intelligently about Science and Art: Kurt Vonnegut's *Galápagos* and *Bluebeard*," *Extrapolation* 38 (1997): 292–301.

7. On this point, see Klaus Theweleit, *buch der könige* (Basel: Stroemfeld/Roter Stern, 1988).

8. As William Rothman points out, the idea that Uncle Charlie is a vampire runs "throughout the film," showing up, for example, in Charles's aversion to being photographed. See his *Hitchcock: The Murderous Gaze* (Cambridge, Mass.: Harvard University Press, 1982), p. 182.

9. Edgar G. Ulmer, *Bluebeard*, Collector's Edition DVD, Allday Entertainment, booklet accompanying DVD.

10. L. M. Montgomery, *The Blue Castle* (New York: Bantam, 1988), p. 134. Subsequent page references in the text are to this edition. Despite the multiple references to Bluebeard, Genevieve Wiggins does not refer to the fairy tale at all in her listing of fairy-tale allusions in *The Blue Castle*. See *L. M. Montgomery* (New York: Twayne, 1992), p. 130.

11. That there is some trouble in this domestic "paradise" is underscored by Sasha Mullally, who notes that Valancy has the power to choose her friends, her husband, and her entertainment, but she does not have the power "to transform the gendered sphere of work and her dependent station within the household."

See " 'Daisy,' 'Dodgie,' and 'Lady Jane Grey Dort': L. M. Montgomery and the Automobile," in *L. M. Montgomery and Canadian Culture*, ed. Irene Gammel and Elizabeth Epperly (Toronto: University of Toronto Press, 1999), p. 122.

12. Max Frisch, *Bluebeard: A Tale*, trans. Geoffrey Skelton (San Diego: Harcourt Brace Jovanovich, 1983), p. 34. Subsequent page references in the text are to this edition.

13. For Zoran Konstantinovic, Frisch engages repeatedly with men's feelings of guilt toward woman. See "Die Schuld an der Frau: Ein Beitrag zur Thematologie der Werke von Max Frisch," in *Frisch: Kritik, Thesen, Analysen*, ed. Manfred Jurgensen (Berne: Francke, 1977), pp. 145–55. For more on this issue, see Marian E. Musgrave, "Frisch's 'Continuum' of Women, Domestic and Foreign," in *Perspectives on Max Frisch*, ed. Gerhard F. Probst and Jay F. Bodine (Lexington: University of Kentucky Press, 1982), 109–18.

14. Wulf Koepke suggests that Schaad, an "obsessed diarist," may have a chance of surviving and forging an identity "by producing a text." See *Understanding Max Frisch* (Columbia: University of South Carolina Press, 1991), p. 115. Frisch himself points out that the use of the term "Bluebeard" was ironic. See *Blaubart: Ein Buch zum Film von Krzysztof Zanussi* (Frankfurt a.M.: Suhrkamp, 1985), p. 146.

15. As Casie Hermannson points out, the title "cannot be trusted. Instead, the presupposition that Schaad is guilty by intertextual reference alone becomes the question." See Casie Hermansson, *Reading Feminist Intertextuality through Bluebeard Stories* (Lewiston, N.Y.: Edwin Mellin, 2001), p. 249.

16. Kari E. Lokke, "*Bluebeard* and *The Bloody Chamber*: The Grotesque of Self-Parody and Self-Assertion," *Frontiers* 10 (1988): 7–12.

17. Mary E. Stewart, "Max Frisch's *Blaubart*: A Trivial Pursuit?" *Forum for Modern Language Studies* 24 (1988): 254.

Epilogue

1. William J. Bennett, *The Book of Virtues* (New York: Simon and Schuster, 1993), p. 127.

2. Winfried Menninghaus, *In Praise of Nonsense: Kant and Bluebeard*, trans. Henry Pickford (Stanford: Stanford University Press, 1999): 202–3.

3. Henry Louis Gates, Jr., writes about literature as affording "the lure of the forbidden." See "Borrowing Privileges," *New York Times* (2 June 2002): 18.

4. Roland Barthes, *S/Z: An Essay*, trans. Richard Miller (New York: Hill and Wang, 1974), p. 19.

5. Ibid., p. 137.

6. Keisuke Nishimoto, *Japanese Fairy Tales*, trans. Dianne Ooka (Torrance, Calif.: Heian, 1998), p. 30.

BIBLIOGRAPHY

Primary Literature

Asbjørnsen, Peter Christen and Jørgen Moe. "The Hen Is Tripping in the Mountain." In *Folktales of Norway*. Ed. Reider Thorwald Christiansen, trans. Pat Shaw Iverson. Chicago: University of Chicago Press, 1964. Pp. 228–33.

Atwood, Margaret. *Bluebeard's Egg and Other Stories*. New York: Ballantine, Fawcett Crest, 1983. Pp. 144–84.

———. *Power Politics*. Toronto: Anansi, 1972.

———. *The Robber Bride*. New York: Doubleday, 1993.

———. *True Stories*. Toronto: Oxford University Press, 1981.

Bachmann, Ingeborg. *The Book of Franza and Requiem for Fanny Goldmann*. Trans. Peter Filkins. Evanston, Ill.: Northwestern University Press, 1999.

Barthelme, Donald. "Bluebeard." In Barthelme, *Forty Stories*. New York: Putnam, 1987. Pp. 92–97.

Bartók, Béla. *Duke Bluebeard's Castle*. Trans. John Lloyd Davies. In *The Stage Works of Béla Bartók*. London: John Calder, 1991.

Bausch, Pina. *Blaubart—Beim Anhören einer Tonbandaufnahme von Béla Bartóks Oper in einem Akt*. Premiere: Wuppertal, 1 August 1977.

Bødker, Lauritis, Christina Hole, and G. D'Aronco, eds. "Blue-Beard." In *European Folk Tales*. Copenhagen: Rosenkilde and Bagger, 1963. Pp. 158–60.

Book of the Thousand Nights and One Night, The. Trans. Powys Mathers. London: Routledge, 1986.

Brontë, Charlotte. *Jane Eyre*. 2nd ed. New York: W.W. Norton, 1987.

Burnett, Frances Hodgson. *The Secret Garden*. New York: Signet, 1986.

Byatt, A. S. "The Story of the Eldest Princess." In *Caught in a Story: Contemporary Fairytales and Fables*. Ed. Christine Park and Caroline Heaton. London: Vintage, 1992. Pp. 12–28.

Cain, James M. *The Butterfly*. New York: Knopf, 1947.

Calvino, Italo, ed. "Silvernose." In *Italian Folktales*. Trans. George Martin. New York: Harcourt Brace Jovanovich, 1980. Pp. 26–30.

Campion, Jane, and Kate Pullinger. *The Piano*. New York: Miramax, 1994.

Carryl, Guy Wetmore. "How the Helpmate of Blue-Beard Made Free with a Door." In Carryl, *Grimm Tales Made Gay*. Boston: Houghton, Mifflin & Co., 1902.

Carter, Angela. "The Bloody Chamber." In Carter, *The Bloody Chamber and Other Stories*. New York: Penguin Books, 1979. Pp. 7–41.

———. "Notes from the Frontline." In Carter, *Shaking a Leg: Collected Writings*. Ed. Jenny Uglow. New York: Penguin, 1997. Pp. 36–43.

———. *The Sadeian Woman and the Ideology of Pornography*. New York: Pantheon, 1978.

Cave, Emma. *Bluebeard's Room*. London: Coronet, 1995.

Chase, Richard. "Mr. Fox." In Chase, *American Folk Tales and Songs: A Treasury of Lively, Old-Time English-American Lore*. New York: Signet, 1956. Pp. 37–42.

Cooke, Rose Terry. "Bluebeard's Closet." In *American Women Poets of the Nineteenth Century*. New Brunswick, N.J.: Rutgers University Press, 1992. Pp. 267–69.

Copus, Julia. "Bluebeard's Wife." In Copus, *The Shuttered Eye*. Newcastle upon Tyne: Bloodaxe Books, 1996. P. 24.

Crane, Thomas Frederick. "How the Devil Married Three Sisters." In *Italian Popular Tales*. Boston: Houghton, Mifflin, & Co., 1885. Pp. 78–81.

Dawkins, R. M., ed. "The Lord of the World Below." In *Modern Greek Folktales*. Oxford: Clarendon Press, 1953. Pp. 89–95.

Dickens, Charles. "Nurse's Stories." In *The Uncommercial Traveller. The Oxford Illustrated Dickens*. Oxford: Oxford University Press, 1989.

———. *The Pickwick Papers*. Harmondsworth: Penguin, 1972.

Döblin, Alfred. "Der Ritter Blaubart." In *Erzählungen aus fünf Jahrzehnten* (Olten: Walter, 1979). Pp. 79–86.

du Maurier, Daphne. *Rebecca*. New York: Avon, 1971.

Ellesmere, Francis Egerton. *Bluebeard; or, Dangerous curiosity & justifiable homicide*. London: T. Brettell, 1841.

Fowles, John. *The Collector*. Boston: Little, Brown, 1963.

France, Anatole. "The Seven Wives of Bluebeard." In *Spells of Enchantment: The Wondrous Fairy Tales of Western Culture*. Ed. Jack Zipes. New York: Viking, 1991. Pp. 566–82.

Frisch, Max. *Blaubart: Ein Buch zum Film von Krzysztof Zanussi*. Frankfurt a.M.: Suhrkamp, 1985.

———. *Bluebeard: A Tale*. Trans. Geoffrey Skelton. San Diego: Harcourt Brace Jovanovich, 1983.

Frost, Gregory. *Fitcher's Brides*. New York: Tom Doherty Associates, 2002.

Grimm, Jacob and Wilhelm Grimm. "Fitcher's Bird" and "The Robber Bridegroom." In *The Annotated Brothers Grimm*. Ed. and trans. Maria Tatar. New York: W. W. Norton, forthcoming.

Hamilton, Patrick. *Angel Street*. New York: Samuel French, 1939.

Holland, Sarah. *Bluebeard's Bride*. Toronto: Harlequin, 1985.

Iles, Francis. *Before the Fact*. New York: Doubleday, 1932.

Irish, William. *Bluebeard's Seventh Wife*. New York: Popular Library, 1952.

Jackson, Shirley. "The Honeymoon of Mrs. Smith (Version I)" and "The Honeymoon of Mrs. Smith (Version II): The Mystery of the Murdered Bride." In *Just an Ordinary Day*. Ed. Laurence Jackson Hyman and Sarah Hyman Stewart. New York: Bantam Books, 1997. Pp. 70–88.

Jacobs, Joseph. "Mr. Fox." In *English Fairy Tales*. Ed. Maria Tatar. New York: Norton, 1999. Pp. 154–56.

Keene, Carolyn. *The Bluebeard Room*. Nancy Drew Mystery 77. New York: Minstrel, 1988.

Kilmer, Aline. "The Case of Bluebeard." In Kilmer, *Hunting a Hair Shirt and Other Spiritual Adventures*. New York: George H. Doran, 1923. Pp. 93–98.

King, Stephen. *The Shining*. New York: Signet, 1978.

Lang, Andrew. *The Blue Fairy Book*. Ed. Brian Alderson. New York: Penguin, 1987.

Lardner, Ring. "Bluebeard." In Lardner, *What of It?* New York: Scribner's, 1925. Pp. 70–73.

Ludlam, Charles. *Bluebeard: A Melodrama in Three Acts*. In *The Complete Plays of Charles Ludlam*. New York: Harper & Row, 1989. Pp. 116–41.

Maeterlinck, Maurice. *Ariane and Blue Beard: A Lyric Story in Three Acts*. New York: Rullman, 1910.

Maugard, Gaston. "The White Dove." In Maugard, *Contes des Pyrénées*. Paris: Érasme, 1955.

Melville, Herman. *Moby-Dick*. Ed. Harrison Hayford and Hershel Parker. New York: W. W. Norton, 1967.

Meuss, Ruth E. K., trans. "Comorre." In *Breton Folktales*. Ed. Ré Soupault. London: G. Bell & Sons, 1971. Pp. 165–74.

Millay, Edna St. Vincent. [Untitled Bluebeard sonnet]. In *Collected Poems*. Ed. Norma Millay. New York: Harper, 1956.

Millet, Lydia. "The Wife Killer." In *Mirror, Mirror on the Wall: Women Writers Explore Their Favorite Fairy Tales*. Ed. Kate Bernheimer. New York: Anchor Doubleday, 1998. Pp. 230–46.

Montgomery, L. M. *The Blue Castle*. New York: Bantam, 1988.

Nabokov, Vladimir. *The Annotated Lolita*. Ed. Alfred Appel, Jr. Rev. ed. New York: Random House, Vintage Books, 1970.

———. *Lolita*. New York: Putnam's, 1955.

Nishimoto, Keisuke. *Japanese Fairy Tales*. Trans. Dianne Ooka. Torrance, Calif.: Heian, 1998.

Oates, Joyce Carol. "Blue-Bearded Lover." In Oates, *The Assignation: Stories*. New York: Ecco, 1988. Pp. 184–86.

———. "In Olden Times, When Wishing Was Having: Classic and Contemporary Fairy Tales." In *Mirror, Mirror on the Wall: Women Writers Explore Their Favorite Fairy Tales*. Ed. Kate Bernheimer. New York: Anchor Doubleday, 1998. Pp. 247–72.

Naylor, Gloria. *Linden Hills.* New York: Penguin, 1986.

Plath, Sylvia. "Bluebeard." In Plath, *The Collected Poems.* Ed. Ted Hughes. New York: Harper & Row, 1981.

Régnier, Henri de. "Le sixième mariage de Barbe-Bleue." *Entretiens politiques et littéraires* 32 (November 1892) : 221–32.

Reichart, Elisabeth. "Die Kammer." In Reichart, *La Valse: Erzählungen.* Salzburg: Otto Müller, 1992. Pp. 103–16.

Ritchie, Anne Thackeray. "Bluebeard's Keys." In *Bluebeard's Keys and Other Stories. The Works of Miss Thackeray.* London: Smith and Elder, 1905. Vol. 5, 1–118.

Rühmkorf, Peter. "Blaubarts letzte Reise." In Rühmkorf, *Der Hüter des Misthaufens: Aufgeklärte Märchen.* Reinbek: Rowohit, 1983. Pp. 110–22.

Shelley, Mary. *Frankenstein or The Modern Prometheus.* New York: Oxford University Press, 1980.

Sherman, Cindy. *Fitcher's Bird.* Photography by Cindy Sherman, based on a tale by the Brothers Grimm. New York: Rizzoli, 1992.

Strauss, Gwen. "Bluebeard." In Strauss, *Trail of Stones.* Illus. Anthony Browne. New York: Knopf, 1990. Pp. 20–21.

Struck, Karin. *Blaubarts Schatten: Roman.* Munich: List, 1991.

Suniti, Namjoshi. "A Room of His Own." In Suniti, *Feminist Fables.* London: Sheba Feminist Publishers, 1981. P. 64.

Süskind, Patrick. *Das Parfum: Die Geschichte eines Mörders.* Zurich: Diogenes, 1985.

Thackeray, William Makepeace. "Barbazure." 1847. *Thackeray's Miscellanies.* Vol. 5: *Burlesques.* London: Smith, 1877.

———. "Bluebeard at Breakfast: An Unpublished Manuscript." Ed. Juliet McMaster. *Dickens Studies Annual* 8 (1981): 197–230.

"Bluebeard's Ghost." In *Spells of Enchantment: The Wondrous Fairy Tales of Western Culture.* Ed. Jack Zipes. New York: Viking, 1991. Pp. 337–56.

Tieck, Ludwig. *Ritter Blaubart: Ein Ammenmärchen in vier Akten.* In Tieck, *Werke.* Ed. Richard Plett. Hamburg: Hoffmann und Campe, 1967.

Tong, Su. *Raise the Red Lantern: Three Novellas.* Trans. Michael S. Duke. New York: Penguin, 1993.

Trakl, Georg. *Blaubart: Ein Puppenspiel* (Fragment). In Trakl, *Dichtungen und Briefe.* Ed. Walther Killy and Hans Szklenar. Salzburg: O. Müller, 1969. Vol. 1, 435–45.

Updike, John. "George and Vivian." In Updike, *The Afterlife and Other Stories.* New York: Knopf, 1994. Pp. 154–89.

Vonnegut, Kurt. *Bluebeard.* New York: Delacorte, 1987.

Warner, Sylvia Townsend. "Bluebeard's Daughter." In Warner, *The Cat's Cradle-Book.* New York: Viking, 1940. Pp. 157–80.

Weldon, Fay. "The Journey to Mr. Fox." In Wilson, *Mirror, Mirror on the Wall: Women Writers Explore Their Favorite Fairy Tales.* Ed. Kate Bernheimer. New York: Anchor Doubleday, 1998. Pp. 318–41.

Welty, Eudora. *The Robber Bridegroom.* New York: Harcourt, 1942.

Wilson, Romer. "Bluebeard." In Wilson, *Red Magic: A Collection of the World's Best Fairy Tales from All Countries.* London: Jonathan Cape, 1930. Pp. 45–49.

Wright, Richard. *Black Boy.* New York: Harper & Row, 1966.

Secondary Literature

Aarne, Antti. *The Types of the Folk-tale: A Classification and Bibliography.* Trans. and enlarged by Stith Thompson. 2nd edition. Helsinki: Suomalainen Tiedeaka-temia, 1964.

Anderson, Graham. *Fairytale in the Ancient World.* London: Routledge, 2000.

Anderson, William C. *Lady Bluebeard: The True Story of Love and Marriage, Death and Flypaper.* Boulder: Pruett, 1994.

Antokoletz, Elliott. "Bartók's *Bluebeard*: The Sources of Its Modernism." *College Music Symposium* 30 (1990): 75–95.

Apostolidès, Jean-Marie. "Des choses cachées dans le château de Barbe-bleue." *Marvels and Tales* 5 (1991) : 179–99.

Ashman, Mike. "Around the Bluebeard Myth." In *The Stage Works of Béla Bartók.* London: John Calder, 1991. Pp. 35–44.

Asper, Kathrin. " 'Fitcher's Bird': Illustrations of the Negative Animus and Shadow in Persons with Narcissistic Disturbances." Trans. Elizabeth Burr. *Psyche's Stories: Modern Jungian Interpretations of Fairy Tales.* Ed. Murray Stein and Lionell Corbett. 2 vols. Wilmette, Ill.: Chiron, 1991. 1: 121–39.

Atwood, Margaret. "Grimms' Remembered." In *The Reception of Grimms' Fairy Tales: Responses, Reactions, Revisions.* Ed. Donald Haase. Detroit: Wayne State University Press, 1993. Pp. 290–92.

Auerbach, Nina. *Daphne du Maurier: Haunted Heiress.* Philadelphia: University of Pennsylvania Press, 2000.

Beauman, Sally. "Rereading *Rebecca.*" *New Yorker* (8 November 1993): 130–31, 133–34.

Bacchilega, Cristina. *Postmodern Fairy Tales: Gender and Narrative Strategies.* Philadelphia: University of Pennsylvania Press, 1997.

Banks, Paul. "Images of the Self: 'Duke Bluebeard's Castle.' " In *The Stage Works of Béla Bartók.* London: John Calder, 1991. Pp. 7–12.

Bardens, Dennis. *The Ladykiller: The Life of Landru, the French Bluebeard.* London: Davies, 1972.

Barthes, Roland. *Image Music Text.* Trans. Stephen Heath. London: Fontana, 1977.

———. *S/Z: An Essay.* Trans. Richard Miller. New York: Hill and Wang, 1974.

Bayley, Amanda. *The Cambridge Companion to Bartók.* Cambridge: Cambridge University Press, 2001.

Bazin, André. "The Myth of Monsieur Verdoux." In Bazin, *What Is Cinema?* Vol. 2. Trans. Hugh Gray. Berkeley: University of California Press, 1967. Pp. 102–23.

Beauman, Sally. "Rereading *Rebecca.*" *New Yorker* (8 November 1993): 130–31, 133–34.

Beckwith, Marc. "Italo Calvino and the Nature of Italian Folktales." *Italica* 64 (1987): 244–62.

Benedict, Barbara M. *Curiosity: A Cultural History of Early Modern Inquiry.* Chicago: University of Chicago Press, 2001.

Benjamin, Walter. "The Storyteller: Reflections on the Works of Nikolai Leskov." In Benjamin, *Illuminations.* Ed. Hannah Arendt. Trans. Harry Zohn. New York: Schocken, 1968. Pp. 83–109.

———. "The Flaneur." In Benjamin, *Charles Baudelaire: A Lyric Poet in the Era of High Capitalism.* Trans. Harry Zohn. London: New Left Books, 1973. Pp. 35–66.

Bennett, William J. *The Book of Virtues.* New York: Simon and Schuster, 1993.

Benson, Stephen. "The Afterlife of 'Bluebeard.' " *Marvels and Tales* 14 (2000): 244–67.

———. *Cycles of Influence: Fiction, Folktale, Theory.* Detroit: Wayne State University Press, 2003.

Bettelheim, Bruno. *The Uses of Enchantment: The Meaning and Importance of Fairy Tales.* New York: Knopf, 1976.

Bevan, David G. "Tournier's Photographer: A Modern Bluebeard?" *Modern Language Studies* 15 (1985): 66–71.

Botting, Fred. *Gothic.* London: Routledge, 1996.

Bourguignon, Thomas, and Michel Ciment. "Entretien avec Jane Campion." *Positif* (June 1993): 6–11.

Boyle, Alistair. *Bluebeard's Last Stand.* Santa Barbara, Calif.: Allen A. Knoll, 1998.

Briggs, Katharine M. "Perrifool." In *A Dictionary of British Folk-tales in the English Language.* London: Routledge & Kegan Paul, 1970. Vol. 1, 446–47.

Broer, Lawrence R. "*Bluebeard*: Redemption and Unwavering Light." In Broer, *Sanity Plea: Schizophrenia in the Novels of Kurt Vonnegut.* Ann Arbor: UMI Research Press, 1989). Pp. 161–75.

Bruzzi, Stella, "*The Piano* Debate: Tempestuous Petticoats: Costume and Desire in *The Piano,*" *Screen* 36 (1995): 257–66.

Cadars, Pierre. "Sept compositeurs pour une Barbe-Bleu." *L'avant-scène opéra* 149–50 (November/December 1992): 82–85.

Carpenter, Humphrey, and Mari Prichard. *The Oxford Companion to Children's Literature.* London: Oxford University Press, 1984.

Caswell, Austin B. "Maeterlinck's and Dukas' *Ariane et Barbe-Bleue*: A Feminist Opera?" *Studies in Romanticism* 27 (1988): 203–20.

Cather, Willa. *O Pioneers!* New York: Penguin, 1994.

Cavell, Stanley. *Pursuits of Happiness: The Hollywood Comedy of Remarriage.* Cambridge, Mass.: Harvard University Press, 1981.

Chaplin, Charles Spencer. *My Autobiography.* New York: Simon and Schuster, 1964.

Clemens, Valdine. *The Return of the Repressed: Gothic Horror from* The Castle of Otranto *to* Alien. Albany: State University of New York Press, 1999.

Clément, Catherine. *Opera, or the Undoing of Women.* Trans. Betsy Wing. Minneapolis: University of Minnesota Press, 1999.

Clover, Carol J. *Men, Women, and Chainsaws: Gender in the Modern Horror Film.* Princeton: Princeton University Press, 1992.

Cook, Nathalie. *Margaret Atwood: A Biography.* Toronto: ECW Press, 1998.

Cooper, J. C. *Fairy Tales: Allegories of the Inner Life.* Wellingborough, Northamptonshire: Aquarian Press, 1983.

Cowie, Elizabeth. "*Film Noir* and Women." In *Shades of Noir: A Reader.* Ed. Joan Copjec. London: Verso, 1993. Pp. 121–65.

Curran, Ronald T. "Complex, Archetype, and Primal Fear: King's Use of Fairy Tales in *The Shining.*" In *The Dark Descent: Essays Defining Stephen King's Horrorscope.* Ed. Tony Magistrale. Westport, Conn.: Greenwood, 1992. Pp. 33–46.

Darmon, Pierre. *Landru.* Paris: Plon, 1994.

Davey, Frank. *Margaret Atwood: A Feminist Poetics.* Vancouver: Talonbooks, 1984.

Davies, Mererid Puw. " 'Du bist in einem Mörderhaus': Representing German History through the *Märchen* of 'Blaubart' and 'Der Räuberbräutigam' in Works by Dieter Hildebrandt and Helma Sanders-Brahms." In *Representing the German Nation.* Ed. Mary Fulbrook and Martin Swales. Manchester: Manchester University Press, 2000.

———. " 'In Blaubarts Schatten': Murder, '*Märchen*,' and Memory." *German Life and Letters* 50 (1997): 491–507.

———. "Laughing Their Heads Off: Nineteenth-Century Comic Versions of the Bluebeard Tale." *German Life and Letters* 55 (2002): 329–47.

———.*The Tale of Bluebeard in German Literature: From the Eighteenth Century to the Present.* Oxford: Clarendon Press, 2001.

Delarue, Paul. *Le conte populaire français.* Paris: Erasme, 1957.

———. "Les contes merveilleux de Perrault et la tradition populaire: Barbe-Bleue." *Bulletin folklorique de l'Ile de France* 13 (1952) : 348–57.

Disraeli, Isaac. *Vaurien: or, Sketches of the Times: Exhibiting Views of the Philosophies, Religions, Politics, Literature, and Manners of the Age.* London: T. Cadell, Junior, and W. Davies, 1797.

Djikstra, Bram. *Idols of Perversity: Fantasies of Feminine Evil in Fin-de-Siècle Culture.* New York: Oxford University Press, 1986.

Doane, Mary Ann. *The Desire to Desire: The Woman's Film of the 1940s.* Bloomington: Indiana University Press, 1987.

Duncker, Patricia. "Re-imagining the Fairy Tales: Angela Carter's Bloody Chambers." *Literature and History* 10 (1984): 3–12.

Dyson, Lynda. "The Return of the Repressed? Whiteness, Femininity, and Colonialism in *The Piano.*" *Screen* 36 (1995): 267–76.

Edmundson, Mark. *Nightmare on Main Street: Angels, Sadomasochism, and the Culture of Gothic.* Cambridge, Mass.: Harvard University Press, 1997.

Ellis, Kate Ferguson. *The Contested Castle: Gothic Novels and the Subversion of Domestic Ideology.* Urbana: University of Illinois Press, 1989.

Elsaesser, Thomas. "Tales of Sound and Fury: Observations on the Family Melodrama." In *Home Is Where the Heart Is: Studies in Melodrama and Woman's Film*. Ed. Christine Gledhill. London: British Film Institute, 1987. Pp. 43–69.

Estés, Clarissa Pinkola. *Women Who Run with the Wolves: Myths and Stories of the Wild Woman Archetype*. New York: Ballantine Books, 1992.

Forster, Margaret. *Daphne du Maurier*. London: Chatto & Windus, 1993.

Foucault, Michel. *Discipline and Punish: The Birth of the Prison*. Trans. Alan Sheridan. New York: Random House, Vintage Books, 1979.

Freedman, Carl. "Towards a Theory of Paranoia: The Science Fiction of Philip K. Dick." *Science-Fiction Studies* 11 (1984): 15–24.

Fulford, Robert. *The Triumph of Narrative: Storytelling in the Age of Mass Culture*. Toronto: Anansi, 1999.

Garrard, Mary. *Judith: Sexual Warrior. Women and Power in Western Culture*. New Haven: Yale University Press, 1998.

Gates, Henry Louis, Jr. "Borrowing Privileges." *New York Times* (2 June 2002): 18.

Gilbert, Sandra M. and Susan Gubar. *The Madwoman in the Attic: The Woman Writer and the Nineteenth-Century Literary Imagination*. New Haven: Yale University Press, 1984.

Gillett, Sue. "Lips and Fingers: Jane Campion's *The Piano*." *Screen* 36 (1995): 277–87.

Gilot, Françoise, and Carlton Lake. *Life with Picasso*. New York: McGraw-Hill, 1964.

Godard, Barbara. "Tales within Tales: Margaret Atwood's Folk Narratives." *Canadian Literature* 109 (1986): 54–84.

Gosse, Edmund. "Bluebeard among the Authors." *Silhouettes*. New York: Scribner, 1925. Pp. 11–20.

Goulden, Joseph C. *The Best Years: 1945–1950*. New York: Atheneum, 1976.

Grace, Sherrill E. "Courting Bluebeard with Bartók, Atwood, and Fowles: Modern Treatments of the Bluebeard Theme." *Journal of Modern Literature* 11 (1984): 245–62.

Grant, Julian. "A Foot in Bluebeard's Door." In *The Stage Works of Béla Bartók*. London: John Calder, 1991. Pp. 25–34.

Griffiths, Coleman R. "The Psychological Adjustments of Returned Servicemen and Their Families." *Marriage and Family Living* 4 (1994): 65–67, 87.

Halprin, Sara. "A Key to *The Piano*." *Women's Review of Books* (July 1944): 35–36.

Haraszti, Emil. *Béla Bartók: His Life and Work*. Paris: Lyrebird Press, 1938.

Harper, Glen. "Interview with Cindy Sherman." *Art Papers* (July/August 1995): 7.

Harris, Nick, and Helene Rico. "The Modern Bluebeard." In *In the Shadows: Thirty Detective Stories Showing "Why Crime Doesn't Pay": A Series of Famous Cases*. Los Angeles: Times-Mirror, 1923. Pp. 307–20.

Hartland, E. Sidney. "The Forbidden Chamber." *Folk-Lore Journal* 3 (1885): 193–242.

Heckmann, Emil. *Blaubart: Ein Beitrag zur vergleichenden Märchenforschung*. Schwetzingen: A. Moch, 1932.

Hempen, Daniela. "Bluebeard's Female Helper: The Ambiguous Role of the Strange Old Woman in the Grimms' 'Castle of Murder' and 'The Robber Bridegroom.' " *Folklore* 108 (1977): 45–48.

Heppenstall, Rayner. *Bluebeard and After: Three Decades of Murder in France.* London: Peter, 1972.

Hermansson, Casie. *Reading Feminist Intertextuality through Bluebeard Stories.* Lewiston, N.Y.: Edwin Mellin, 2001.

Hoile, Christopher. "The Uncanny and the Fairy Tale in Kubrick's *The Shining.*" *Literature-and-Film Quarterly* 12 (1984): 5–12.

Holland, Norman N., and Leona F. Sherman. "Gothic Possibilities." *New Literary History* 8 (1977): 279–94.

Huang, Mei. *Transforming the Cinderella Dream : From Frances Burney to Charlotte Brontë.* New Brunswick, N.J.: Rutgers University Press, 1990.

Huysmans, J. K. *Là-bas.* Trans. Keene Wallace. New York: Dover, 1972.

Jameson, Vere. *Bluebeard.* London, Ont.: Hunter Printing, 1954.

Jenkins, Stephen. "Lang: Fear and Desire." In Stephen Jenkins, *Fritz Lang: The Image and the Look.* London: BFI Publishing, 1981. Pp. 38–124.

Johnson, Barbara. "Muteness Envy." In *Human, All Too Human.* Ed. Diana Fuss. New York: Routledge, 1996. Pp. 131–48.

Jones, Steven Swann. "Folk Characterization in *Lolita.*" *Western Folklore* 39 (1980): 269–83.

Jordan, Elaine. "The Dangers of Angela Carter." In *New Feminist Discourses: Critical Essays on Theories and Texts.* Ed. Isobel Armstrong. London: Routledge, 1992. Pp. 119–31.

Kahane, Claire. "Gothic Mirrors and Feminine Identity." *Centennial Review* 24 (1980): 43–64.

Kast, Varena. "Bluebeard: On the Problem of the Destructive Animus." In *Witches, Ogres, and the Devil's Daughter: Encounters with Evil in Fairy Tales.* Ed. Mario Jacoby, Varena Kast, and Ingrid Riedel. Trans. Michael H. Kohn. Boston: Shambhala, 1992. Pp. 86–104.

Katsavos, Anna. "An Interview with Angela Carter." *Review of Contemporary Fiction* 14 (1994): 11–17.

Keith, W. J. "Interpreting and Misinterpreting 'Bluebeard's Egg.' " In *Margaret Atwood: Writing and Subjectivity. New Critical Essays.* Ed. Colin Nicholson. New York: St. Martin's Press, 1994. Pp. 248–57.

Kelly, Richard Michael. *Daphne du Maurier.* Boston: Twayne Publishers, 1987.

Kilgour, Maggie. *The Rise of the Gothic Novel.* London: Routledge, 1995.

Koepke, Wulf. *Understanding Max Frisch.* Columbia: Univ. of South Carolina Press, 1991.

Konstantinovic, Zoran. "Die Schuld an der Frau: Ein Beitrag zur Thematologie der Werke von Max Frisch." In *Frisch: Kritik, Thesen, Analysen.* Ed. Manfred Jurgensen. Berne: Francke, 1977. Pp. 145–55.

Kopper, Edward A. "Abstract Expressionism in Vonnegut's *Bluebeard.*" *Journal of Modern Literature* 17 (1991): 583–84.

Kudszus, Winfried G. "The Bluebeard Affection." *Disease and Medicine in Modern German Cultures*. Ed. Rudolf Kaser and Vera Pohland. Ithaca, N.Y.: Cornell University Press, 1990. Pp. 108–19.

Kuntzel, Thierry. "The Film-Work, 2." *Camera Obscura* 5 (1980): 6–69.

Langlois, Janet L. "Belle Gunness, the Lady Bluebeard: Symbolic Inversion in Verbal Art and American Culture." *Signs* 8 (1983): 614–17.

———. *Belle Gunness: The Lady Bluebeard*. Bloomington: Indiana University Press, 1985.

———. "Belle Gunness, the Lady Bluebeard: Community Legend as Metaphor." *Journal of the Folklore Institute* 15 (1978): 147–60.

———. "Belle Gunness, the Lady Bluebeard: Narrative Use of a Deviant Woman." In *Women's Folklore, Women's Culture*. Ed. Rosan A. Jordan and Susan J. Kalcik. Philadelphia: University of Pennsylvania Press, 1985. Pp. 109–24.

Leafstedt, Carl. *Inside* Bluebeard's Castle: *Music and Drama in Béla Bartók's* Opera. New York: Oxford University Press, 1999.

Leigh, Olivia. *The Fifth Wife of Bluebeard*. London: Hale, 1969.

Leroux, Gaston. *The Phantom of the Opera*. New York: Harper, 1987.

Levy, Diane Wolf. "History as Art: Ironic Parody in Anatole France's *Les Sept Femmes de la Barbe-Bleue*." *Nineteenth-Century French Studies* 4 (1976): 361–70.

Lewis, Philip. *Seeing Through the Mother Goose Tales: Visual Turns in the Writings of Charles Perrault*. Stanford: Stanford University Press, 1996.

Light, Alison. *Forever England: Femininity, Literature, and Conservatism between the Wars*. London: Routledge, 1991.

Lokke, Kari E. "*Bluebeard* and *The Bloody Chamber*: The Grotesque of Self-Parody and Self-Assertion." *Frontiers* 10 (1988): 7–12.

Lotman, Jurij M. "The Origin of Plot in the Light of Typology." *Poetics Today* 1 (1979): 161–84.

MacCannell, Dean. "Democracy's Turn: On Homeless *Noir*." In *Shades of Noir: A Reader*. Ed. Joan Copjec. London: Verso, 1993. Pp. 279–97.

Madoff, Mark S. "Inside, Outside, and the Gothic Locked-Room Mystery." *Gothic Fictions: Prohibition/Transgression*. Ed. Kenneth W. Graham. New York: AMS, 1989. Pp. 49–62.

Maio, Kathleen L. "Had-I-But-Known: The Marriage of Gothic Terror and Detection." *The Female Gothic*. Ed. Juliann E. Fleenor. Montreal: Eden, 1983. Pp. 82–90.

Maland, Charles J. *Chaplin and American Culture: The Evolution of a Star Image*. Princeton: Princeton University Press, 1989.

Maltby, Richard. "Film Noir: The Politics of the Maladjusted Text." *Journal of American Studies* 18 (1984): 49–71.

Mank, Gregory William. "Bluebeard." In Mank, *Hollywood Cauldron: Thirteen Horror Films from the Genre's Golden Age*. Jefferson, N.C.: McFarland & Co., 1994. Pp. 265–92.

Marcus, Jane. "Bluebeard's Daughters: Pretexts for Pre-Texts." *Feminist Critical Negotiations*. Ed. Alice A. Parker and Elizabeth A. Meese. Amsterdam: Benjamins, 1992. Pp. 19–32.

Massé, Michel. *In the Name of Love: Women, Masochism, and the Gothic.* Ithaca, N.Y.: Cornell University Press, 1992.

McCarthy, Cliff. "*Bluebeard* and the Abstract Expressionists." In *The Vonnegut Chronicles: Interviews and Essays*. Ed. Peter J. Reed and Marc Leeds. Westport, Conn.: Greenwood Press, 1996. Pp. 164–77.

McClary, Susan. "Introduction: A Material Girl in Bluebeard's Castle." In McClary, *Feminine Endings: Music, Gender, and Sexuality*. Minnesota: University of Minnesota Press, 1991. Pp. 3–34.

McGilligan, Patrick. *George Cukor: A Double Life*. New York: St. Martin's, 1991.

McLaughlin, James. "All in the Family: Alfred Hitchcock's *Shadow of a Doubt*." In *A Hitchcock Reader*. Ed. Marshall Deutelbaum and Leland Poague. Ames: Iowa State University Press, 1986. Pp.141–52.

McMaster, Juliet. "Bluebeard: A Tale of Matrimony." *Room of One's Own* 11 (1976): 10–19.

Menninghaus, Winfried. *In Praise of Nonsense: Kant and Bluebeard*. Trans. Henry Pickford. Stanford: Stanford University Press, 1999.

Messent, Peter. "Introduction." In *Literature of the Occult: A Collection of Critical Essays*. Ed. Peter B. Messent. Englewood Cliffs, N.J.: Prentice-Hall, 1981. Pp. 1–16.

Miller, D. A. *The Novel and the Police*. Berkeley: University of California Press, 1988.

Millet, Lydia. "The Wife Killer." In *Mirror, Mirror on the Wall: Women Writers Explore Their Favorite Fairy Tales*. Ed. Kate Bernheimer. New York: Doubleday, Anchor Books, 1998. Pp. 230–46.

Minghella, Anthony. *The Talented Mr. Ripley: A Screenplay*. New York: Hyperion, 1999.

Modleski, Tania. *Loving with a Vengeance: Mass-Produced Fantasies for Women*. Hamden, Conn.: Archon Books, 1982.

———. *The Women Who Knew Too Much: Hitchcock and Feminist Theory*. New York: Routledge, 1988.

Moglen, Helene. *Charlotte Bronte: The Self Conceived*. New York: W.W. Norton, 1976.

Moreux, Serge. *Béla Bartók*. London: Harvill Press, 1953.

Morris, Catherine. *The Essential Cindy Sherman*. New York: Harry N. Abrams, 1999.

Morse, Donald E. "Thinking Intelligently about Science and Art: Kurt Vonnegut's *Galápagos* and *Bluebeard*." *Extrapolation* 38 (1997): 292–301.

Mowshowitz, Harriet. "Bluebeard and French Literature." Ph.D. diss. University of Michigan, 1970.

———. "Gilles de Rais and the Bluebeard Legend in France." *Michigan Academician* 1 (1973): 83–92.

Mullally, Sasha. " 'Daisy,' 'Dodgie,' and 'Lady Jane Grey Dort': L. M. Montgomery and the Automobile." In *L. M. Montgomery and Canadian Culture*. Ed. Irene Gammel and Elizabeth Epperly. Toronto: University of Toronto Press, 1999.

Mulvey, Laura. *Fetishism and Curiosity*. Bloomington: Indiana University Press, 1996.

———. "A Phantasmagoria of the Female Body: The Work of Cindy Sherman." *New Left Review* 188 (July/August 1995): 136–150.

Musgrave, Marian E. "Frisch's 'Continuum' of Women, Domestic and Foreign." In *Perspectives on Max Frisch*. Ed. Gerhard F. Probst and Jay F. Bodine. Lexington: University of Kentucky Press, 1982. Pp. 109–18.

Mustazza, Leonard. "The Genesis Gang: Art and Re-Creation in *Bluebeard*." In *The Critical Response to Kurt Vonnegut*. Ed. Leonard Mustazza. Westport, Conn.: Greenwood, 1994. Pp. 291–300.

Onley, Gloria. "Power Politics in Bluebeard's Castle." *Canadian Literature* 60 (1974): 21–42.

Ostria, Vincent, and Thierry Jousse. "Entretien avec Jane Campion." *Cahiers du cinéma* 467/8 (1993): 17–20.

Pastoureau, Michel. *Blue: The History of a Color*. Princeton: Princeton University Press, 2001.

Pell, Nancy. "Resistance, Rebellion, and Marriage: The Economics of Jane Eyre." *Nineteenth-Century Fiction* 31 (1997): 397–420.

Perrault, Charles. "La Barbe Bleue." In Perrault, *Contes*. Ed. Marc Soriano. Paris: Flammarion, 1989. Pp. 257–62.

Perrot, Michelle, ed. *From the Fires of Revolution to the Great War*. Vol. 4 of *A History of Private Life*. Cambridge, Mass.: Harvard University Press, 1990.

Peterson, Nancy J. " 'Bluebeard's Egg': Not Entirely a 'Grimm' Tale." In *Margaret Atwood: Reflection and Reality*. Ed. Beatrice Mendez-Egle and James M. Haule. Edinburgh: Pan Am University, 1987. Pp. 131–38.

Polan, Dana. *Power and Paranoia: History, Narrative, and the American Cinema, 1940–1950*. New York: Columbia University Press, 1986.

Pomeroy, Sarah B. *Goddesses, Whores, Wives, and Slaves*. New York: Schocken, 1975.

Radway, Janice. *Reading the Romance: Women, Patriarchy, and Popular Literature*. Chapel Hill: University of North Carolina Press, 1984.

Rampton, David. "Into the Secret Chamber: Art and the Artist in Kurt Vonnegut's *Bluebeard*." *Critique: Studies in Contemporary Fiction* 35 (1993): 16–26.

Raphoz, Fabienne. *Les femmes de Barbe-Bleue: Une histoire de curieuses*. Geneva : Metropolis, 1995.

Renov, Michael. "The Male System of Hitchcock's *Notorious*." *Wide Angle* 4 (1980): 30–37.

Richter, David. "Murder in Jest: Serial Killing in the Post-Modern Detective Story." *Journal of Narrative Technique* 19 (1989): 106–13.

Rigney, Barbara Hill. *Margaret Atwood*. London: Macmillan, 1987.

Robinson, David. *Chaplin: His Life and Art*. New York: Da Capo, 1985.

Roe, Steven C. "Opening Bluebeard's Closet: Writing and Aggression in Hemingway's *The Garden of Eden* Manuscript." *Hemingway Review* 12 (1992): 52–66.

Roemer, Danielle M. "The Contextualization of the Marquis in Angela Carter's 'The Bloody Chamber.' " *Marvels and Tales* 12 (1998): 95–115.

Rosen, Marjorie. *Popcorn Venus*. New York: Avon, 1974.

Rothman, William. "Alfred Hitchcock's *Notorious*." *Georgia Review* 4 (1975): 884–927.

———. *Hitchcock: The Murderous Gaze*. Cambridge, Mass.: Harvard University Press, 1982.

Rowe, Karen E. " 'Fairy-born and human-bred': Jane Eyre's Education in Romance." In *The Voyage In: Fictions of Female Development*. Ed. Elizabeth Abel, Marianne Hirsch, and Elizabeth Langland. Hanover, N.H.: University Press of New England, 1983. Pp. 69–89.

Rushdie, Salman. *Haroun and the Sea of Stories*. London: Penguin, 1990.

Russ, Joanna. "Somebody's Trying to Kill Me and I Think It's My Husband: The Modern Gothic." *Journal of Popular Culture* 4 (1973): 666–91.

Sage, Victor, and Allan Lloyd Smith, eds. *Modern Gothic: A Reader*. Manchester: Manchester University Press, 1996.

St. Andrews, Bonnie. *Forbidden Fruit: On the Relationship between Women and Knowledge in Doris Lessing, Selma Lagerlöf, Kate Chopin, and Margaret Atwood*. Troy, N.Y.: Whitson, 1986.

Sanders, Ivan. "Symbolist and Decadent Elements in Early-Twentieth-Century Hungarian Drama." *Canadian-American Review of Hungarian Studies* 4 (1977): 23–42.

Schechter, Harold. "The Bloody Chamber: Terror Films, Fairy Tales, and Taboo." In *Forbidden Fruits: Taboos and Tabooism in Culture*. Ed. Ray B. Browne. Bowling Green, Ohio: Bowling Green State University Popular Press, 1984. Pp. 67–82.

Sconce, Jeffrey. "Narrative Authority and Social Narrativity: The Cinematic Reconstitution of Brontë's *Jane Eyre*." In *The Studio System*. Ed. Janet Staiger. New Brunswick, N.J.: Rutgers University Press, 1995.

Shattuck, Roger. *Forbidden Knowledge: A Landmark Exploration of the Dark Side of Human Ingenuity and Imagination*. San Diego: Harcourt Brace & Co., 1996.

Sheets, Robin Ann. "Pornography, Fairy Tales, and Feminism: Angela Carter's 'The Bloody Chamber.' " *Journal of the History of Sexuality* 1 (1991): 633–57.

Sine, Nadine. "Cases of Mistaken Identity: Salomé and Judith at the Turn of the Century." *German Studies Review* 11 (1988): 9–29.

Skenazy, Paul. "Poking Holes in the Social Fabric." In *Critical Essays on Kurt Vonnegut*. Ed. Robert Merrill. Boston: G. K. Hall, 1990. Pp. 64–66.

Soriano, Marc, ed. *Charles Perrault: Contes*. Paris: Flammarion, 1989.

Spoto, Donald. *The Dark Side of Genius: The Life of Alfred Hitchcock*. New York: Ballantine Books, 1983.

Steiner, George. *In Bluebeard's Castle: Some Notes towards the Redefinition of Culture.* New Haven: Yale University Press, 1971.

Stewart, Mary E. "Max Frisch's *Blaubart*: A Trivial Pursuit?" *Forum for Modern Language Studies* 24 (1988): 248–55.

Stone, Lawrence. *The Family, Sex, and Marriage in England, 1500–1800.* Abr. ed. New York: Harper & Row, 1977.

Stoneman, Patsy. *Brontë Transformations.* London: Prentice Hall, 1996.

Suhrbier, Hartwig. *Blaubarts Geheimnis.* Cologne: Eugen Diederich, 1984.

Suschitzky, Anja. "*Ariane et Barbe-Bleue*: Dukas, the Light, and the Well." *Cambridge Opera Journal* 9 (1997): 133–61.

Tatar, Maria. *The Hard Facts of the Grimms' Fairy Tales.* Princeton: Princeton University Press, 1987.

Theweleit, Klaus. *buch der könige.* Basel: Stroemfeld/Roter Stern, 1988.

Tolkien, J.R.R. "On Fairy-Stories." In *The Tolkien Reader.* New York: Ballantine, 1966. Pp. 3–84.

Truffaut, François. *Hitchcock.* Rev. ed. New York: Simon and Schuster, 1985.

Valenzuela, Luisa. *Symmetries.* Trans. Margaret Jull Costa. London: Serpent's Tail, 1998. Pp.145–51.

Vellay-Vallantin, Catherine. *L'Histoire des contes.* Paris: Fayard, 1992.

Vincent, Louis. *Gilles de Rais: The Original Bluebeard.* London: A. M. Philpot, 1926.

Vizetelly, Ernest Alfred. *Bluebeard: An Account of Comorre the Cursed and Gilles de Rais.* London: Chatto & Windus, 1902.

Wakefield, H. Russell. *Landru: The French Bluebeard.* London: Duckworth, 1936.

Waldman, Diane. " 'At last I can tell it to someone!': Feminine Point of View and Subjectivity in the Gothic Romance Film of the 1940s." *Cinema Journal* 23 (1983): 29–40.

Walker, Cheryl. "In Bluebeard's Closet: Women Who Write with the Wolves." *Literature Interpretation Theory* 7 (1996): 13–25.

Walker, Michael. "Secret beyond the Door." *Movie* 34/35 (1990): 16–30.

Walsh, Andrea S. *Women's Film and Female Experience: 1940–1950.* New York: Praeger, 1984.

Walz, Robin. "Murder, Mirth, and Misogyny: The Dark Humor of Henri Desiré Landru, the Bluebeard of Gambais." In Walz, *Pulp Surrealism: Insolent Popular Culture in Early Twentieth-Century Paris.* Berkeley: University of California Press, 2000. Pp. 76–113.

Ward, Catherine C. "Gloria Naylor's *Linden Hills*: A Modern Inferno." *Contemporary Literature* 28 (1987): 67–81.

Warner, Marina. "Bluebeard's Brides: The Dream of the Blue Chamber." *Grand Street* 9 (1989): 121–30.

———. *From the Beast to the Blonde: On Fairy Tales and Their Tellers.* New York: Farrar, Straus and Giroux, 1994.

———. *Monuments and Maidens: The Allegory of the Female Form.* New York: Atheneum, 1985.

Watson, Daphne. *Their Own Worst Enemies: Women Writers of Women's Fiction.* London: Pluto Press, 1995.

Weigel, Marta I. "I Have No Language for My Reality: The Ineffable as Tension in the 'Tale' of *Bluebeard." World Literature Today* 60 (1986): 588–92.

White, Alfred D. "Max Frisch Revisited: *Blaubart." Monatshefte* 78 (1986): 456–67.

Wiggins, Genevieve. *L. M. Montgomery.* New York: Twayne, 1992.

Williams, Linda. "When the Woman Looks." In *Re-vision: Essays in Feminist Film Criticism.* Ed. Mary Ann Doane, Patricia Mellencamp, and Linda Williams. Los Angeles: American Film Institute, 1984. Pp. 83–99.

Wilson, Sharon R. "Bluebeard's Forbidden Room: Gender Images in Margaret Atwood's Visual and Literary Art." *American Review of Canadian Studies* 16 (1986): 385–97.

———. *Margaret Atwood's Fairy-Tale Sexual Politics.* Jackson: University of Mississippi Press, 1993.

———. "Sexual Politics in Margaret Atwood's Visual Art." In *Margaret Atwood: Vision and Forms.* Ed. Kathryn VanSpanckeren and Jan Garden Catro. Carbondale: Southern Illinois University Press, 1988. Pp. 205–14.

Wilson, Thomas. *Bluebeard: A Contribution to History and Folk-lore, Being the History of Gilles de Retz of Brittany, France.* New York: Putnam's, 1897.

Winter, Douglas E. *Stephen King: The Art of Darkness.* New York: Signet, 1984.

Wood, Robin. "Rebecca Reclaimed." *Cineaction* 29 (1992): 97–100.

Yearsley, MacLeod. "Bluebeard and the Forbidden Chamber." In *The Folklore of the Fairy-Tale.* 1924. Detroit: Singing Tree, 1968. Pp. 121–37.

Zeitlin, Froma. "Travesties of Gender and Genre in Aristophanes' *Thesmophoria-zousae.*" In *Reflections of Women in Antiquity.* Ed. Helene B. Foley. New York: Gordon and Breach, 1981. Pp. 169–217.

Ziolkowski, Theodore. *The Sin of Knowledge: Ancient Themes and Modern Variations.* Princeton: Princeton University Press, 2000.

Zipes, Jack David, ed. *The Oxford Companion to Fairy Tales.* Oxford: Oxford University Press, 2000.

Žižek, Slavoj. *Looking Awry: An Introduction to Jacques Lacan through Popular Culture.* Cambridge: MIT Press, 1992.

———. " 'The Thing That Thinks': The Kantian Background of the *Noir* Subject." In *Shades of Noir: A Reader.* Ed. Joan Copjec. London: Verso, 1993. Pp. 199–226.

Zlotnick, Susan. "Jane Eyre, Anna Leonowens, and the White Woman's Burden: Governesses, Missionaries, and Maternal Imperialists in Mid-Victorian Britain." *Victorian Institute Journal* 24 (1996): 27–56.

Films

Bluebeard. Dir. George Méliès, 1901.

Bluebeard's Eighth Wife. Dir. Ernst Lubitsch, 1938.

Rebecca. Dir. Alfred Hitchcock, 1940.

Suspicion. Dir. Alfred Hitchcock, 1941.

Shadow of a Doubt. Dir. Alfred Hitchcock, 1943.

Bluebeard. Dir. Edgar G. Ulmer, 1944.

Dark Waters. Dir. Andre de Toth, 1944.

Gaslight. Dir. George Cukor, 1944.

Jane Eyre. Dir. Robert Stevenson, 1944.

Spellbound. Dir. Alfred Hitchcock, 1945.

Experiment Perilous. Dir. Jacques Tourneur, 1945.

Undercurrent. Dir. Vincent Minnelli, 1946.

The Two Mrs. Carrolls. Dir. Peter Godfrey, 1947.

Monsieur Verdoux. Dir. Charles Chaplin, 1947.

Secret beyond the Door. Dir. Fritz Lang, 1948.

Caught. Dir. Max Ophuls, 1949.

Bluebeard. Dir. Claude Chabrol. 1963.

Bluebeard. Dir. Edward Dmytryk, 1972.

Deutschland, bleiche Mutter. Helma Sanders-Brahms, 1980.

Raise the Red Lantern. Dir. Zhang Yimou, 1991.

The Piano. Dir. Jane Campion, 1993.